The Winds of Jeju Island
제주섬의 바람

The Winds of Jeju Island — Jeju PEN Mook①

Publication(2004.12.30)

editor • Sung-Chan Oh
compiler • Prunsasangsa
responsible editing • Jeju PEN Publication's Suhcommittee

Jeju PEN Mook ❶

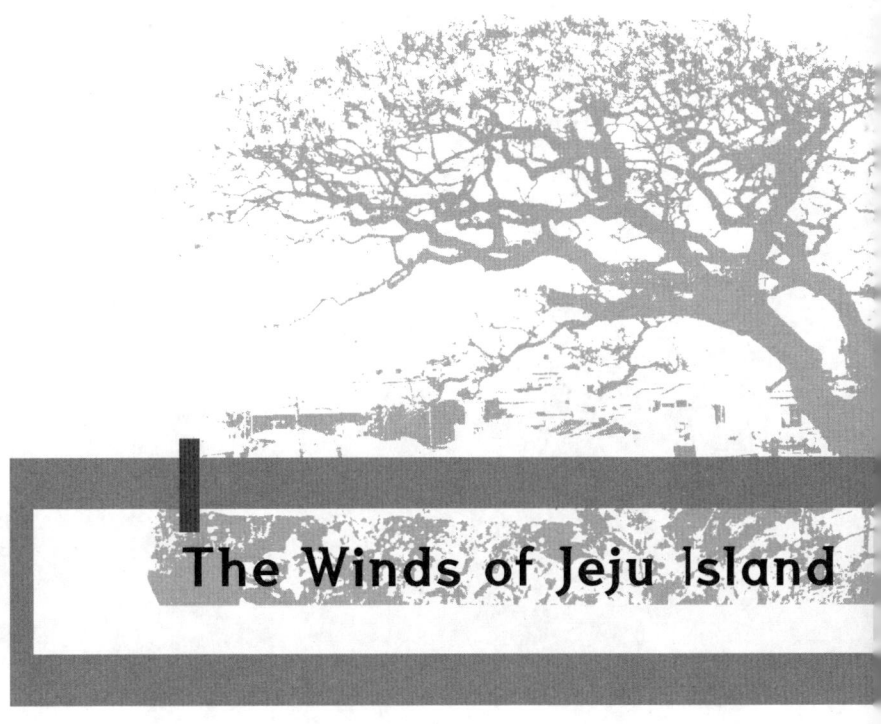

The Winds of Jeju Island

Translated by Bang-young Kang etc

푸른사상

Preface

I would like to congratulate the members of Jeju PEN (the Jeju Branch of the Korean Headquarters of the International PEN Club) on publishing this book of their works in English. This book is a result of their long-fostered wishes and plans to introduce 'Jeju Literature' to the world in this global age.

The translated works of Jeju authors comprise some poems, novels, and legends translated into English or Japanese and published in our country. As for translated anthologies, Professor Omura Mathuo, who worked as a director of the Korean Language and Literature Research Institute at Waseda University, published *Tamra Stories-Selected Literary Works of Jeju Island,* in Japan. It was a work of individual interest, and it might be the first foreign introduction to Jeju Literature.

We are living in a global age and profess our island to be an international free zone. But until now, the literature of Jeju was not known to the outside world, and is only just now beginning to toddle its way to the world. At this time, we are publishing poems, short stories, children's stories, essays, and criticism by Jeju PEN members. I think it can be a new opportunity for our island literature.

At the same time I feel sorry because this is only our first step toward the world. With this book as a start, I hope 10 or 100 more books of Jeju Literature will be translated into several foreign languages, and that there will be many people who continue their efforts to rank highly in world literature.

I would like to thank the Jeju PEN members who worked hard to plan and get funding for this book and the Jeju Provincial Government and Jeju City for providing money for publication. Also I thank to Professor Bangyoung Kang and her team at Jeju Halla College who completed the hard work of translation.

In addition I'd like to highlight the committee of Il-Hong Jang, Seung- Lip Kim, Young-Joo Jang, which carried forward the plan for this book's publication.

Sung-Chan Oh
(The Chairman of Jeju PEN)
December, 2004

◻ Contents ◻

publish — Seong-Chan Oh • 5

■ Poetry · Poem

- Joong-Hae Yang 13
    On the Ridge • 14   The Horizon • 16
- Tong-Won Kang 19
    The Jeju Island Ⅰ • 20   The Snow Flowers of Mt. Halla Ⅰ • 22
- Seung-Lip Kim 24
    About the Door • 25   Island • 27
- Yang-Soo Kim 28
    Who Were You • 29   The Lost and Gone • 31
- Yong-Kil Kim 33
    Resolution • 34   Wailing Eulalias • 35
- Gi-Cheol Na 38
    A Prayer • 39   Reminiscences • 40
- Choong-Seong Moon 41
    The Birds • 42   The Horizon • 43
- Tae-Gil Moon 44
    The Bell • 45   Azaleas • 46

◻ Contents ◻

- **Jeon-Hyong Yang** 47
  - My Wife • 48   A Love Song from the Woodo-Hill • 49

- **Young-Ho Oh** 51
  - In the Field of Eulalias • 52   In Front of the Sunset • 53

- **Bong-Taek Yoon** 54
  - On a Windy Day • 55   The Wind, 6 • 56

- **In-Soo Jeong** 58
  - A Woman Diver • 59   The Eulalia Flowers • 60

- **Gi-Pal Han** 61
  - The Pasturing of the Stars • 62   From There Unknown • 63

■ Novel

- **Hyon-Sik Choi** 67
  - Salvia • 68

- **Si-Hong Koh** 97
  - The City Under Martial Law • 98

- **Sung-Chan Oh** 121
  - People Thrown Away • 122

Contents

■ Children's Literature

- **Young-Ki Kim** 143
  - The Light House • 144
  - Mount Halla 2 • 145
- **Jong-Doo Kim** 146
  - The Isle of Mara • 147
  - Mount. Halla • 149
- **Soon-Bok Kang** 150
  - A Paper Piano • 151
- **Jae-Hyong Park** 158
  - Meeting the Sun • 159
- **Young-Ju Jang** 166
  - Seolmoondae-halmang • 167

■ Drama

- **Il-Hong Jang** 173
  - Invocation Dance • 174

■ Essay

- **Tae-Gook Kang** 205
  - A Fly-Swatter • 206

▫ Contents ▫

• Ga-Young Kim 211
　The Star-Pouring Night • 212

• Myong-Chul Cho 215
　The Tiny Life In the Orchid Pot • 216

■ Literary Criticism

• Seung-Haeng Shin 223
　Narrative: The Heritage of the Ceremony for Water and Imagination • 224

Poetry · Poem

On the Ridge / The Horizon
The Jeju Island I / The Snow Flowers of Mt. Halla I
About the Door / Island
Who Were You / The Lost and Gone
Resolution / Wailing Eulalias
A Prayer / Reminiscences
The Birds / The Horizon
The Bell / Azaleas
My Wife / A Love Song from the Woodo-Hill
In the Field of Eulalias / In Front of the Sunset
On a Windy Day / The Wind 6
A Woman Diver / The Eulalia Flowers
The Pasturing of the Stars / From There Unknown

Joong-Hae Yang

On the Ridge
The Horizon

The Introduction of the writer
First recognized in 〈Sahsahnggye〉. Past president of the Jeju Branch of the Korean Writers' Association and of the Jeju Branch of The Federation of Artistic and Cultural Organizations of Korea. Currently president of the Jeju Branch of the Federation of Korean Cultural Centers, board member of P.E.N. Korea
Publications : 〈Waves〉 〈Songs of Halla〉 〈The Horizon〉
Address : 108-306 Hyundai Apts, 943-3 Geonip-Dong, Jeju, Jejudo, Republic of Korea / Phone : 064) 722-0523

On the Ridge

by Joong-Hae Yang

At the ridge
The white cloud parted
After a pause,
Today, I am taking a rest
As a white cloud.

Those rivers and mountains
That I recollect
As beautiful memories...
Again those green woods and ridges
That I will visit...

The mountain from afar
Answered my shouts of yearning
Only with its echoes.
Today I sit on its ridge,
Calling out as an echo myself.

Sometimes, throwing away everything,

I wish to fall into a death-like sleep.
But at the sounds of the wind blowing,
And of the cloud gathering,
I must leave again and again.

On which ridge next
Shall I stop to take a rest?
On which ridge shall I call
To this mountain of today
Out of my yearning?

The Horizon

by Joong-Hae Yang

The people of Jejudo live
Surrounded by the horizon.

Since olden days
They settle anywhere on the foothills of Mt. Halla,
Sometimes facing the mountain with the horizon behind,
Sometimes facing the horizon with the mountain behind.
They all live their lives,
Long or short,
Contained within the horizon.
They all live and die
Surrounded by the horizon.

The people of Jejudo believe
There's the I-eo Island
Somewhere beyond the horizon,
But no one has been there.

The closeness within the horizon sometimes

Lead them to seek after the I-eo island on a boat.
But after rowing the boat awhile in that direction,
They find the horizon
Retreating itself as much further.
No one
Of the people of Jejudo
Has ever crossed the horizon once,
Has ever been to the I-eo Island.

In Jejudo,
The sun and the moon
Rise on the horizon.
And both plunge into the horizon.
Clouds, too, arise from the horizon.
After being pushed around within the horizon,
They disappear over the horizon.

The horizons of Jejudo look
So beautiful,
So calm outwardly,

But there at the horizon right now
Mighty waves are rolling up.
The joys and tears
Of the people of Jejudo,
Their life's pulsation
Incessantly upsurges at the horizon.

That horizon,
The fate of the people.
Their limited universe,
Leaving no other choice to them.

Tong-Won Kang

The Jeju Island I
The Snow Flowers of Mt. Halla I

The Introduction of the writer

Graduated from the Department of English Language and Literature at Jeju National University. Honorary Ph.D in Literature First recognized in 〈Poetry〉 in 1977. Past president of the Jeju Branch of The Federation of Artistic and Cultural Organizations and of the Jeju Branch of the Korean Writers' Association. Currently Central Committee Member of Korean Modern Poetry Association, Advisory Committee Member of Korean Poetry Association, Professor Emeritus at Jeju National University.
Publications : 〈The Fog Horn〉, 〈Upstream and Downstream〉, 〈Jeju Island Eulalia Flowers〉, etc.
Address : 255-18, Yongdam 1-Dong, Jeju, Jejudo, Republic of Korea
Phone : 064) 753-1732

The Jeju Island I

by Tong-Won Kang

Fire arises, fire blazes,
Bursting into great flames.
A fantasy, or my hallucination?
Some god's anger or curse?
Is it a fire of extermination
Or creation?
Of what myth or legend?
Is that a fire of life burning thus furiously?
Flames are soaring sky high.
The whole Island of Jeju is burning.
Did heaven and earth begin burning like that?
Whence did the seeds of fire fly over?
When did they?
In the remote universe
Ere the Creation,
Some five billion years ago,
What a thrilling firework there was,
Breaking, exploding, soaring,
Shooting up flames immeasurable.

From dark veins down the earth,

Gushing out again like a huge mountain range,

Fire burns up the earth and the sea altogether,

Spreading all over the space an entrancing festival of fire.

Is God thus drinking his toast of ecstasy

At this feast of fire?

The imponderable fire of the pre-history!

Once again the sea is torn,

The earth split.

Mountains are broken and gone.

So are meadows.

Wither is Jeju Island disappearing?

From the dust of ashes blown throughout the space,

From roaring clouds of fire shaking the whole heaven and earth,

From the growing pile of ashes like Mount Halla,

Is the eve of Jeju dawning?

Fire burns, fire blazes.

Again comes out the life-bud,

The breath and writhing of life,

Is it the eve of Jeju dawning?

Fire burns, fire blazes.

The Snow Flowers of Mt. Halla I

by Tong-Won Kang

Leaves are gone from the wood.

Snow flowers are in bloom

Over the dream of the wood,

Along the edge of long hibernation.

Whose hands sowed the seeds?

Blown in the cold wind,

These flowers come

Without being planted.

Though they bloom, therefore,

They bear no fruit.

Whose hands are tending this flower bed?

Creatures like butterflies and bees

Have forgotten about their garden.

Now they too are roaming

Along the dreamy paths

In the remote wintry sleep.

Only a poorly feathered bird in the mountain

Thinks idly

Of her loves and dreams.

Some day
In their chilly dreams
They will see the bright sun,
And hear the ponies neighing
On the hills in its dazzling shower.
The cold wings of the bird
And the frozen wrists of the trees thawing,
They will come out on the road to greet spring.

Seung-Lip Kim

About the Door Island

The Introduction of the writer
Address : 402-11 2-Do 2-Dong, Jeju, Jejudo, Republic of Korea
Phone : 064) 753-3185, 019-9101-3185

About the Door

by Seung-Lip Kim

With the doors unwilling to open,
We looked rather unfamiliar to each other.
We were happy, then.

What a sordid affair love is,
When we exchange our souls swiftly
Through accustomed handshakes and hugs
With painted faces under its name.

When we grew a tree of anguish,
Before the closed door,
From the seed of yearning for the inside,

Even with the wind and rain
Thrashing on the up-reaching branches,
The sleep breathing under the tree
Kindled up the fiery flowers.

Now the doors gone,
We just stand weeping,
And the familiar strangeness also gone,
We just keep standing there.
With faces of indifference.

Lost in the strangeness,
Lost and forlorn.

Island

by Seung-Lip Kim

1.
After a night of an uncomfortable sleep,
The sorrow purely Korean
Oozes up.

I hear the rain-fall in the yard.

2.
What will open your eyes,
With only the artificial flowers
Growing thickly in your armpits?
Having lost your scales for an age,
You couldn't swim around.
That lulled the sea to fall asleep,
Falling deeper and deeper
Into an indigo sleep.

Yang-Soo Kim

Who Were You
The Lost and Gone

The Introduction of the writer
First recognized in 〈Shimsahng〉 in 1990.(New Writers' Award).
Vice president of the Jeju Branch of P.E.N. Korea, member of the Korean Poets' Association and of the Shimsahng Poets' Association
Publications : 〈Wind, Too, Would Yearn for Rest〉, 〈Thanks to You, Mother, Despairs Turn into Hopes〉, 〈In the Shadow of Xylophone Music Playing〉
Address : 255-18, Yongdam 1-Dong, Jeju, Jejudo, Republic of Korea
Phone : 064) 753-1732

Who Were You

by Yang-Soo Kim

At the beginning we were
Like budding leaves on an empty branch.
Or like water and fire.
Or were we like clouds reflected on the river?

The imponderable distance of our relation
Rears impatience much
As does the weight of the sky.

Sealing off your mouth, you make me jealous.

What were you and I, originally?
Were we not like
Light and shadow?
Or like a button and its hole
On a prisoner's jacket?
Being unable to measure
The brightness of sunlight
Pouring down on your lonely back,
My heart breaks.

I know

You would not return for all the world.

Who were you?

When we meet where no nametags are worn,

You might not recognize me.

Here I hang on the wall of darkness,

A face that once wandered around in your dark pupils.

Come the new day,

Let you and I revive as cicadas

And cry ourselves out

All summer long.

The Lost and Gone

by Yang-Soo Kim

What were they?
Which were they
That we felt sure we had?
As does a net unable to contain wind,
The wood only struggles more fiercely,
Swaying its chest of holes.

Did we know
Or even suspect it
That things we kept are
Only as bleak as the smoke
Rising from the burning of autumn leaves?
At the end of the rock-heavy parting,
There remains nothing even to be erased.

If you must go away,
And if I knew like sensing the approaching rain,
That you'd abandon me
No rubbing off of your shadows should make me hollow.

Alas, I didn't build a pen to keep you in,
Who were like a rhinoceros.
Nor I did a pond
Where I could check
My cascading tears.

Empty-handed,
Trying to grasp the fading yearning
Only to feel my hands more hollow,
I lament at the hallucinative voice
Deeper than darkness
And wish that you take away with you
Even that trace of loss left behind.

Yong-Kil Kim

Resolution
Wailing Eulalias

The Introduction of the writer

Jejudo Culture Award (Division:Art) and Seogwipo Civil Culture Award. Past president of the Seogwipo Branch of the Korean Writers' Association
Publications : 〈Duet of Sea and Island〉
Address : 206 Jungbang Villa, 118 Seogwi-Dong Seogwipo, Jejudo, Republic of Korea / Phone : 064) 762-4943, 011-694-9229

Resolution

by Yong-Kil Kim

Along your lonely riverbank
I won't recall the names of wild flowers,
Nor I call to the stars blue as separation.
I won't sing with birds chirping,
Dangling their blank name-tags,
The stories of their sweet first love.

Where human odors linger,
I will hide my tearful eyes of pity and pain.
I won't seed my old furrows of truth
With empty shells of deception.

Now I will hold your name in my bosom.
In this land of mercy and peace,
I will not take off the bolt from the door to time.
Nor I will erect a gravestone bearing a new epitaph,
In front of the lonely grave where you lie buried.

Wailing Eulalias

by Yong-Kil Kim

1.

In the Jeju Island,
Eulalias bloom everywhere.
Along the gravel roads in the field,
On the bare volcanic mounds,
They bloom white and white
And wail in the wind.

When swayed, they sway themselves.
When trod down, they suffer.
They wail, lying low in the shaking.
They wail, standing up after their fall.

2.

In the field, they become birds and weep.
Along the thorny trails to the mounds,
They weep like motherless roe.

They sob with throats burning,
In the dry dales
Where sunlight alone echoes it.

When the dusk falls down the slopes,
They ululate
With their hair disheveled in the moonlight.

3.
They scream as billows
Surfing and shattering
The dreams on the cliff edges.

Surrounding the Jeju Island,
Waves are wailing.
Like sea gulls,
The birds of soul,
They wail, leaving for an eternal trip
Wound with white bands.

4.

In their hearts they moan,
Reducing themselves
To light bodies.
And turn into seeds like butterflies.

They soar up
And fly far and near,
They light on whatever they bump against,
And there they moan in their hearts.

Wherever they could stick their roots,
Even a single strand of a thin thread,
The life-line of fate,
There they would bloom and moan.

Gi-Cheol Na

A Prayer
Reminiscences

The Introduction of the writer

Born in Seoul in 1953, Graduated from the Department of Korean Language and Literature at Jeju National University. First recognized in 〈Poetry〉 in 1987. Member of 〈Poems of Awakening〉.
Publications: 〈Longstanding Dreams of Islands〉, 〈Namyang Inn〉
Address : Gah-106, Cheonil Apts, 1699-4 Ara 1-Dong, Jeju, Jejudo, Republic of Korea / Phone : 064) 702-2726, 016-692-9652 / E-mail : nagc0914@hanmir.com

A Prayer

by Gi-Cheol Na

In my death, I would visit the Sara Hill.
In a dale near the Byoldo Hill,
I would collect the sound of the waves.
Even in my death, I would look after my love.
Breaking the grave at eleven at night,
I would like to come out in the street,
I would braid her hair on the pillow.
A basket of chrysanthemums I would leave behind me.

Reminiscences

by Gi-Cheol Na

'Me', the seven stars of the Big Dipper, the evening horizon, a cold, an epitaph, La Boheme, a field of reeds, birthday, a picnic, 'A Bell', meanness, 'A Blue Flower' fool······fool.

Dry snow pellets piling up on the evening horizon.

A voice of pity,
Deep blue,
Is being covered with the snow grains.

Choong-Seong Moon

The Birds
The Horizon

The Introduction of the writer
Born in Jeju. Ph.D in French Language and Literature at Korean Foreign Languages University. First recognized in 〈Literature and Intellect〉.
Publications: 〈Seas of Jeju〉, 〈Rainbow Growing Out of My Palm〉, 〈Song Last Sung on an Island〉, 〈French Symbolist Poetry and Korean Modern Poetry〉, etc.
Address : 301 Cheonglim Villa, 52-23 Donam-Dong, Jeju, Jejudo, Republic of Korea / Phone : 064) 753-2449, 011-699-2448 / E-mail : mcs2449@yahoo.co.kr

The Birds

by Choong-Seong Moon

Numerous birds were flying away in the blue.
They were flying in the blue glaciers.

They were pushed by the icy wind,
The boundless expanse.
I could do nothing but let them fly away.

You, birds, wandering in the wind!
Haven't you secured a little place to land with your bare feet?
Come back then, folding your tired wings, my birds!
But my bosom was only an empty skin.

My shadow was disappearing into your weeping, the land of hard hearing,
Birds having soared up in the blue were now falling, falling,
Each holding a piece of my cry in its beaks.

The Horizon

by Choong-Seong Moon

How innumerable the horizons are in this world!
One of them surrounds my life,
Inducing me to tremble
Always with new beginnings in yearning.
One day fishing in the sea
I found another horizon with loving strokes
Lulling the land of men into sleep.
Another, embracing the lights of men,
Stands as a mountain.
It comes rushing through the wind,
Encircling my life with a white line.
Even when a dark storm engulfs the horizon,
It appeases the darkness, awakens the dawn,
And leads the blind sun to rise in my heart,
Letting me sing about the waves of the ocean.

Tae-Gil Moon

The Bell
Azaleas

The Introduction of the writer
Past president of the Jeju Branch of the Korean Writers' Association, Jeju Branch.
Jeju Civil Award (Division: Art and Culture).
Publications : 〈Mara Island Lighthouse〉, etc.
Address : 315-7 2-Do 2-Dong, Jeju, Jejudo, Republic of Korea

The Bell

by Tae-Gil Moon

Always my voice will fly
Through the sky as much as it likes,

When it meets the clouds,
With a smile it will just pass.

When struck by a gust,
My voice will be shattered
Only more loudly.

Being tired of crying,
It will wet its throat
In the stream,

Until the stray people
regain their paths,

My voice will ring
And ring again
Against the hills of agony.

Azaleas

by Tae-Gil Moon

To make our love
Eternal one,

We should leave
This gorgeous garden as it is.

For an earnest dream
That will bloom
On the other side of the mist.

Your heart gets wet,
Not by the spring rain alone.

Shedding off the feather-like rain drops,
You are always going away.

Where longing has collapsed,
Leaving only its trace,
Azaleas will bloom.

Jeon-Hyong Yang

My Wife
A Love Song from the Woodo-Hill

The Introduction of the writer

Member of Hallasan Literature Society.
Yeollin Literature Award and Korean Jayoo Poets Award.
Publications : 〈I Am a Rock〉, 〈Dandelion on a Street〉, 〈Love Is Silent〉, etc.
Address: 38-1 Oilnam-Ro, Ora-1-Dong, Jeju, Jejudo, Republic of Korea
Phone : 064) 725-3960, 016-685-3960 / E-mail : yih3960@hanmail.net

My Wife

by Jeon-Hyong Yang

Though she is so short
That only on tiptoe she can cling to me,
And that she can hardly be seen
Among the crowd of the fifth-day market,
She occupies such a wide space, you know,
With her bearing so dignified,
She fills up closely
Every nook and corner of our house,
Every crack in the hearts of our children,
Every turn of the awkward wandering in my night-outs.
She is really a full moon,
Casting her light all over the world
Grown from the promise of the crescent moon.
She is really a daffodil, fragrant and graceful,
That would stand in bloom even in the blizzard.

A Love Song from the Woodo-Hill

by Jeon-Hyong Yang

The tide is high in the harbor, the boats blowing their whistles.
Time to leave for those transient visitors.
They stand up one by on shaking off their last night's dream.

Leave if you must. Stay if you wish to.
The island has never stopped anyone.
People separate on an island.
Waiting is all that remains there.
Waiting grows into a flower.

When the waves are high or the dawns shrouded by the sea fog,
The bind-weed flowers on the shore open their mouths wider.
Like a cow bereft of its calf, a fog horn lets out screams
For your voyage home after a thousand years,
And the bind-weed flowers, facing seaward,
Turn their throats redder and redder.

You, whose name I've long known!
Come to this light house to the sound of the horn.

Things on the island are all beautiful
Everything left behind on the island will bloom.
Here you and I may also bloom into some flowers.

Young-Ho Oh

In the Field of Eulalias
In Front of the Sunset

The Introduction of the writer
Past president of Jeju Shijo Society. Currently vice president of the Jeju Branch of P.E.N. Korea and board member of the Korean Shijo Poets' Association. Korean Shijo Critics' Award.
Publications : 〈An Insignificant Reason〉
Address : 324-10 2-Do 2-Dong, Jeju, Jejudo, Republic of Korea
Phone : 064) 757-1361, 011-9660-6250 / E-mail: jeju500hamail.net

In the Field of Eulalias

by Young-Ho Oh

The blue wind, having brightened the world

With rolls of the spring light.

Hovers above the wings of time

That covered the blue grass in the olden days.

Today, there grows the fruit of silvery words, murmuring.

In the revelation of the trees

Standing with empty hands day and night,

The noise of the bustling white hairs

Sounds sharply across the space.

A cock-pheasant flitters. Untying the knot of life?

In Front of the Sunset

by Young-Ho Oh

In an evening of late autumn,
On the shore of Bomokni, Seogwipo,
Having invited the dozing Moon Island nearby,
Poets were fishing in the ebbing water,
Trying to catch some shi-os* escaping in the tide.
At the sublime moment of the mass of the sun falling down slowly
Over the islands of Sae and Seop, and over the horizon,
They closed their hearts, catching their breath.
Right then, the blood-red sea whispered,
Back to the beginning, Back to the beginning,
Taking off your black attire of vanity!
Burn it all and go on living.

*shi-o: a homonym for herring and poetic words.

Bong-Taek Yoon

On a Windy Day
The Wind, 6

The Introduction of the writer
Born in Seogwipo.
New Writers' Award by 〈Literary Trends〉 with 〈Island Wind〉, etc.
Publications : 〈Farmers Also Yearn〉, 〈Every Wild Flower Has a Name〉
Address : 4316-5 Gahngjeong-Dong, Seogwipo, Jejudo, Republic of Korea
Phone : 064) 739-2332, 011-9662-2340 / E-mail : seogwipo@hamail.net

On a Windy Day

by Bong-Taek Yoon

On a windy day, I miss the island.
You, my dearest!
If it is a sin
To miss,
If it really is a sin
To miss a person,
If it is a sin
To leave, looking for a person of one's longing,
I'd rather live on committing the sin.

Even if I don't wait for you,
You become the mist of love,
Bathing me in the river of our childhood.
Sorrowful you, my dearest!
If I let myself flow with the river,
Perhaps we might meet together on the island.

As time is raising the transparent sea-spray
On the quiet shore of the remote remembrance,
On a day like this when the wind is blowing,
I miss the sea of the island.

The Wind, 6

by Bong-Taek Yoon

Oh, the land!
Having sold you and abandoned you,
Now I am sowing the seeds of the wind
On you, the island, where even wild flowers can hardly bloom,
Where only the wind and seaweeds may take root.
We were at breakfast, a family of four.
When mother departed for her long journey,
Gathering rice grains her grandson dropped.
The wind of Jejudo shook her wet bosom
Exhausted from persisting through hard knots of her life.
Now that wind of Jejudo is stirring again,
Blowing away the darkness overdue.
Snow falls heavy this winter for the places lower and warmer.
In the villages sad for no piling snowfalls,
People cough and spit out blood
At every other house in every other neighborhood.
The sleepless eyes open this morning
And it's the New Year's Day today.
Yet, sorrows are borne on the waves

Like falling petals of the citron flowers.
You, attached anchor! You, wind!
Why can't you leave the island?

In-Soo Jeong

A Woman Diver
The Eulalia Flowers

The Introduction of the writer
New Writers' Award by 〈Korean Literature〉 in 1974, Jejudo Culture
Award Publications: 〈Samda Island〉
Address : Gah-602, Samboo Jahngmi Apts, 1601-11 Samyang I-Dong,
Jeju, Jejudo, Republic of Korea
Phone : 064) 756-1846, 018-350-1846 / E-mail : jung40@paran.com

A Woman Diver

by In-Soo Jeong

A woman diver opens her eyes and mouth
Only in the water.

Once taking off her clothes out of sight,
She readily entrusts the water with her life.

What she can't really trust
Is the world
Beyond
The whistling sound
Of her drawing breath.

The Eulalia Flowers

by In-Soo Jeong

Watching my wife's careworn eyelids,
I went out to pick an armful of eulalias,
And put them in an earthen jar.

My grandmother's once,
Long since the jar emptied its mind.
With its big mouth, poor-looking,
It is finally met with its better half.

In a world where the plain water alone
Cannot cure its hunger,
The jar suddenly looks affluent and plentiful,
Holding in her arms the bunch of eulalias.

The living room brightens up at once.
Lo and behold,
The wrinkles are gone from her eyelids!

Gi-Pal Han

The Pasturing of the Stars
From There Unknown

The Introduction of the writer
First recognized in 〈Shimsahng〉 in 1975. Past president of the Jeju Branch and the Seogwipo Branch of the Korean Writers'. Association
Jeju Culture Award, Seogwipo Civil Award, Jeju Literature Award
Publications : 〈Between Words and Silence〉, etc.
Address : 681 Bomok-Dong, Seogwipo, Jejudo, Republic of Korea
Phone : 064) 732-4138 , 011-694-4138

The Pasturing of the Stars

by Gi-Pal Han

Those with warm souls
Live always with some stars kept
By their windows.
Like descendants of the nomads of old,
They pasture stars
In the huge meadow of the sky.
Though lonely are our souls,
We talk about our past life
With the stars every night.
The cloud hanging on the mountain
Is our shepherd boy,
When you go out to the pond,
He drives a herd of stars to it
Like a flock of sheep.
After some splashing, he drives them back.

From There Unknown

by Gi-Pal Han

1.

Over the hill
Lies the blue sea.
There the mysterious wind
Arises.

There lingers the voice
Of the person of my yearning.
There the mysterious snow
Falls.

2.

On the way back,
I realized I forgot the blue sea.
The sea that turns into
A drop of tear,
A little shiver.

Then your whispering
In my ears.

Novel

Salvia
The City Under Martial Law
People Thrown Away

Hyon-Sik Choi

Salvia

The Introduction of the writer

Born in Hongwon, Hahmkyungnahm-Do in 1924. Awarded in the Spring Literature Contest of Josun Daily Newspaper in 1957 with 〈Deer〉. Member of the Korean Writers' Association, Korean Novelists' Association, Korean Writers' Association, Jeju Branch.
Publications : 〈Red Dress〉, 〈Black Cat Diary〉 〈Mountain at a Distance〉, etc.
Phone : 064) 757-4525

Salvia

by Hyon-Sik Choi

"Who cut this? Chadol!"

I woke up to a strong Hamkyungdo (a North Korean dialect) accent. The door was open toward the flower garden and I could catch the shrill chirp of a cicada within my muddled head.

'It was mother's voice', I thought. But Chadol's usual answer in Jeju (a southern Korean island) dialect of, "I don't know, I didn't do that!" was not heard.

Although the sunshine on the yard was much more weaker than before I had fallen asleep, a butterfly was hanging around the abundant scarlet salvia, then disappeared fast, zigzagging into the blue over the fence.

'It was a dream, an odd dream that consisted of a voice only, without the story before or after.'

After watching the soaring butterfly to the last, I turned my eyes to the wristwatch on the table. It was ten to five. It was around two that I had left the hospital with mother, helping her, and it was around three before I took a nap. So it might have been for two hours that I had slept. I drank too much Soju, which I had bought on my way home. I felt serious thirst so I drank cold water from the kettle, pouring it into a glass. The thirst was gone but the throbbing in my chest remained.

In K hospital, after her medical examination, mother came back to a sofa in the waiting room. She used her mouth and eyes to express that she was thirsty. I asked the nurse to take care of mother and went to the consulting room.

"It is flu but⋯".

Dr. K did not talk for a while, and then asked me, hesitating,

"Has your mother said anything about pain in her chest?"

"No, she hasn't"

I answered and told him that her digestion had been bad since the spring and began alopecia.

"Though I need to do more tests, it seems to be gastric cancer."

"A gastric cancer?"

An electric fan was spinning and blowing wind on the desk. I took out my handkerchief and wiped sweat from my forehead.

"It is big enough to be held in one's hand and it seems to be in the upper part.".

"Held in one's hand?"

"Yes, that's why I asked you about the pain."

"Never⋯"

"She is lucky then. When the patient knows⋯"

"How about taking an X-ray?"

"Although it could cause pain to the patient, we will take an X-ray. It could be cirrhosis of the liver, but the prescription would be the same. Let's see her again after treating the flu".

"If it is true, that it's gastric cancer, how long could she last?"

"Considering her age, it could be around 6 months."

"6 months⋯."

I could not find any words and left the consultation room. She was getting a shot in the surgery room.

"It is flu. After being treated 3 or 4 days, you will be OK."

She made a sign with her eyes, saying, "Mm⋯I got it."

We left K hospital. I wanted to look for another hospital and see another doctor, but gave up because it would cause too much strain to mother. After returning home, I had mother lie down. I took my wife out of the house and talked to her about the diagnosis, asking her to keep it a secret.

"She has been drinking Whalmyongsu (a digestive) and saying her heart felt heavy since January⋯"

My wife could not hide her wary face.

"Nothing is clear yet, so please look after her", I said and began to drink Soju, pouring three cups, five cups⋯

Maybe for my own consolation, I remembered a lesson in Confucius' Teachings: 'A true gentleman should not be afraid of disaster or be pleased with luck'.

Into the scarlet salvia, a white butterfly came again. It might have been the one which had disappeared over the fence. The butterfly disappeared, surging busily along the same way in short time, without resting in the flowers.

"There are ways for butterflies. They have their own ways to travel changelessly."

Last summer I went to hike Mt. Halla to pray. My party and I drove a car to the Eorimok mountain villa on a Saturday afternoon, spending the night there. We asked the owner of villa to join us and left early the next morning. We went to the reservoir and had lunch at the edge, then went down to Gaemidoeng. (a small hill on the climbing path)

During the night it had rained but the weather changed to fog in the early morning, then was fine when we arrived at around 1,000 meters above sea level. The sky was wide open and the mountain road was filled with hydrangea flowers and the sounds of Jeju's whispering birds' song. My back was wet with sweat where my rucksack covered it.

"You will see a great view after ten minutes' more walking," said Mr. S, who had hiked the mountain more than 150 times. I stopped, panting, and asked,

"What is that?"

"It would not be as wonderful if I told you first",

S went straight in front of us, smiling. Finally, we reached the great viewpoint. On the right there was a slope covered with lots of brown flowers.

"Yahaa," I cheered for a while. I was more surprised at the group of butterflies than at the flowers.

"Yahaa," I cheered again, then, at that moment, I saw a small, thin green snake slither straight, as if flying, over the flowers shining with rain drops. It was only I who was surprised. Butterflies were flying, flowers were shining, and Mr. S was smiling still.

"Was that a venomous snake?".

"No, it does not have poison but I don't know the name…"

I gave a cigarette to Mr. S.

'Flower, flower, flower/ Butterfly, butterfly, butterfly/ The seven color rainbow hanging over the leaves/ Don't hurt them/ Roars a striped snake…,'

I composed a clumsy poem, forgetting myself, then I asked Mr S, "What is the elevation of this place?".

"Around 1600 meters…".

After we hiked 365 meters more, we came close to Baengnokdam, the lake on top of Mt. Halla. While I got up and packed my rucksack, Mr. S shared his knowledge on the ways of butterflies. He also told me watching the life of spiders could be fun.

"If butterflies could be compared to dancers, spiders are gypsies. There is no constant home for spiders. They say there are hundreds kinds of spiders on Mt. Halla, among them, the long-legged spiders that walk around the grass fast and cast their strong nets across the butterflies' way."

We left the flower field. After passing the Korean firs and fields of wild orchid, we reached the top of Mt. Halla. Stopping, I knelt on the lawn. I collected my hands on my chest and, straightening myself, prayed to the deep blue sky over the peak. After a few minutes I stood up slowly.

"What kind of prayer was it?" I heard Mr. S's joking voice behind my back and I sent him a smile with my eyes.

"Guess."

"It must be for the peaceful unification of South and North Korea."

"That is rubbish. Come on! Guess. I will treat you if you guess the right answer".

Mr. S smiled and we faced each other for a while, then I told him my prayer was to have a son.

"Come on! You are a manager of a big newspaper company, and pray for such a thing! Nowadays, people do not care about having a baby, son or daughter".

"Ha ha ha⋯"

We had a big laugh and I told him the prayer was for my mother⋯ (mother insisted the forth granddaughter's name be 'Chadol', meaning quartz or a hard rock), because, a long time ago, one of grandfather's sons had had a son after giving this name to his last daughter, but in my family it didn't help. Mother had had to calm my crying wife after she gave birth to her fifth baby daughter. She said, "Well, have another baby, you are still young⋯"

And she didn't express the darkness inside her heart. (My wife was due to have another baby this month.)

For 20 minutes we walked toward the peak. I guess my religious beliefs toward the mountains began when I was young.

There was a mountain about 200 meters high in my home town. It was rather a hill but thought to be a noted mountain. It was in North Korea. The hill hugged all the streets in the town and had the shape of a crane sitting down with wings spread, so people named it Hakdubong, meaning 'back of a crane hill'. People could see the charm of royal azaleas in spring around this mountain, and built a Confucian temple and a school attached to it in the woods. Lots of men of ability were cultivated there during the early and later enlightenment. Later, two elementary schools were built at the foot of mountain. I could not remember how old I was when my mother began religious services on this hill. It might have been around May because I remembered hearing cuckoos. Mother had me carry a brass pot on my head, which was filled with boiled rice made early in the morning, and mother and I hiked about 4 kilometers to this mountain. Around 10 o'clock, we walked down the mountain with an armful of royal azaleas. The vitality of the flowers still remained, so I put them in a vase quickly. Then I ate the rice we'd used for the ritual for lunch with mother. Its taste was the greatest I'd ever had. It might have been the 2nd year of school that I went to the hill with some of my friends to cut some azaleas. I fell down while climbing a cliff when one of my legs slipped. Some pine trees held me and prevented me from falling. Friends put their belts together and pulled me up the cliff. After this accident, I never climbed the hill. The memory of that cliff made me shudder. From then on I got azaleas from my mother every year. I could see the figures of the thick branches and trunks of pine trees for 40 years.

I hiked Baeknokdam to pray to have a son. Having 5 granddaughters in a row, Mother's frustration would be as deep as the lake itself. I wiped sweat from my forehead.

It was three days after climbing. I drank so much and came home at night. When I entered, mother greeted me hastily and signaled me to be careful with her eyes. I realized intuitively the situation from the sounds of my wife's suffering in mother's room so I went into my room, then fell asleep at once.

"My boy…"

I opened my eyes at mother's voice. I heard that in my muddled brain and raised my head to the direction of the sound.

"Yes…", I answered.

"It is a grandson".

A low voice shuddered a little, then the door was closed silently.

"What time is it?", I raised my head and asked.

"About one a.m."

I heard an urgent voice from the outside. Then mother's steps went away. I heard a baby's crying break the heavy silence. I smiled for a while and slept again.

The next morning, mother suggested the new grandson's name 'Gaettong' (dog's dung), referring to a tradition that, for a dear son, people used an indecent name. People believed a baby named humbly would grow well without meeting bad luck.

"Good," I agreed and went to work.

That was the 4th of July, the day so-called, "I have been to Pyongyang." At 10 o'clock all my colleagues were watching television in a tea shop. The joint communique of the 4th of July between South and North Korea! The streets were filled with excitement and the people looked, expecting that the whistling sound of a train to North Korea would be heard. I could not calm down all day. Taking in all the colleagues' blessings without hesitation, I couldn't work properly. I tried to concentrate on the work but couldn't control myself-peaceful unification of country, handshakes between the leaders of both governments, their travels between Seoul and Pyongyang, and the joint declaration with toasts from both sides···what majestic events !

I examined myself to know why I was excited. Was it because of what was happening then? No. I couldn't settle down as I was a mean person who couldn't distinguish an important affair from a trivial thing.

"It is a grandson", mother's shaky voice and busy steps, the birth of Gaettong, those trivial matters I couldn't forget or put out of my head.

Darkness fell on the salvia garden. The cicada was still singing and kids' shouts of joy from the playground broke the silence. From the back of the house I heard the sound of dishes, maybe my wife making dinner, carrying Gaettong on her back. I got up and entered mother's room. Mother was lying down.

"How do you feel, mother?"

"Feel a little dizzy—less headache, but feel heavy in the chest…"

She touched her chest in the middle. "After treatment for a few days…".

I sat down near mother's head. I felt mother's forehead to see if she had a fever. It was not so hot.

"Would you like to eat something?"

"I lost my appetite."

Mother wrinkled her brow.

Only 6 months left. If she withstood it well…

I turned my eyes from mother. She seemed to be having difficulty breathing because of something heavy in her chest (which mother touched).

I cannot stand sitting like this…

I wished I didn't know. I touched my chin with my hand and counted 6 months. August, September, October, and then the hour of death. I wanted mother to die in peace. I wished God's call would be like sleep for her. I remembered hearing my father asking mother about mercy killing, as spending long autumn nights was too difficult for him to stand.

I had never seen anyone's death. When father died, I was working as an elementary school teacher in the country. He kept mother from sending mail to call me back for his dying hour. He thought a teacher should not vacate the position earlier than usual, even though his father was dying. It was September by the lunar calendar and late autumn in North Korea. The day before receiving the letter from my hometown, I dreamed a big snake came into my room and guessed my father was dying. As a chief mourner, aged 19, for the first time I learned to wail, kneeling in front of father's corpse. My lament was too fast to hear so one of the aunts standing behind me advised me do it slowly. Then father's body was placed in the coffin. I cried bitterly. We had endured grandmother's death 5 years before father's. It was the 11th month of the lunar calendar, a very cold winter, when father died. 5 years before grandmother's death, we had buried grandfather in the hot summer. For 9 days people prepared for the funeral and had noodles, pork and gruel like at a festival. Mosquitos around the dim candlelight made humming sounds. That sound never disappeared from my head. I had lost my only younger sister before I lost my grandfather. Mother used to put an apple in front of the small tomb in the public cemetery early morning on Korean Thanksgiving day every year. 30 years after father's death, I came to South Korea with mother. It was the year of Korean liberation, so I didn't witness the deaths of many relatives. My grandfather on my mother's side might be dead, the sister of my father also might have died; if she were alive, her age might be⋯

When I talked to mother about these things, the loneliness of being cut off from her family often showed in mother's face. I turned my eyes from mother. She was sleeping with her hands on her chest.

> Ah, ah
> Life is born in eternity
> Dies in eternity
> The fact that life is the only thing is,
> Human beings' unique honor
> A living thing's unique's sorrow

I thought of 'Revelation' by a Japanese poet and left mother's room quietly. One month passed while I visited 3 hospitals with mother. All 3 hospitals had the same diagnosis. I avoided taking the X-ray, because I believed it could only give pain to mother.

After being treated for the flu, mother helped with laundry and took care of flowers in the yard. But that was due to mother's personality—she hated to sit down, doing nothing, and only in the early morning could she move; she had to lie down for the rest of the day.

One day, I invited an artist, Mr. C, to drink with me in order to ask him to do mother's portrait. Willingly, Mr. C consented to draw it. I picked out three pictures from our album; one picture of her was black and white, in her fifties, and the others were color pictures with Chadol in Seogwipo the previous spring. Combining the three pictures, we decided to get a face in her sixties, 6.4 inches by 9.2 inches.

"I would use the colors made in France".

"It is too good for me".

I appreciated him from my heart.

"It will take one month, but don't expect too much",

Then he asked about mother's disease. I told him not to worry about it too much, because she would survive more than one month. I gave a pot of Jeju orchids to him despite his refusal. "This is too much to take," he hesitated.

I hailed a taxi and put it in with him.

Mother should not know about her portrait···

I came back to my room and, adjusting the album, decided to keep it secret in my heart. Her keen heart seemed to know about her body's condition already.

A few days before, I had found out something unbelievable. Mother had taken care of a flower garden of about 20 square yards. Usually I bought plants but never cared for them after getting them home and washing my hands. For 9 years it had been mother who had watched over plants. All the work in the garden was for mother's hands. Sometimes my wife was nervous about that and criticized me. But mother didn't mind and said, "Don't blame him. He cannot even drive in a nail with a hammer."

She had never learned gardening before, but every plant— magnolias, gardenias, camellias, a tangerine tree in the back yard—grew well. In my memory, mother's favorite flower was the rose moss. Then, living in Seoul, it changed to the morning-glory. Moving to Jeju, it became the salvia. For the last 10 years the salvia flowers(which mother called sesame flower) had painted our front yard with a bright orange color every year. In mother's words, salvia flowers had not only a bright color but also vitality strong enough to continue to grow new flowers for three months. I got two yulan trees from Seogwipo and planted them near the salvia last spring. The roots were strong to grow well. But one day a mouse had bitten the tree near the root. Mother couldn't hold her anger. She bought an iron net and installed it to protect the root. However, it must have been bitten seriously. The tree began to die slowly in early summer. When mother went to bed with her disease, the tree had only three leaves on the branches.

Mother told me to remove the sick yulan tree. She used to stop me from throwing away the hopeless plant, suggesting I wait until the next spring. But now she wanted to throw it away even though there were some leaves left on the tree. I felt a lump in my throat and couldn't find any words. But after some minutes, I decided to remove it. It was not difficult work. I broke the branches into 2 or 3 pieces and put them away at the back of the house.

"Now it is nice."

From the living room, looking toward the salvia flowers, mother smiled. I sat next to her. In the sky flowed some clouds and the evening twilight was deep.

"I wanted to travel a lot—to see Japan and the USA⋯",

she said suddenly.

"Travel?".

"No— just like⋯"

She hid her smile. Maybe she was sorry to have said that because it looked foolish.

"Maybe there are not many people who have seen many other places like you, mother".

"Ya⋯"

She smiled again.

"Well, in North Korea, you have been to Hamheung, Wonsan and Pyongyang, then, in the South, Seoul, Mokpo, Jeju and Seogwipo, which is located in the southernmost part of Korea. You have even boarded planes. When you recover you can go sightseeing from Busan to Kyongju, then you can tour all parts of Korea. But visiting foreign countries is not easy for most people".

"Yes, yes, I have been on the airplanes", she said joyfully.

"Mother, Did you feed me mother's milk until I was 7?"

I wanted to change the subject, so I asked her coaxingly.

"You didn't want to be cut off from it—later you said the milk was bitter. You were so fretful, someone had to pick you up; only then could others eat their meal".

Always, mother was happily reminded of my childhood.

For me, I could not remember that time or how fretful I was, what the milk tasted like. What I remembered vividly was her face, like a bright spark in ash.

A spring day of very bright sunshine. I was on the roadside outside the neighborhood. Acacia were in full bloom. I squatted, looking at the main road, waiting for mother. I came there to see mother after I was crying at home. Finally, she appeared on the road full of sunshine. I couldn't remember how and from where she walked; suddenly she was on the road. Only the big smile on her face, something on her head, and her holding my hand. I remembered.

When I told the story above, she explained I was 5 years old (she was 29 years old) at that time and she was carrying a sewing machine on her head. Then I asked her why I couldn't remember being fed milk until the age of 7, although I could remember earlier times, and I thought it was an illusion. But she always told me it was absolutely real.

The memory of her face and the distance between her head and mine, the height of her and the holding of our hands, looking up at the natural location of her from me… Those memories made me stand strong and be stable in difficult situations.

Our big house was sold for father's maritime affairs and our family moved to a small property, then mother decided to support father's drinking with sewing. She suffered, working on the sewing machine for decades. And after all that, father ended his life at the age of 40 because of his heavy drinking.

Salvia in the garden got discolored, chrysanthemums had buds full of wetness around the salvia. Every Sunday, people from the church visited mother with the Bible and prayed for her. On such a day, she regained a little vitality. She showed Gaettong how to use a spoon as he sat on her knees and practiced 'Hal' to call his grandmother. But that vitality was only for the morning. I could see her health was getting worse by her face and her uneasy breathing when she slept.

One day her portrait arrived.

"I'm so sorry for the delay. I had to make an unexpected trip."

I thanked Mr. C for the picture he showed me. It was a real masterpiece. Mother was shown as a person in her sixties. I drank with Mr. C. When I drained a glass and saw her portrait on the table, I realized father's portrait was seedy. Putting on his black and white Korean overcoat, father showed himself in front of the family three times a year, on New Year's Day, Thanksgiving Day and his death anniversary, the 12th of September by the lunar calendar. Put with mother's portrait, father's picture looked really poor.

His status is not so good.

I stopped, shaking my head, and passed a glass to Mr. C. I remembered father, he might have been 35 or 36 years old then. He ordered me, 'Get the picture'. I ran straight to S studio. I knew the owner of studio was a drinking companion of my father. The studio and my father seemed to have settled the picture's charge because I went there with empty hands. There I met a man whose words I never forgot. The guy saw my father's picture near the owner, and muttered to himself,

"Is it a woman?"

I remembered the owner's height and the shape of his long face dimly but couldn't catch the other guy's face or what shape he was. But I remember his words, "Is it a woman?"

Woman?—What was that meaning? It might mean father was not good-looking or in good shape or rather too handsome. I came home gasping and gave him the picture and told him about the words of the guy. I watched his face carefully; he only smiled and explained to me the guy meant father looked like a girl.

'Girl?'

I laughed and went to the playground. I played with friends but felt embarrassed. If the guy thought of father as a girl, the point was that father was not looking good, not in good shape. He could have been right. I couldn't concentrate on or enjoy playing.

Really, father was like a woman. According to mother's explanation, he spent too much money on workers to continue his business. That proved it. I also estimated father was like a woman from the fact he couldn't refuse friends or drinking at a suitable time. At the end, he was fatally addicted to alcohol.

I had no idea how the size of father's original photo had been enlarged to a bigger one and used on the ceremony table. Father's picture was only as big as a business card when carried in mother's bosom, crossing the 38th parallel to South Korea. 20 years later, it might have been enlarged at a studio somewhere on Jeju Island. And that would have been the same time we settled down in Jeju.

"O.K. Cheer up"

I gave Mr. C one more drink and asked my wife to bring another small bottle. We drank three and half bottles, talking about how to take care of the plant in the pot. I almost said, "There is father's picture…", but I didn't. I drank at a breath and passed the glass to Mr. C, hiding my awkward feeling. And I held my breath to calm myself down. It would be enough to see father in his youth , it would be enough to have a photo of him in a white Korean overcoat. If I could change him to his sixties in a painting, it would not fit with mother's, or it would be worse. The thing lacking in father's picture was just its small size. I would enlarge it to the same size as mother's portrait and change the frame.

It was autumn one Sunday around sunset. I saw off the people who visited our house to pray. Mother was looking at the garden. She looked to have a little vitality. I began to water the plants.

"Son, let the salvia be thrown away. It is almost withered ···"

I stopped and turned my eyes to the flower garden at her fastidious voice. The salvia still had some flowers and leaves at the edge of their branches, near chrysanthemums half-blooming.

"Let's leave them. We can throw them away after picking the seeds."

"Seeds? I've already taken them."

"When?"

"Long ago."

Where did you put them?, I almost asked her, but I didn't say that. I repented making a careless mistake. She kept silent for a while, but, guessing my thoughts, said quietly,

"I put the bag of seeds on the shelf over a desk of the childrens' room".

I sighed deeply. Something hot was surging and digging up my heart.

"Tell Chadol not to hurt the chrysanthemums."

Her voice was dry again.

"Yaa, I got it. Never let her abuse them"

I answered with a bitter smile because it reminded me of an event a few days before. Two chrysanthemum buds were cut and thrown down in the yard. Mother picked them up then threw them away, calling Chadol. She blamed her with glaring eyes.

"You tomboy, why did you do such a naughty thing?"

"Gaettong asked me to cut them…"

Chadol stood calmly, showing a different attitude. Befor,e she used to run away saying, "I don't know, I didn't do that."

The young girl knew grandmother's serious fondness forand partiality to Gaettong. Grandmother always said Gaettong looked like her, with good sense and diligence. As Chadol expected, mother's voice became lower.

"Gaettong wanted them …"

I moved the orchid pots into the room, then sat down near mother on the living room floor.

"The chrysanthemums are late to bloom."

I lit a cigarette and looked at her face.

"It is too warm. Chrysanthemums bloom on cold days,"

she told me, looking at them.

The chrysanthemums bloom when it is cold, I thought.

No, it can't be true. They should bloom when it is warm. But maybe, she is right. No, she is wrong…

I laughed to myself inside my heart because it was funny that I couldn't get a conclusion or an answer.

"If I could live 'til this September, I would live 3 years more…", she muttered.

"Mother, what are you talking about?"

"No, you'd never understand that."

And she began to count the people who'd died in September, including my father and other relatives.

"It is almost built."

I pointed to the 19-floor K Hotel with my hand to change the subject.

"Mm…"

She looked up. They were working on the huge building (K Hotel), which was obstructing the eastern view. We could see their welding fires and hear the metallic sounds of iron reinforcing rods.

Mother often looked up at K Hotel unsatisfied. The 19-floor building had been built on the highest point of the city in the heart of downtown. The community didn't expect it to be so huge and imposing until it appeared. K Hotel was, they said, a cooperative venture with some Japanese plutocrat. People began to complain that its location was wrong because the hotel looked higher than Mt. Halla as days went by. They said it should be built outside the city. One day, mother asked me what that building was and I told her it was a hotel. Then she asked me again what the hotel was and I explained that it was a kind of inn. She understood that it was a restaurant.

"Hotel? Bullshit!"

She sneered again.

"Is it bad to earn money by building a 19-floor hotel?", I asked her with curiosity.

"To earn money? How much do they get?"

"As much as like raking in money".

"Mm—like raking?".

She laughed at my expression. Her face looked as if she was biting her molars and she said, "Everything is good when money comes? Looking down from the top of that building, they can see everything in our yard, even the figures sitting here."

"Ya, it's true—but who cares? They have to earn money from foreigners."

"Money is everything, money from foreigners, the owner of the hotel wants to become a fat pig".

I was sure that she was angry by the wrinkles around her eyes.

"A fat pig? You are speaking in a refined style."

I smiled.

She also had a smile but entered her room feeling cold. I sat there smoking. Mother had never been to school. Her resume would be written like this: Born on the 1st of July, 1900, married at twenty, had a son and a daughter, became a Christian in her fifties. She could not read even a phrase of the Bible but could be proud of herself for being faithful. The year 1900 was the start of the 20th century and she experienced 4 wars in Korea; the Russo-Japanese, the 1st and the 2nd World Wars and the Korean Civil War of June 25th, 1950.

During the Civil War of June 25th, she changed her name from Lee Hwoe Son to Geom Soon. It happened while I was away from mother for 4 years after the January 1st retreat.

"Mother, you have changed your name."

I was surprised.

But she said only, 'it happened,' and no more talking about that. The name, 'Geom Soon', felt a little funny because it reminded me of a popular song which was about a girl by that name. The song was popular at the shelter in Pusan, but I thought the name 'Geom-sun' sounded better than the name 'Hwoe Son'. It was easy to call and sounded soft. When I wrote it in Chinese characters, it had graceful lines, too. Anyway, the name, 'Geom Soon', was used when she became Christianized. When she asked me, "Please write my name clearly on the envelope", I used to pick up a pen and write that name on the envelope, first of all my work, even if I was busy. She needed that kind of envelope in many cases; when I won a literary prize, finished the military service, when Sung-ran and the other girls, including Chadol, were born. All the time, she wanted me to write her name 'Lee Geom Soon' under the title 'Thank You'. Then she put some clean bills into the envelop and kept it in a clean enclosure in a high place which children couldn't reach, and went to church, keeping it with her.

Her faith in God was the foundation of her simple personality, of which I was always proud, and I believed that was her virtue. This virtue of hers seemed to me as excellent as those of heroes all over the world. It might sound exaggerated, but her sense of reality and her ability to see the world looked much better than those of patriot leaders after the Korean liberation. I have some unforgettable words of hers:

'Too much greed is an injurious thing, trouble will follow behind you certainly'.

She confessed to shameful episodes from throughout her whole life. The first was in 1946; she was a victim of fraud. At that time I was in Seoul. She left her hometown and started a business with town friends. She traded some marine products with people in Pyongyang, receiving necessities of life such as rubber shoes and cereals during times when obtaining food was difficult. It was a very good business. But she lost all her money and had to stop the business. One day, after selling her products, she was walking along a street with stalls, then she met a man who sold good cloth for suits, very cheaply. All the people around him bought as much cloth as they could, so she bought 5 yards of that cloth in a hurry. Coming back to her inn and unrolling it, she found out its size was very small, only enough to cover a desk. She fell into a panic and went straight back to the street, but the peddler had gone. She realized she had been a victim of fraud.

The second unforgettable story of being cheated was in Seoul. During the '1.4 retreat', mother didn't leave Seoul. She earned some money by selling rice on a street stall at Dongdaemun market. One early spring day it was near sunset and she was going to her room at Won-seo dong with fast steps, passing along the uphill path on the west side of Changkyung-won. A young woman in clean clothes called to mother on the uphill path. The woman had a pretty face and looked around twenty-four. Smiling, she said,

"Excuse me, would like to buy high quality make-up powder from the PX at a cheap price?"

She explained to her that the PX was a part of the US army, the powder was made in USA, the price really cheap, someone would pay double to buy it. Then the woman took out a powder pack from her bosom and made mother smell its fragrance. It smelled so good that mother followed her to the place where the powder was and bought an armful of powder packs, using all of her money. Mother came back home and discovered that wheat flour filled the inside of powder packs. She didn't go to find the woman because of her Pyongyang experience. She was surprised.

"How could she do this with such a pretty face?"

She decided not to stop on the street in any case.

I have one more episode to add. I thought she had relished this event for long time.

During the Civil War of 6 · 25, I left Seoul as a soldier. Around October mother had to move to a relative's house at Wonseo-dong from the room in

Sungbook-dong. That relative's family left Seoul, except for a 70-year-old grandma. I thought it would be good for mother and the grandma to stay with each other, rather than being alone. Mother continued her business selling rice. She made kimchi, preparing for winter, and had no concern for water because there was a well in the yard. She thought they could survive the winter.

There were no people in ruined Seoul during the first month of the year. There was no one even to sweep the street, so the snow piled up. Chinese and North Korean soldiers entered those streets, covered with snow. They hurried to find a well because the water main was broken. Mother's house was not safe. Five North Korean soldiers, with two women soldiers, occupied the house. Mother and grandma gave the main room and the guest room to them and stayed in the room beside the entrance. Two women soldiers were in charge of cooking. The white winter went on, and around February, there were offensive and defensive battles between the sides across the Han River. Shells from the river smashed the north side of the mountain ridge near Changkyong-won night and day. Carriages of injured soldiers who were not taken care of properly, in tattered clothes, showed their defeat. One day, the soldiers searched the wardrobes in the house and separated only the white clothes, packing them in their knapsacks. At night, the two women solders came to mother.

"Please eat this!"

One of them, from mother's home town, Chungjin, opened the window and brought soup with beef. It was not the first time. Mother and grandma received that kind of gift several times, and they invited her, with the same Hamkyungdo accent,

"Thank you, please come in".

"Thank you",

Four women in a small room in candlelight in the middle of the room. The woman from Chung-jin said, "Thank you for your kind help during our stay".

"Help?"

Mother was surprised. The young woman told mother about their defeat without hesitation.

"We will leave early next morning!"

Then she begged pardon about the white clothes from the wardrobes, explaining their use as camouflage in battles in snowfields. She asked mother to forgive them. After some silence, the young woman proposed that mother go to North Korea with her,

"You are like my aunt! Would you like to go to North Korea with us?"

"How could I go? I even do not know if my only son's alive or not, who is in the South···"

The young lady could not talk any more, and, with a vacant look, she started to cry very sadly.

The next day they left in a hurry, their backpacks filled with white cloth.

"How sadly she cried ···."

Whenever mother talked about that episode, she was choked with sorrow. With tears falling in drops, mother worried about them; how they could walk those snowy roads again? According to her, even during the Summer Retreat their legs had swollen badly because of exhaustion and hunger. At that time they had eaten only durra powder until they reached the Tuman river.

After the retaking of the capital by South Korea, the relative's family came back to the house in Wonseo-dong, but mother continued to stay there in the room near the gate. In a military uniform, I met her in that room. I had sent her letters, but it had been four years since I had seen her last. The day before, the young woman from Chung-jin had wept and gone away from there, and the next day mother was weeping there, grabbing my hands.

September 17th was my father's memorial day. I had argued with my wife about the memorial service. I suggested that we should skip it this year because the process would be burdensome for mother when we prepared for it. My wife, however, refused because all neighbors knew about it and skipping the ceremony would have been ridiculous. So we decided to ask mother what to do. She wanted to invite only a few close neighbors and keep it simple.

During the memorial service mother, in a vivid voice, taught me many things, such as where I should put a liquor glass or fruit.

"You aren't like a Christian."

I said it for fun.

"Your father wasn't a Christian⋯but on my memorial day, you shouldn't⋯"

She spoke in a stiff manner.

Next day, I called my office, informing them that I would be late, and slept late. My wife woke me up. According to her, mother suffered from diarrhea, then vomited. She needed a doctor right away.

In pajamas, I went out. She was moaning. She said she needed to go to the bathroom again and she sat up. My wife helped her up. I told my wife to bring a chamber pot so that she could use it in the room.

Mother turned her eyes sharply to me and murmured that she was not that miserable yet. I insisted on her using it and called Dr. K. I told him about mother's condition briefly, and asked him to see her. In about 10 minutes, Dr. K showed up with a nurse who had Ringer's solution. He took her pulse and blood pressure and felt the lump in her chest, then made his nurse give mother two injections. Then Dr. K and I left her room.

"It's a miracle. She's still supporting herself."

He wasn't sure what made mother remain patient, her nature or something else, but he wondered at her great endurance. I offered him a cup of coffee my wife brought.

"How long will she⋯?"

I kept my voice down.

"Maybe this time will be the last chance. She has low blood pressure. I recommend that you not go far away⋯"

"But she doesn't feel any pain, then⋯?"

"Sometimes cancer doesn't cause pain. The patient might never feel any pain."

"Thank you for coming."

"Not at all⋯"

Because my wife was able to take care of things, including Ringer's solution, Dr. K and the nurse left. While mother was asleep, I called the telephone office man and moved the phone from her room to mine. I had suggested that before but postponed it because she seemed not to like it.

The next day mother recovered a little vitality. It was Sunday, so I could sit all day by her bed. The TV was turned on at a low volume.

"How are you feeling?"

"Hmm⋯getting better⋯"

She felt thirsty and asked for water. I poured some tea into a small cup from a kettle and started to put water in her mouth with a teaspoon. A sip, two sips⋯my hands trembled.

Her body used to be small but firm, but not anymore. Her earlobes, formerly large and prosperous-looking, now had shrunk. Only her high nose was still high because her face has dwindled to half its former size.

A blood vessel was beating in her throat. I braced myself.

"Is it enough?", I asked.

"Yaa⋯"

She answered with her eyes,

"Can't someone open my chest and clean it up?"

She stared at me.

"What are you talking about?"

I bit my lips.

"Doctor don't give me straight information⋯."

She talked to herself and closed her eyes quietly.

"There is a war again, right?"

Listening to her voice, I came close to her bed.

"Yes, but far from here. Many young men are dying."

"Young people? There aren't any Koreans, are there?"

"No, there aren't. Israel and Egypt, very far from here."

"Hmm⋯ water please⋯."

She asked for water again.

'Young people are dying.'

I said it unintentionally, but a purpose was contained. I hoped she would get some comfort knowing 'young men are dying'. I had had a similar conversation with my father long ago. He had been suffering an incurable illness for five months before he died. According to the death certificate, he had died of laryngeal tuberculosis, but he had got many kinds of illnesses. He probably had lung problems because of liquors including gastroptosis, At that time, the Second World War broke out. One day, I told him young people were dying. Father had gotten the meaning and said with smile.

"Yes⋯."

Dying at the age of forty⋯much happier than death in his twenties⋯he didn't say that. At that time he only showed me his smile, but mother asked me,

'There aren't any Koreans, are there?'

She felt sorry but consoled herself with the fact that they were not Koreans. She was worrying about neighbors, beyond herself; in other words, larger and broader than herself, 'country.'

I poured water in her mouth again and I couldn't stop my hand from trembling with many kinds of thinking.

Chrysanthemums were in full bloom. We had had the first snow on the top of Mt. Halla, but yellow butterflies were in our flowerbed.

"Who cut this? Hey, Chadol!"

Before long we would not be able to hear her speaking any more, I thought in front of the chrysanthemums. Next year, by whose hands would Salvia seeds be sown? My wife's or mine then. The paper bags of seeds were hanging on the shelf over my children's desks. Once sown, they would fill all the yard as scarlet as they were.

But before next year, I should have to handle mother's death. An old man in a village once said every death and birth in the world happened at ebb tide, then she would pass away at a low ebb of the Jeju sea⋯ at midnight or dawn⋯

'Mother, mother⋯'

I would call her name a few times⋯let her eyes close quietly, my children would stir, and then her body⋯an incense fire. Oh, at time all order would collapse. But I wouldn't be thrown into confusion. I kept it in mind not to forget to put a chrysanthemum jar before her departed spirit.

I would discuss the procedure of funeral service with church people, put a scripture phrase on the gravestone. Which would be nice? 'Whomsoever believes in him shall not perish but have eternal life', 'You will grieve, but your grief will turn to joy', 'To dust you will return.' They didn't satisfy me. Then what should I do?

A tiny yellow butterfly was flickering near chrysanthemums. Right, there was an eulogy for a graveyard by poet K.

Ye departed this life leaving only an insignificant sacrificial day.
No more past is in the world, you are making past.
By chance, a yellow butterfly is flying low over a grave,
This autumn the butterfly says repeatedly,
'There is a following beyond the sky.'

Si-Hong Koh

The City Under Martial Law

The Introduction of the writer

Graduated in 1972 from the Department of Korean Language and Literature, Jeju. National University New Writers' Award by 〈Monthly Literature〉 Member of Korean Writers' Association, Jejuhak Research Center.Commissioner of Jeju City Board of Education. Tamla Culture Award.
Publication : 〈A Handkerchief of the President〉, 〈The City of Commandments〉, etc.

The City Under Martial Law

by Si-Hong Koh

I opened my eyes with severe thirst. The telephone was ringing. The inside of my mouth was as dry as a paper cup. I picked up the telephone, closing my eyes.

"Hello…"

A clatter, then followed by a metallic sound like the powder of iron. With no words my answer was intercepted, one-sidedly. It was second time. It might be a wrong number. I had no one to call me in the early morning. I got out of the bed awakened by the ringing telephone and thirst. Trying to wet my throat with saliva I felt like vomiting because of the rotten dishwater.

What I remembered was, with someone's help, I got out of President Ji Yong Park's house. Holding my chin up under the tap I turned it on. Heat collected at the pit of stomach was washed out with the running water.

"Are you a deadly enemy of liquor, trying to drink all of it in the world? You are already fifty. You should know better."

"Don't worry about me. You'd better practice to be a widow."

"Venomous mouth. Your lips should be poisoned. The messenger from the underworld would take you, leaving out of your mouth!"

Wife entered mother's room, saying that speaking could be the seeds of trouble. The room was empty. Mother might go to the countryside. Her bed was not made. A strand of white hair on the pillow caught my eye. The room had repulsive smell.

"What's that?"

I asked my wife pointing with my chin to a bowl by the pillow.

"I didn't know how much malice she had······"

After wiping the floor wife went out of the room, bringing a bowl full of onion and garlic slices. Through the precipices of hotel buildings came the ridge of Mt. Halla. The window was ajar. I opened it wide. The scene of my hometown enveloped in flames was erased. It was dazzling. —Please, don't set the house on fire—the voice of mother, weighed down under the walkers, choked down a shot. The odour of garlic turned to the stinking smell of a rotten body. The people used garlic instead of disinfectant and deodorant. Holding funerals in hot summer, the pallbearers singing dirges used to take garlic in their mouth like candies.

"Didn't you hear me? Let's eat."

"I don't want to eat. Give me something to drink."

"There is no medicine and no doctors for grinding one's teeth. What should we do?"

Those days it was getting worse.

"After taking that, is it getting better?"

"She doesn't eat them, only breathe on them."

I smiled grimly standing in front of the mirror. The phone rang again. I stopped wearing a tie. I saw the reflection of wife on the mirror. I tried to listen to the voice from the handset.

"It's not needed, only tell him what I'm saying. I drank with Han-Goo Yang, so I'm giving him a piece of advice. Let him take care of himself. Anyway our country is an anti-communist nation. You tell him that, then he will understand."

I came out of the room leaving a metallic sound of locking. Last night at the house of Mr. Park, the voices heard from the opposite room, all were buried under the blowing horns. —Don't do a useless thing, Mr. Park. You'll get hurt. It would be no good to dig open an old grave left forgotten without posterity……

"What's the matter with you?"

Wife followed me, opening the entrance door.

"You don't need to know," I said turning my face away.

I smiled intentionally, seeing her scared face.

"What do you mean? You heard the telephone call, didn't you?"

"You don't need to worry."

I walked to the gate, glancing at wife furtively. She looked be struck dumb.

"I wanted to quit three or four years from now, but you insisted on me staying home, then I don't know what are you doing…"

When I started my business, I had my mind made up to do such and such things. —You will be killed! Do you want to die? Prepare to die! —From my childhood I became immune to death and the fear of dying. My chest bone was hardened by being kicked and struck with fists. On the contrary, I was afraid of silence. Silence seemed to me more than violence, more than fear.

A cement mixer truck came into the narrow side street. On the gate stairs I happened to open the mail box. A yellow envelope was there, folded in half.

Opening the envelope, I tried to read the sender's name, but there was no address or name. Inside the envelope there was a black plastic bag. A lot of black shadows passed in my brain.

Putting my hand into the plastic bag I shrank. I felt a shuddering more horrible than silence hit the pit of my stomach.

After a good while I spat at the gray thing dropped in the tire rut then went out of the side street. Looking around the street.

—Let's get rid of mice, today is exterminating day, put rat poison… —My brain was full of rumors about people and dogs killed by rat poison.

A "STOP" sign was written in white paint on the road like a barricade. I stood in front of the red light but I could not get rid of the after-image of the gray thing. A swallow sitting on the wire dived behind a building. Trying to forget about the dead rat, I crossed the side street.

The bus ran, turning widely on the slanted road. No Urinating. Post no bills here. No Parking. Keep off the gras…… I passed the department store, decorated with colorful curtains, buildings in the marketplace. To get out of the bus I moved to the rear. Don't Touch. A sticker was on the entrance wall of the bus. —The Five-Day Marketplace is always full of life. —Surged the voice of Mr. Park like the sound of the sea.

We quit, climbing Mt. Halla on the way. After eating lunch we descended the mountain. When we got the downtown it was fine again. Sending other employees home I and President Park got out of the at the entrance of the Five-Day Market. 'This landscape could be a feature article,' I thought.

"Hey, director Yang, how about running a risk?"

"You mean a penniless trip abroad?"

"I'd like to dig up 4 · 3 in full-scale. What's your opinion?"

I looked about instead of answering. Some people were getting in. It felt like being hit on the face defenselessly.

"Are you scared? Going to jail again?"

Mung-bean pancakes and raw rice wine were put on the table. 'What made him behave so haughtily- I wondered. 'Referring to 4 · 3, he is talking about revealing its truth, bringing 4 · 3. to light, even at the crowded marketplace···' I couldn't understand his innermost thoughts. To me, his attitude and speaking felt like urination on the road.

"I'm concerned for my wife and children."

The night sky of my childhood, with gunshot and bursting flames, obstructed my view.

"Surprising."

President Park put down his glass of rice wine on the table.

"Your referring to 4 · 3. was surprising, too. No kidding? You don't take 4 · 3. as one of multiplication rules, do you?"

"Frankly speaking, I thought it could be a sales policy. To increase circulation income. Another reason, the voice of the leftists growing stronger. But you make final decision as a chief editor, regardless of my idea."

I felt a tickle in my eyes from the sunlight through a hole in the tent. It looked like a searchlight. On the low benches were displayed weeding hoes, sickles, kitchen knifes, charcoal tongs, and shovels.

—I could get rid of you without leaving any trace, and no one could complain. By whom were you enticed to organize a club to reveal the truth of 4 · 3?

—We got together voluntarily, believe me. Only for those under a false accusation···

Again the foot in a military shoe kicked me in the shin. I bit my words between back teeth. Only a glow lamp was hanging in my vacuous brain. — Hey, a sophomore in a college, why are you frivolous without knowing anything?··· I almost shouted then what you knew and carried, a coup d'état, you are only in your thirties.

"Editor Yang, are you doing a memorial service with two glasses of wine in front of you?"

"Oh that's right. We need to create an atmosphere to erect a memorial tower at least."

I stirred the white dregs in the rice wine glass with chopsticks.

"Let me think. Well, it was an old grave left for forty years, we need at least forty days to prepare for its excavation."

—In this busy world it's not easy to wash off the dirt from one's throat. Why do you want to dig up a cemetery in the prohibited area? What can you get, except bones?— but I didn't say anything,

"I'm not imposing a burden on you, just I think you can pay off an old grudge by doing it."

Hearing him I understood this risky attempt could be a trap.

"If you start full-scale work I would be a windscreen for you. I already dropped a hint to the persons in the Anti-Communist Division."

He said he was ready to give up the copyright of the magazine house with his press.

I stared at his pupils through his glasses. What I had learned keenly from my past life was a need for taking strict precautions with the persons who knew me best. I had known Park for almost twenty years. When I was a reporter we were on a first-name basis, before I became one of his ink-smelling employees.

"What's your genuine design? You are not placing stones in strategic positions preparing for local autonomy, are you?"

"I want to find some ways for you to be tortured, through water and electricity."

President Park stopped laughing and assumed a solemn air.

"Before he died last year my father told me about his last wish. He wished me to collect data on 4·3 and write a book even though I would have to quit my printing work because of it. I wondered if I didn't know some secret in my family affairs. But there was nothing serious. Then father told me his story about 4·3. with some neighbours. One day father went to a high hill, near now White Horse Ranch, with a punitive force. They got information from a prisoner of war. They surrounded the hill and went toward the rioters' agitating point. But in a cave under the bush there were only a blood stained bamboo spaer and a sneaker without a sole. They were coming back without any gain then heard the crying of a baby. The punitive force searched around a stream for an hour, catching only a woman with a baby. Grabbing her by the hair they questioned her a lot. But her repeated answer was she had come to find her husband. A man in the punitive force disguised himself as a rioter, snatched the baby from the woman, and threw it to another man. They laughed saying something in North Korean dialect my father didn't understand. They passed the baby among four men as if they were playing basketball."

I puffed smoke for a long time.

"Let's go."

"Oh, how about one more bottle of rice wine?"

"I feel tired and need to go home and rest."

A woman carrying a baby on her back went away, buying a potted plant as small as a rice bowl.

"Don't you have courage to dig out a notice board in the prohibited area?"

"Testifying falsely in favour of the others is like murder itself.

Let's think for a while······ How about drinking some tea and going home?"

On the first day I went to work as a chief editor at a magazine my wife asked me to live silently. ─This is not a world in which you live alone, dear. Please, try to stay calm.─ I wanted to ask her if I had lived eloquently, but gave up.

I didn't work for a year and ten months after being fired from the newspaper publishing company. The summer in 1980 was especially boring, humid and hot. According to the laws enacted to control press activities, Hangdo Sinmoon─ a daily newspaper─ was to cease publication and I was deprived of my job. I killed time day after day with a pack of cigarettes and one-thousand bill my wife handed me going to work. Smelling wife's body odor mixed with chalk was the only joy left for me then. ─How long are you going to live on your wife's back? These days even one-year babies go around. I'd like give you some proofreading work at my office if you could put your pride in your pocket.─ I accepted President Park's offer. I had no other choice. I needed to stop being a unemployed husband and father. It was from that day I began to use honorific language toward him. After one year, President Park took over the publishing house which was under pressure of heavy debt. I'll entrust the magazine to you, so do it at your discretion. But President Park went to gather news with other employees, took pictures when the cameraman was busy, even did proofreading when it was short-handed.

They had already begun printing at the factory. On my way to the editorial room along the outdoor stairs I stopped at the entrance.

"You may think like that… But it would be an extreme view you insist that we have defeatism, a history of opportunists, need a mass struggle… You sound young, confined in your thinking. That would be killing the 4 · 3. generation twice."

I sat in a chair, greeting reporter Kim, talking on the phone, and others around him with my eyes.

"As I said earlier, we started in that way after working hard on how we should tell the story. So we are checking the collected data and doing on-the spot inspections. In the villages we are listening to their insistences, victims of both sides. You may know after participating in the last seminar, we were trying to edit their voices in our magazine this month."

I closed my eyes propping my face with my elbow on the desk. I was apt to be hunchbacked, internally and externally.

"It seems we need to hire some guards."

After hanging up, reporter Kim brought an envelope to me.

"Who was it?"

"He didn't give his name, only revealed he was a college student."

"What's the problem?"

"He looks like a student belonging to a social reform movement."

"It could be. I'm worried about them because they, the young, could be out of the original point of view."

Suddenly I remembered the fairy story of a sold donkey.

"They look very much interested in our article, but I wonder if we can gather the materials smoothly.

"Why? Is there anything wrong?"

"After you went home, President Park and his father-in-law got into a hot discussion. They both were drunk, the father-in-law even talked about taking his daughter from him. It was an almost fistfight."

"Seobook Cheongnyon Dan (one of punitive forces consisting of Northen Korean young men) might be their point of dispute, I think."

I muttered, opening the envelope. President Park once bragged at a drinking party that his wife was a daughter of the last royal family exiled to Jeju Island. During the 1 · 4 Retreat the family came to Jeju and continued staying here, so the family had no hometown.

"Can we ask him to donate this album to our company?"

I asked reporter Kim lifting the album.

"Oh, no way. He even didn't want to show it because it was the most important family treasure. I pleaded to borrow it. We have to give it back at least by tomorrow evening."

The album was an article left by the grandfather of reporter Kim's friend. I began to look the photos closely again from the cover as if I was examining antiques. The album was a record of the second regiment among the punitive force stationed in Jeju Island during 4 · 3. About 40 pages were printed with a black cover. A contour-line map plated with gold was on the middle of the cover. Turning the musty first page, five portraits were printed crosswise. His excellencies, the President, the Minister of National Defense, the Capital Defense commander, the regimental commander with a steel helmet, and the vice commander of the U.S. Military Advisory Group. All of them were in uniforms.

"By the way, it's the earlier site of the agricultural school."

Looking around me I found five or six reporters were surrounding me. On the gate and entrance of the building in the picture appeared signboards, saying it was headquarters of the second infantry regiment. Turning the next page I felt my heart beating fast, blood flowing into the crown of my head. Smoking a cigarette I took my eyes away from the album. The letters in "Announcement to the Brothers in the Mountain" scattered in the smoke.

> Brother, why don't you submit now? It's almost one year that you haven't seen your families and your hometown suffering snowy and rainy weather on the mountain. It's because you didn't know better and were deceived by one or two cruel and wicked communists. Think that we are all the descendents of Tangun, the founding father of Korean nation······

"I wonder you have already prepared pictures for tomorrow's news." I sent away the reporters surrounding me.

> But the benign president felt pity on your foolishness and came to this island with his esteemed lady. He ordered the Minister of National Defense to guarantee your lives······
>
> May 9, 4282 in the Tangun Era
> Seong-Mo Shin
> the Minister of National Defense

There were three photos under that announcement. In one picture a man with a white armband was thrusting his fist into an old woman bent with years. Another woman next to the old woman was hiding her eyes with her hand. Men in pictures all had their heads shaved, from kids to grownups. It looked like a playground in a school. Next day the 'brothers on the mountain' attacked a village, they usually forced the people to get together at a public hall.

I moved my hands fast. I had no time to read the explanations about the picture. Nightmare-like days in my memory went past by as if scenes in a film. In another picture, a jeep with a megaphone was running across the field, old men were making a coffin in front of a sharp pointed tower.

"Don't go to bed! crack, crack, crack······"

The night watchmen went around the village from 8 o'clock to curfew. The village people themselves formed and maintained the night watch system. We heard their voices all night as if good news. The nights were especially long. At first we imitated their words in the beds and enjoyed it like a funny game. Later it became boring. My brothers asked me to tell them fairy stories, I used to make new stories from the ones my teacher told. But only three or four stories I repeated. My brothers and I wondered how we could not sleep, they thought we were gods··· But our complaining to the night watchmen disappeared gradually. When the 'brothers on the mountain' came to the village throwing us into confusion, we could not hear the night watchmen.

As months went by and seasons changed, the words 'Don't go to bed!' sounded like 'If you sleep, you shall die!' to me. Sometimes, under the eaves of the houses on the street side, we could see a sack hooked like a flag with strange phrases and sentences: **Only traitors vote! No unitary government, no unitary election!**

As soon as the morning broke the elders removed that sack flag. I didn't understand what the words meant, but asking my father didn't solve the question. The elders only wanted us to be silent and give no answer to the police officers if they asked anything. I was afraid of the elders, they were like some monsters. Every night they lighted signal fires on the peak of the volcanic humps near village. Our village was a little far from downtown. Only in daytime police came to our village. At night it was the world of 'the brothers on the mountain'. Two days before the election village people were driven away from the neighbourhood by 'the brothers on the mountain'.

"This is like a homerun……"

President Park came into the editorial room and gave me an envelope. It was an envelope of condolence money.

"What is it?"

I looked at him suspiciously.

"Open and look what is inside."

His face hardened. I took out a piece of paper, it reminded me of the black plastic bag in the morning. With shuddering fingers I unfolded the paper. Two 10,000 won notes and a short letter came out.

> Mr. Park, the 4 · 3. riot was only a story of unhappy history. I got an impression that you are abusing police and punitive forces including Seobook Cheongnyon Dan chasing the story without considering the situation of the victims and the bereaved families. I think you are clever enough to do no more harmful things for yourself. Don't you think you need not make trouble?

I read it again. It might be one among the condolence callers, yesterday was the first anniversary of father's death and of President Park's. The handwriting was beautiful.

"Do you have anyone in mind?"

"Oh, you believe we have installed a fluoroscope in our house? I will hand down this to posterity."

"We should modify our way of collecting and reporting 4 · 3······ It seems to me."

"Hey, Miss Moon, two coffees, please."

President Park led me to the resting place. Building a darkroom they left an L-shaped room, and we used it as a resting place. There was a table between two sofas, and President Park and I used to sit and drink tea or discuss about editing. Other employees called it a secret room.

"Mr. Yang, did you mean it?"

"The adverse wind is too strong, I think."

"Oh, they say time is a medicine··· you became wise or weak?"

I put down my tea cup saying I was weak.

"Then why did you start the project?"

"In fact I had something bad this morning······"

Drinking coffee I told about the envelope without a sender's name on it, and the black plastic bag in it. I wouldn't let it known at first.

"I suspected. Before I woke up, someone called my wife and wanted to talk with me. Then the caller asked for the editor's number and she gave him your number. But don't take it seriously. As long as human beings rule the earth, violence continues"

After silence for a while the President spoke and advised me to push on. Absent-mindedly, I looked at him walking downstairs.

"Reporter Kang, can you give me the tapes, June and next month?"

"Which tape do you want?"

Reporter Kang brought keys and asked me. Everything about 4 · 3. we had recorded.

"Egg happening."

"Egg happening? Oh, yes."

I turned on the recorder, opening the magazine. I had not listened to the tape recording before editing, only read the scripts. After that issue was published I didn't read the article. It made me nervous now.

After some noise my voice heard. As an emcee I was explaining the background and the purpose of the meeting.

—This seminar is held by our Yongju Province Governor and Baekrok Research Institute attached to J university. This seminar can be called one of our groping efforts to reveal the truth of 4 · 3. after 40 years. After the April 19th Student Revolution some students had organized a group to find out the truth of 4 · 3. and began to collect data on it. But it had been dispelled by the 5 · 16 military revolution. After that some individuals had attempted to reveal the truth of 4 · 3. but had been forced to keep silence. Even some suffered physically···.—

I stopped and wound the tape forward.

—Here we have three guest speakers whose opinions are different. Let me introduce Dr. Gwan-Jong Yoo on the right of you. Dr. Yoo is now the director of the Research Institute for Far Eastern Problems, and he himself, belonging to regiment 2, participated the military operation to quell the riot during 4 · 3. The next is Mr. Doo-Man Choi, once a police officer. He was born in Hamkyong Do (North Korea), and from the year 4 · 3. happened, he has worked as a police officer here and retired here. And the next is Mr. Ong — Chan Kim, the director of Baekrok Research Institute. And we have three other speakers who didn't want their introductions······

It was a Saturday afternoon and the 300-seat hall was full. We installed a loud speaker for the crowd of people outside the building and on the street. First, when we considered holding a seminar on 4 · 3. I myself hesitated. Even though the gymnasium voting system had changed into a computer system, they would not leave people to rake up old prohibited ground. I'd rather mitigate the voice of the ultra-left and interview the victims of 'the brothers on the mountain'. I didn't want to draw sarcastic remarks that I was making an opportunity for my own personal affairs.

—To refer to 4 · 3. the rightists and the leftists use different words. From the view of the rightists 4 · 3. is a riot, armed revolt, incident. From the opposite side 4 · 3. is a mass struggle, public fighting, armed campaign.

The number of the victims are different. Government data looks

reduced, the other party's data looks magnified. The number of the 4 · 3. victims is from 4,200 to 100,000. And the population of Jeju at that time is not clear, from 276,000 to 300,000. And then, by whom, why, and how the 4 · 3. happened and progressed. One party insists that 85% of Jeju people were communists, and the other party asserts 4 · 3. was a public struggle of Jeju people and 85% of them participated it. The difference between their opinions is that it was a riot by the communists or it was a Jeju people's public struggle against outside influence. For your information, 6 persons in 10 were illiterate then. According to records, in every village in Jeju, public committees were organized first after Korean Liberation. They say Jeju was a nursery of the socialist movement. They also say Jeju people became communists 20 years after the liberation because villages were based on blood ties and the laborers, come back home from Japan, and the student soldiers gave them a communist's reverie. Byong- Ok Jo, the superintendent general at that time, suggested government should burn the whole island of Jeju drenched with gasoline to kill the 300,000 people there and protect the nation. Jin-Kyong Park, a regimental commander of the 11th regiment which stationed first in Jeju, gathered numerous Jeju people at the old agricultural school ground and announced them if any man did something for the enemy he would be executed by shooting immediately, and even he said they could kill all the communists by burning Mt. Halla by spraying some gasoline. He was a student soldier for the Japanese army before liberation and he knew well Jeju Island. I would like relate an episode before finishing my speech. Summer in 1949, Seong Mo Shin, the minister of national defence at that time, came to Jeju and at Gwandeokjeong square announced to the people his opinion that the officers and police from the mainland and Seobook Cheongyon Dan oppressed Jeju people and caused 4 · 3. The great reaction of Seobook Cheongyon Dan made the minister of national defence take shelter on a naval vessel. Seobook Cheongyon Dan was privately established, and came to Jeju in spring of 1947. It led an important role in driving out the public committees. About 200 persons in Seobook Cheongyon Dan were killed during the 4 · 3. subjugation process. The arrogance and aggressiveness of Seobook Cheongyon Dan irritated Jeju people badly. There were only 35 Japanese officials and 70 police officers to administer Jeju island under the rule of Japanese imperialism. During 4 · 3. 5 regiments and many other independent companies including Arirang, Baekgoldan, and Doksoori, were stationed in Jeju with assistant troops. And only in 1954 was the prohibition order against the entrance to Mt. Halla lifted, and it's very suggestive······

I felt the tape recorder stop, and quit looking out of the window. I finished reading through the magazine but couldn't help doubting the interpretation of 4 · 3. It felt like a puzzle. What was the use of this kind of work, and what kind of help history could it give an individual life, if restoring history like a broken jar was possible. I felt sudden 'spring fever'.

— At that time I cursed myself for being born as a human being. Nights were heaven for 'the brothers on the mountain' and the world of ghosts. After the black shadows stirred the silence the number of the lost men grew. The Kings of Hell, 'the brothers on the mountain', took only young men. They took everything to eat, wear and cover them. Many chickens and pigs, cows and horses were taken to the mountain and became communists. "Eat, eat more, in this world we can expect nothing, let's eat everything we can." Father killed our hens and often slaughtered pigs with neighbours. They thought feeding their children was better than being robbed of domestic animals by strangers. Two days before the election the people were taken to the Black Hill by 'the brothers in mountain' and came back home after the election day. They slept wearing clothes and practiced running away and hiding in their dreams.

In daytime it was the same as the night; people felt fear. The punitive forces and the police looked to be afraid of 'the brothers on the mountain' and came to the village only in daytime. They blamed people for their failure in defending the village, giving salt and bean-paste to 'the brothers on the mountain', being robbed of domestic animals. Some people were taken by the punitive forces and came back as dead bodies. The village road was a death road.

Village people kept sentinel duty at night because of 'the brothers on the mountain', and watched in the daytime to see if the police or the punitive forces came to the village. Children, 12-14 years old, usually watched in the daytime. We children played with the flags at the top of the pine tree in the back hill of the village. We played like monkeys moving from tree to tree and grownups worked. Then we laid down the flags saying 'here comes the black dog, here comes the yellow dog', then everybody stopped working. Some young men went away from the village and came back after the police left. To stop my youngest brother's crying mother used to say, "Look out, the rioters are coming!" at night, and in daytime, "Stop, or the police willcome and catch you." At the end of that year mother changed her words: "Rice with soy-sauce." We didn't have enough food so rice with soy sauce sounded as good as delicious meat and was enough to make us stop crying.

I pressed the button to hear the last tape. I wanted to confirm the recorded contents for a most unexpected situation. The seminar was begun at two but after three hours it continued, much longer than we expected. The last speaker was the director of the Research Institute for Far Eastern Problems, we had spent a lot of money to invite him.

—I won't try to discuss what the other speakers said, but I'm worried because they seemed to believe blindly the record written by the persons who participated in the revolt at that time and who now live in Japan. Toward the end of April, 1945 the Japanese army planned to move children, women and old men from Jeju to the mainland because the Japanese army wanted to prepare an advanced base for the landing of U.S. forces. But the first ship bound to Mokpo sank with 280 passengers on board because of the U.S. air force attack. So the plan was cancelled. Consider the situation in those days of liberation and the war; you can understand that Jeju would be a second Okinawa if the U.S. army landed at Jeju and fought with the Japanese. Based on the result the U.S. army saved the lives of Jeju people······ As far as I know, the candidate for the presidency from the Peace Party referred to 4 · 3. officially on November 30, last year. He came to Jeju during his speaking tour and declared if he became the President he would reveal the truth of 4 · 3. as well as other revolts in Geochang and Inhyokdang on the same level as Gwangjoo situation. He told us openly that he would have redeemed the honor of the falsely charged. But he failed to be President, and I'm really sorry for the victims of 4 · 3. and ···

The shouts outside the hall changed into curses. But the speaker continued indifferently. The atmosphere outside the building was unusual. Taking out my handkerchief I wiped sweat off my brow.

— One said that to reveal the truth of 4 · 3. in our history we should bring a lawsuit to the International Court of Justice, because among 300,000 Jeju people, 100,000 were killed during 4 · 3. I think it's a terrible misunderstanding. Even if we had democracy, the revolt by the Southern Communists could not be changed into a worthy and noble undertaking. Jeju

Island is highlighted as a sightseeing spot all around the world, so there should not be any tragedy like the second 4 · 3. revolt······

With the sound of breaking windows, yellow things flew in and the inside of the hall became a scene of confusion.

"Oh, you should not do this, oh, don't do that please······"

But the volley of eggs continued, with shouts and broken glass in wild disorder. The line of the microphone was already cut. Two police officers escorted the director of the Research Institute for Far Eastern Problems through the back door.

─Please, please··· I remembered my mother··· Please don't burn the house, please spare the lives of the children··· in my brain my hometown was in flames.

Bang, bang, bang···

"The rioters attack!" Father looked around stopping repairing the kitchen door with a hammer in his hand. "I don't care. I think they also have their ancestors so they will understand we are preparing for a memorial service." Mother continued grinding grain in a stone mill. "Hey, Han-Gu, hide quickly. Whenever the rioters attacked our village father made me hide in the forage pile. He thought I should survive even if all our family died because I was like a girder in our family. Here and there the neighborhood burst into flame, screaming and wailing spread.

"Ah, what are you doing now? We had order to evacuate the mountain villages, so go to the seaside village immediately."

Soldiers with torches burned the eaves of our house.

"Can you do this without notifying in advance?" "Would you please save the barn? Tomorrow is our memorial service day, so please······" Mother clung to the leg of the soldier going to the barn but she was kicked and fell down. "Oh, rather kill me!" Mother hung on the soldiers shoulder and the two rolled over the ground. The muzzle of the rifle came out through the armpit of mother then a shot was heard. I ran to mother screaming.

"Daddy! daddy!" my younger brothers shouted, crying like fire crackers. Then I found out father was lying dead in front of the barn. The cows, untied of reins, ran out of the barn treading on father.

"Oh, my dear!" Mother hugged father in her arms with her disheveled hair. Blood spread on the ground like Chinese ink.

"You, loathsome creatures, make my husband live again!"

"You touched the trigger, don't blame anyone!"

"This woman, isn't she a communist?"

Another soldier pointed mother with his gun.

"Oh. save the children, please!" Mother shouted crying.

The village was collapsed as the fire burned low. Gradually sounds of a child crying and women wailing stopped. The sky over the village was as bright as at midday. Somewhere from a seaside village a rooster crowed. Sitting like a statue, mother put father's head off her knees. I realized father couldn't go with us. I thought that hell might be like our burning village.

Mother threw sweet potatoes out of the storage pit. In the pit there appeared a room where we, mother and my two brothers and me, could sit down.

"Han-Gu, take the body of father there." Suddenly I was afraid of mother with her cold voice. Mother and I pulled the body of father with a rope and put it into the pit where the sweet potatoes had been stored. The body of father was curved like a shrimp.

"Dear, my dear, don't blame me for leaving you without giving any money or food for your travel to the world beyond. Don't ask me why your road to the other world begins with this pit for sweet potatoes. Forget this village, don't look back on this house where you and I raised our children, sometimes happily, sometimes sadly. Be a star in the night sky, be a sun and moon over the clouds and then look after our children……"

Using her both arms and hands, mother filled the pit with sandy soil.

For next month's magazine our staff and I finished an interview in the J village about 4 · 3. and arrived downtown late at night. I and President Park met reporter Kim's friend and his father. But our effort to get the album reporter Kim had borrowed was useless. We separated at midnight.

"Mr. Han-Gu Yang!"

"Who is it?"

I couldn't see anyone. Turning around I saw headlight at the beginning of the street attack my body between two walls with iron window bars along the narrow street. Instinctively I leaned my body against the wall and covered my head with two arms. Darkness like the black plastic bag wrapped my consciousness. The light of the car felt like a search-light, then the sound of walking feet with shoes on began to strain my heart.

Sung-Chan Oh

People Thrown Away

The Introduction of the writer

Born in Seogwipo, Jejudo.
Awarded in the Spring Literature Contest by Shinah Daily Newspaper (Division: Novels) Past newspaper reporter and museum curator. urrently president of the Jeju Branch of P.E.N. Korea, runs a publishing company, 〈Panseok〉 Yosan Literature Award, Korean Novel Award, Korean Literature Award, etc.
Publications : 〈Halla Mountain〉, 〈Portraits of a Dark Era〉, 〈Reborn as a Butterfly〉
Phone : 064) 721-1202, 011-9589-2134 / E-mail : ohsungchan@hanmail.net

People Thrown Away

by Sung-Chan Oh

Ms. Seong Sook Lee, in the Department of Women's Welfare in the municipal office, arrived at work at five to nine. She usually felt as if she had done a part of day's work already as she went to work after helping her husband and children.

The chair of her boss, the head of the department, was empty; he might have gone to a staff meeting. The chief of the department, who had worked for the ruling party during the last election campaign and been appointed, was fixing up her make-up using her compact. The chief greeted her with her eyes.

"Oh, Ms. Lee, could you go to the police station in Gangdam Dong? I'm too busy to go there…"

Ms. Lee felt a lump in her throat but she kept patient. Being patient had become common for her those days. She stopped unbuttoning her coat and looked down on the shiny desk; there many faces flickered, appearing then disappearing. All the faces looked worn with the burdens of life. As the business of the department was dealing with abandoned or missing children, loafers and vagabonds, it was not unusual for the staff to visit those kinds of places in the early morning. But recently it had been too often, never so frequently in the last 15 years. She wondered who was thrown away that day and how.

Ms Lee picked up her handbag on the desk and came out of the office, looking back the chief, who showed relief. Chief Kang at the children's department pouted her lips, glaring with her eyes when she met Lee's eyes. Like an auditory hallucination, Lee heard her soundless slander, 'Busy, busy, every day she says she is busy……'

Arriving at the police station, Ms. Lee saw an old woman with white hair. The old woman was sleeping crumpled and stuck on the bench near the wall. Lee realized immediately that the old woman would be her business.

"So what? I drank with my own money, What's wrong?"

A man, being questioned at the other side of the room, shouted, thrusting his fist at the police officer sitting in front of him. The officer was trying to soothe then asking him something. His voice was too low for Lee to understand.

"Don't you think so? What kind of wrong did I do? Why should I be here?" the man shouted again in a very clear tone. So his exaggerated attitude looked intentional

"You are still behaving wrong, huh?"

The voice of the police officer became louder. Then the man said nothing, lowering his head.

A police officer whose face was familiar to Lee came into the office through the side door. He looked like he was finishing his nightly duty and washed his face.

"Oh, you've come. A taxi driver found the woman crying alone near Dragon's Head and brought her here,"

he said to Lee, pointing to the old woman. The woman was still sleeping and her clothes looked tidy as if she had been planning to travel. Looked at closely, she was not so old, except for her white hair.

"What did the driver say?"

Ms. Lee needed any hint to find her tie-in. A tug-of-war between people throwing away their burdensome relatives and the government policy of putting them back in their places as much as possible, and it's usual and never-ending, Lee thought.

"According to the driver it was evening and he had a newly-married couple on a sightseeing trip. He was leading them to Dragon's Head, thinking that would be his last work for that day, then he found her crying alone sitting facing the sea. She might be touched in her head…"

The police officer drew a circle with his extended index finger around his ear. Nodding, Ms. Lee looked down at the old woman with sympathy.

"She said she had come here with her husband by ship. Her newlywed husband left her, saying he would come back after drinking a glass of rice wine, so she should wait for him there, looking at the sea. She was sitting there a whole day but he didn't come back. A newlywed husband at her age …… she might have some stories. She looked very hungry so I gave her instant noodles. She is only sleeping……"

'Some one had thrown her away,' Lee thought. The old woman reminded her of abandoned children.

—You play here, I'll come back after getting something delicious.—

Then a father or mother never came back. Ms Lee had experienced numerous cases and heard so many stories. This island, a place of exile long time ago, had changed to a strange place.

"I can take her, right?"

"Of course, We have a lot of trouble. You go through many hardships, too."

"Oh, that's my job."

But Ms Lee got a feeling of self-scorn that morning. She remembered the face of the chief putting on make-up. She erased her image, coming closer to the old woman. She was almost sorry to wake up her, because the old woman seemed to be in a really sound sleep. But she had no time to wait.

"Grandma……"

Ms. Lee shook her on the shoulder, feeling it gaunt in her thin sweater. She woke up at once, surprised. With bloodshot and almost hostile eyes the old woman looked at Ms Lee.

"Grandma, wake up. We should go…," Ms. Lee said sternly.

She knew by experience some strictness and a calm attitude were necessary to treat most vagabonds. She needed such an attitude to make them cooperate easily. The old woman looked scared at Lee's facial expression and stern attitude, and she got up, and sat down on the bench.

"Grandma, do you have anything to show me?"

Most vagabonds had something in their arms. But the old woman had nothing with her. She shook her head no after looking around the room.

"Did she have anything?"

Ms. Lee asked the police officer.

"I'm not sure if she had something or not before, but when the driver brought her here, nothing. The man she was calling her newlywed husband might have taken everything from her······"

"Thanks, anyway."

"Oh, you're welcome! You should not thank us"

"Then what can I say?"

"Well, ha, ha, ha,···"

Taking the old woman by her arm and coming out of the police stand, Ms. Lee was worried about the man who was shouting and swaying his body.

"Oh, another, again···"

The boss showed disgust when he saw Ms Lee come back with the old woman. He was trimming his fingernails and the chief's chair was empty that time. Ms. Lee didn't answer him, putting her handbag on her desk and taking off her coat. She hung her coat on a hanger.

"Grandma, come and sit here."

Miss Joo called the old woman, she might have felt nervous at Ms. Lee's coming into the office without saying anything and her tight expression. Miss Joo brought the old woman to the window side.

"What has become of her? Did you examine her belongings?"

The boss was much older then Ms. Lee, but his way of talking always made Lee angry.

"Nothing."

"Without any kinds of certificates?"

"No, she looked touched in her head."

Ms. Lee commented on her situation after some hesitation. She looked in the mirror coming back to her desk. As usual after feeling anger or worry she found a shadow around her eyes. She herself couldn't understand why she got such shadow.

"Are you going to make her our guest? Send her here."

Ms Lee thought the boss might be bored then. One of the first-class war-disabled, he always thought the world treated him badly by not paying him enough attention. From the beginning of the year when he had come to the department as a head, he was dissatisfied. His dissatisfaction often broke against the staff as they worked. Miss Joo brought the old woman to the boss with scared eyes. The old woman didn't sit down, even though there was a sofa for visitors. She only looked at it.

"Grandma, where are you from," the boss asked, giving her a searching glance up and down. But the old woman looked at him with hostility. He was not sure if she understood him.

"Hey, where did you come from? Didn't you understand me?"

His voice became louder then. The old woman gave no answer, instead she shook her head.

"Oh, then you are from the mainland, right? Who on earth brought you here by ship? What are they doing at the pier inspection station?"

"She didn't come alone, They said her newlywed husband brought her."

At Ms. Lee's answer some young staff laughed furtively.

"Where was she abandoned?"

The boss seemed to decide the case as a desertion.

"It was not certain if she was abandoned or not, she was crying alone at the seaside late at night and reported to the police station."

"She might be thought of as a ghost⋯", the boss said to himself and stared at the face of the old woman until they felt embarrassed.

"A woman crying alone at a remote place at that time meant something⋯"

"By the way, how many grandmas like her came here this year?"

"Old people… already 5 or 6 cases, maybe."

"We need to collect statistics separately. It is not a common thing, absolutely not. People are throwing away their mothers and fathers like trash. Oh, my goodness…"

"The world is going to the dogs…", the driver Mr. Choi concluded with the boss's usual opinion. The boss agreed.

"Right, everyone knew it…"

The boss looked around the office as if to confirm his opinion. But the staff already stopped their furtive laughter and turned their heads down to their papers like young chick pheasants.

"Miss Joo, check her body."

The boss shouted to her, hesitating near the wall. She came close to the old woman with strict caution as if the old woman would spring on her at any time. Miss Joo touched the sides and chest of the old woman.

"Nothing…"

"You think you would find something in that way? Ah?"

The boss clicked his tongue, showing his dissatisfaction. He stood up suddenly and touched the old woman abruptly in her chest. At his rough manner the old woman seemed startled, but did nothing as if she was tamed. But Ms. Lee saw the old woman's facial expression became dark.

"What should we do with her?"

The boss turned to Ms. Lee, asking how they could handle her.

"Well, we should send her to Somangwon first and then we could try to find her relatives…"

Somangwon was a temporary protection institution for vagabonds in the city. There vagabonds from everywhere, young and old, women and men, were 'protected'. But it was a dirty and miserable place called by another name 'beggars' meeting place'. Somang meant hope, and people wondered why its name was Somang because there was no hope there. Ms. Lee felt it was a terrible paradox whenever she visited.

"How many people are there now?"

"As of yesterday, one hundred and three."

The staff member who was in charge of Somangwon answered quickly.

"It's full, then."

"Right. It could be inconvenient for now. But it's OK."

The staff member showed his belief that such people deserved inconvenience.

"Then, bring her to Somangwon first. You must find her tie-in. We cannot forgive them."

The boss spoke loudly, raising his right hand. He had lost two fingers as a soldier and wore bandage on his right hand.

"Yeah, that's right. But we've got no hints. Grandma, where is your hometown?"

But the old woman didn't answer only looking vacantly at them.

"Don't you know the place you lived, uh?"

The boss pointed out the window over the sea. But the old woman shook her head and even her body.

"Oh, no! She even doesn't know where she lived, where she was born. No certificates. What a pity!"

The boss looked at the indifferent old woman for a while, hopelessly. Then he said, giving up, "Mr. Choi, drive her to Somangwon with Miss Joo."

"OK, give me any papers you're sending there."

"Tell the director to try to find her relatives and bring her back home."

"Yes, sir."

Two people went out, helping the old woman on both sides. Ms. Lee sighed shortly. She got over the second wave of work at last, she thought.

Ms. Lee wondered where the chief was, gossiping and rounding the departments. Ms. Lee worried about that because she could make a false charge against her when she came back. For example, the chief could blame her for making a decision without asking advice. It was the boss who had made the decision, so Ms. Lee could leave the case with him, but she could not help worrying.

After lunch the chief came back and showed no concern about the old woman or decision.

"There is no better way than sending her to Somangwon and trying to find her relatives. Thanks for your trouble."

The chief showed a frank attitude. Ms. Lee admitted the chief was really political. Dividing people into two parts, pushing the other party, taking needy persons, making them the same party,… Ms. Lee could see figuring of the chief clearly.

"You should hurry up trying to find her tie-in. Before long it will be the end of the year. I wish we could make our institutions as empty as possible…"

She had the same wish. It would be nice if they came back to their family before the end of the year. Some families would be anxious to find them, Ms. Lee thought. Diverse ads in the newspapers, 'Darling, come back please, Hyon Bok is crying for you,… The faces of the missing children printed in color on the packs of cigarettess…

Ms. Lee also remembered an unfortunate affinity. When she went to Seoul to receive some education for civil servants she stayed with other workers from a different city. During the stay they ate together, sharing the same room. The other worker was in the women's welfare department, too.

"Do you want to know how we deal with them?"

Her eyes were shining. Ms. Lee didn't answer but was curious about how they were working with the vagabonds.

"At night we go riding the last bus to the border between our province and another province. At the end of a bridge it is another province⋯"

"Then, what?"

Ms. Lee asked her urgently.

"We left them with some money needed to come home."

"Oh, Goodness! How much is that money for homecoming?"

Ms. Lee uttered the word then asked her.

"In fact, our superiors don't want spend money on such things. Building a bridge or institutions would attract public gaze⋯"

"They talk about welfare, only words, without contents. The money should be enough to help them go back home and start again."

"Administrative organizations or religious groups are the same, they had only lip service to offer⋯⋯"

"Don't they come back, the people left at the border?"

"Why not? They go around again and again. At dawn we find many new vagabonds in our province, God knows where they are from."

"Then it is only a first-aid treatment, sending and receiving vagabonds among provinces."

"You got it."

They stopped talking, only looking each other in the eyes rather bitterly.

Ms. Lee called the counseling office at the harbor. She explained what the old woman looked like and asked them when she came to the island.

"The old woman you are talking about didn't enter the island. As you know we always send all the vagabonds on the ship back to their places immediately."

The man on the phone was busy trying to excuse himself with a hoarse voice.

"I'm not blaming you. I need her background to find her relatives and send her back home. If she came here by the ship she might have some certificates."

Ms. Lee was trying to persuade him.

"Well, I don't know anything. The old woman didn't go through the harbor."

"I got it, then."

Ms. Lee realized the empty space between them on the line. She hung up.

There was nothing to talk about with him. After sitting for a while she called an office at the airport. Miss Jeon answered.

"Consultation office at the airport, How can I help you?"

Her feigned voice was ticklish.

"This is the woman welfare department in the municipal office. We had an old woman who had no relatives or tie-in."

Ms. Lee explained about the old woman. But Miss Jeon was smart enough to get out of the affair.

"You know nobody can board the plane without certificates. They are under strict watch."

That was true. As for the old woman, it would not have been possible to travel on the flight. Then, where had she come from……

"OK, I got it. If you find out anything about her let me know, please." Ms. Lee hung up the phone.

"Try to get rid of trouble and end up with twice as much."

Chief Kang at the Children's Department interfered. In the office only she remained with her paperwork. She had been working with Ms. Lee for long time and she understood Lee even though she had an evil tongue.

"Don't try too hard. You have shadows under your eyes again"

"I should have become immune to my work by now. But it always bothers me whenever a new case happens. It hurts me⋯"

"Well, where does this world go?"

Chief Kang threw her pen and went out of the office, dragging her slippers. Ms. Lee telephoned Somangwon.

"Hello"

The director answered. He was always blunt and everybody disliked him. But Lee knew he was a warm-hearted man. Lee asked about the old woman. His voice became louder.

"Oh, that grandma! Her Yukjabaegi (a brisk and lively folk tune with six words to the line) is wonderful, fantastic."

"Really? Does she sing well?"

"You come here and listen to her, then you will understand what I mean."

Any way it was good for the old woman to recover her peace. Ms Lee hung up and Chief Kang came in with two cups of coffee.

After work Ms. Lee went to Dragon's Head Rock. She thought it would be in vain but she went there. Lee remembered a legend about the rock: A long time ago tyrannical government officials killed a commander, then his swift horse became a rock. It was standing in the wind and the waves were beating upon its foot.

Although it was not high season, some travelers were taking pictures on the seashore. On the wall of rock, along the stairs down to the coast, you could see carved coarse letters; most of them were visitors' names.

―Human beings, why do they want to leave the traces of themselves during their short lives. Maybe they are keenly conscious of their short existence in this world······

Ms. Lee wondered where it was that the pupa-like old woman cried, where her newlywed husband ordered her to wait for him looking out the sea. She looked around the empty benches made of artificial stone. But there were no marks of the old woman. Ms. Lee herself knew her expectation was useless.

A telescope was installed there and a newly-married couple passed by it. No one was interested in that telescope. Maybe everybody was too busy to use it. Walking down the stairs to the coast, Ms. Lee stood in front of the telescope. Lee took out a coin from her pocket, then inserted it in the telescope stand. She could watch an enlarged sea gull flying alone over the waves. What does the sea gull's flight mean to me? Lee switched the direction of the telescope and found out an isle far away.

―Oh, that might be the isle named Gwantal (deprivation of an official post). Government officials condemned to exile on our island, they said, came by a ship, on their way they passed that isle and were stripped of their post. Then how could they keep their post until they sailed to that isle?

Maybe they were overwhelmed by the Mt. Halla and its daunting appearance, so they gave up their government posts, taking off their official hats at that site. Hundreds of officials were exiled and came here during the

Lee dynasty. This island was a place to send burdensome people away then, now is a place to send the unfortunate again.—

The island was suddenly open to the mainland in the late 1960s. In New Jeju Town more than one thousand miserable women were selling their smiles and bodies. Ms. Lee also knew in Old Jeju Town, near the east and west piers, a lot still came back again and again in spite of expulsion. Not only the 'migratory birds' but also many other women followed men who wanted them anywhere. Ms. Lee understood their numbers, their lifestyle and way of thinking.

Sexual morality had changed as the island had gotten many visitors. Ms. Lee often got reports of babies abandoned in noodle boxes at a park bench or communal lavatory. Newborn babies, red in towels in inns, were only writhing after a long time crying. No one had cut their umbilical cords. They usually had clenched fists as if showing their hostility toward the world.

Ms. Lee remembered a bad case of an abandoned baby. An owner of a small hotel in downtown notified her about it at dawn.

—Ah, the mother has run away. The baby is dying. Hurry!—

It was not far, so Ms. Lee ran to the hotel. The hotel was isolated at the end of the street. Lee could see marks of blood from the garden through the corridor to the doorsill. In the room a baby was bloodstained on the mattress. The placenta was dropped at the doorsill and still connected to the baby with the umbilical cord. Lee thought the mother might have been scared after giving birth to the baby and run away.

—A woman checked in at midnight. I thought it was strange but didn't expect an incident. We thought some one had been murdered, seeing the blood when we got up in the morning.—

With the talkative owner Lee cut the dry umbilical cord. The baby boy kicked some times. It had well-balanced features and was healthy.

—Ah, what a handsome baby!—

The hotel owner was sorry for the baby. Lee came out of the hotel with the baby wrapped in a hotel towel. Doctor said the baby was unusually strong, one in ten thousand. But the baby had to live dumb and blind because they cut the umbilical cord too late. It was sent to a temporary home for infants, then adopted to the USA.

Ms. Lee came to Yongdam Rotary passing by the elevated bridge and saw a beggar sitting in front of her. Lee couldn't tell if the beggar was a man or woman. The beggar was wearing many layers of clothes and hats and looked like a hairy dog imported from foreign countries. Ms. Lee got a shock on seeing him. Most beggars were familiar to her because almost all the downtown beggars had been to Somangwon. But it was new one. —Where did this beggar come from? How should I deal with it—Ms. Lee was worried without finding any solution. She followed the beggar as if attracted by magnetism. The beggar walked, staggering, then ran toward garbage cans. In the second garbage can the beggar found a coat without a sleeve. After examining it, the beggar put on the coat. Ms. Lee followed the coat, which was stained on the back. But arriving at the another garbage can she ran away, almost vomiting at the sight of the beggar picking up and eating some noodles with bean sauce in a plastic bag from the garbage can.

While running Ms. Lee realized her own tears and worries about the beggar. Instead of the desire to vomit Lee felt a lump at the pit of her stomach. The wind was blowing against her, she was walking in a dust of sand. Lee wanted relief and thought of the director of Cheongsongwon, an orphanage. The director was also an orphan himself, and was once a teacher in a high school. Lee had met him in the high school. In several ways he had helped her. When Lee called him, finding a pay phone on the street, he answered.

"Where are you? I'll meet you there now."

Lee's voice might have sounded urgent to him. Lee named a teashop and hung up. Lee waited in the basement teashop. She could remember only miserable affairs. It was last August she had run to an orchard on hearing news of an abandoned infant. It was a really hot and humid day, Lee was sweating as soon as she got out of the car.

—We thought it was a cat mewing. Although it began the day before yesterday, we didn't think it was a baby……—

The owner of the orchard looked struck dumb. Following the owner, Lee went into the orchard. Through the tree branches Lee felt the strong heat of the sun and heard something like a cat mewing. There was an infant was wriggling on a girl's high school uniform blouse. Some tangerine leaves were on the dry body of the infant, its small heels bruised.

—What a tenacious life—

The owner talked gibberish.

"Oh! Dear me!"

Lee walked back from the infant when she found some maggots hatched in its groin. The owner noticed them also and wiped them out driving out the blowflies and cursing the unknown mother of the infant. She wrapped the baby with the blouse and a towel. Ms. Lee couldn't get rid of a feeling the maggots were eating into her own brain.

The baby survived three days under the hot sun, was sent to a home for infants and was one year old.

— How ruthless life is —

Then in front of Lee the director had a seat, asking what bothered her. He looked at Lee closely. Lee tried to smile but failed.

"Oh, you look lost today……"

— Yes, I got lost. —

Ms. Lee wanted answer him but failed, too. Drinking their tea Lee told him what happened to her in the morning and the whole story about the old woman.

"Really a matter of grave concern… The number of the abandoned children was 8,500 in eighty, it is growing continuously every year, 12,100 in eighty-three, 13,300 in eighty-seven."

The director said gloomily.

"It's not only the children, old people are thrown away these days. What should we do?"

"We need a new policy to support paupers economically, and a new concept for families. I think we urgently need a sense of common solidarity……"

"How can we change the society and people's way of thinking?"

"I must not give up. Religion and education…we should do our best in every field. Working as an orphanage director I often find springs, vivid fountains. There are people helping others without showing themselves."

Ms. Lee was nodding as she watched the director's face. It might be the reason she needed him, not her husband.

"Let's go out and enjoy the cool wind of the evening and have dinner together. We need to save our strength for the dark corners in this world."

Walking to the counter he paid for the tea. Ms. Lee followed him up the stairs.

The woman welfare department inquired about the fingerprints of the old woman. After a week, the investigative section of the police station sent them a report. The address of the old woman was known. Ms. Lee asked the administrative office of that township by long distance. After trying several times she got information on the old woman.

"Oh, that grandma, it's a shame……"

"Why is it so?"

"She has no husband, no child, she's only a pauper……"

Pauperdom would be similar, no difference wherever their home was. Ms. Lee knew the lowest stratum of society was covered with dry leaves—like paupers. During the election campaign, just a bag of rice was enough to get their decision. Lee herself had worked to give them gifts for the election.

"But the old woman insisted her husband brought her here."

Ms. Lee asked the administrative office worker.

"You should not believe her. She had been mentally-handicapped from her childhood. Once she got married but returned soon. We got the report card on her family."

"Then how could she come here, to a far island?" Lee asked.

"She had stayed with her mother, over eighty. These days whenever she had fits she resorted to violence and grabbed her mother by the hair saying she wants her husband. So the relatives got some money and decided to send her to a prayer house. It was her cousin by a maternal aunt." The officer answered. Then Ms. Lee understood the situation. She felt a ringing in her ears, a hard thrashing on the shoulder. She sat down exhausted. The she wrote down the report on the old woman.

"There is no other way. We should reduce the number of the people at Somangwon by the end of the year. You had better go with the old woman to her home town···"

After meeting the deputy mayor, the boss drove Ms. Lee into a corner.

The chief, waiting for the boss at her desk, demanded Ms. Lee to be quiet. Ms. Lee turned to Miss Joo. But Miss Joo was not reliable.

Ms. Lee felt sorry for her husband and children on each occasion. Lee asked her mother to help the family and applied for the money to bring the old woman to her hometown. She got the money but it did not make actual expenses. She had to accompany a mad woman, a risky trip. It was windy when they got on the ship. Did they feel similar, the exiled in old days? Ms. Lee wondered. She was shaking even in her heavy clothes.

When they were far away from the island the old woman, watching the sea leaning against the side of the ship, began to sing Yukjabaegi. Ms. Lee suddenly collected her mind.

— I'm going, going and going — but
— where is the place I can go —

The voice of the old woman sounded clear and she looked not insane.

Ms. Lee wanted to cry, she wanted to pray to the waves. She asked herself what she could do for the old woman.

A couple of sea gulls were struggling lonesomely, flying against the wind and waves.

Children's Literature

The Light House / Mount Halla 2
The Isle of Mara / Mount Halla
A Paper Piano
Meeting the Sun
Seolmoondae-halmang

Young-Ki Kim

The Light House
Mount Halla 2

The Introduction of the writer
New Writers' Award by ⟨Children's Literature⟩ in 1984
Publications: ⟨Dreams of Wings⟩, ⟨An Islet⟩, ⟨Birds' Talk⟩. etc.
Address : 1180-21 2-Do 2-Dong, Jeju, Jejudo, Republic of Korea
Phone : 064) 757-1459, 011-695-1459 / E-mail : yykk99@hanmail.net

The Light House

by Young-Ki Kim

When seagulls
Fly over the sea,
Ducking,

The light-house, too,
Raising waves,
Flies up
Turning into a white bird.

When fathers
Cast nets
Into the night sea,

The light-house also
Casts a net
Into the night sea
To pick up stars twinkling there.

Mount Halla 2

by Young-Ki Kim

She dreams in secret,
Like inner leaves growing in the rain,
About having her own wings.
Her dream grows,
Like bracken sprouting in the mist,
And wishes for flying around in the sky.
She raises behind the down-pour
The dream about the wings
That were once hidden under the armpits
Of the legendary baby-general in old Tamna,
And even tries flying, covered by the fog.

*According to a Jeju legend, there was a baby born with a pair of wings under his armpits. People took him to be a great, powerful man. The local officials thought he would grow to be a dangerous threat to them and that he should be killed immediately. The parents of the baby got rid of his wings by searing them with a hot iron to protect him.

Jong-Doo Kim

The Isle of Mara
Mount Halla

The Introduction of the writer
First recognized in 〈Sonyeon〉. Past president of Jeonnam Province Children's Literature Association and Jeju Province Children's Literature Association. Currently president of the Korean Writers' Association, Jeju Branch.
Korean Children's Literature Award, Socheong Literature Award.
Publications : 〈What Is Life?〉 〈Garden with the Sun〉, etc.
Address : 2423-15, Bonggae-Dong, Jeju, Jejudo, Republic of Korea
Phone : 064) 721-1658, 019-721-1658

The Isle of Mara

by Jong-Doo Kim

On a fine day like this,
She doesn't put up a sail.
Tooting her horns to drive the fog away,
She only wants to take a look
Of Mt. Halla beautified in the day-long sunlight.

On a day like this,
Mt. Halla allures her,
With his ever-changing face of light.
With gently ducking waves,
The smiling eyes of the blue sky
And the dazzling sun,
Mt. Halla seduces the isle of Mara,
An innocent island girl.

On a day like this,
She anchors herself
And sings airs of love,
Enjoying the views of the famous spots in Jeju.

Until his shadow comes over her,

Then she drains hard liquer glasses
With overnight visitors on the grass.

On a fine day like this, with her beacon put out,
The Isle of Mara sweetly falls asleep,
In the bosom of Mt. Halla, her eternal home.

Mt. Halla

by Jong-Doo Kim

The island children grow in the bosom of Mt. Halla.
Whether from the seashore,
Or from the mountain,
They all grow as they look at Mt. Halla
Like the true island children.

Climbing up Mt. Halla everyday,
Walking around in it everyday,
Drinking at its fountains everyday,
And listening to its stories everyday,
The children of Jeju grow.

Mt. Halla raises the children
Who were born on the Jeju Island,
The children who grow,
And settle down there,
Into the people of Jeju.

Soon-Bok Kang

A Paper Piano

The Introduction of the writer

Born in Seogwipo, Jejudo.
Awarded in the Spring Literature Contest by Shinah Daily Newspaper (Division: Novels) Past newspaper reporter and museum curator. Currently president of the Jeju Branch of P.E.N. Korea, runs a publishing company, 〈Panseok〉. Yosan Literature Award, Korean Novel Award, Korean Literature Award, etc.
Publications : 〈Halla Mountain〉, 〈Portraits of a Dark Era〉, 〈Reborn as a Butterfly〉
Phone : 064) 721-1202, 011-9589-2134 / E-mail : ohsungchan@hanmail.net

A Paper Piano

by Soon-Bok Kang

A stir occurred in the theater, Moonyeheogwan, where beautiful music flowed. It was because the marvelous thing happened so quickly. The marvelous event that cannot be was caused by the girl, Banji, who was playing the piano.

Banji, who was deaf, practiced playing the piano so hard that her fingers were numb. She practiced Chopin's Etudes so hard that she could play it even with her eyes closed.

While she was waiting for her turn to play, she kept saying the same prayer again and again. "God! Help me play well. Please, give me wisdom through every knuckle of my fingers and help me to not make a mistake. She prayed, breathing a deep breath, 'Hoo!', until her turn came round.

At last her turn came round. "Now it's the turn of Banji Lee, a 5th-grader at Hahyo Elementary School. She will play Chopin's Etude." After MC said that, Banji went to the piano on the stage. While she was walking to the piano, the audience in front saw her stagger a little. She saw the audience open their eyes wide, but she bowed modestly. Then she put her fingers on the keyboard of the piano. "Hey! Please help me. You, every note and every rest, please, help me," she muttered to the keyboard very softly. She had been thinking of the keyboard and the notes as her friends.

Ding Dong Dang, Ding Dong, Ding Dong Dang.

The sound of the piano Banji was playing began to ring through out the hall. The audience was listening to the music, thinking that the ten-year-old girl played the difficult tune very well.

Then, in a moment, Banji stood up very slowly. Her fingers were not on the black and white keyboard of the piano, but in the air. She moved her fingers very hard in the air. But the strange thing was that still music was flowing.

"What? That... That child······?"

"That's the show. Maybe they are playing a record."

"No. It seems they are not playing a record."

A fuss broke out here and there. Banji's parents and her teacher were in a cold sweat watching her. Some of the audience, listening to the music with their eyes closed, also stood up in surprise.

Banji walked to the center of the stage moving her fingers in the air as if the keyboard was in the air. The impossible which could not be was happening now. How could you believe it if the piano no one was playing sounded by itself?

People in the hall were now standing blankly with their mouths open and Banji continued to play the piano in the air.

Banji was normal when she was in the first grade. She liked the piano unusually much but her family was not rich enough to buy a piano. When she got some money, one thousand won, she said that she was going to buy a piano with her money. Her mother smiled and said, "Do you know how much the piano is? It costs one hundred times as much as one hundred times the bill, one thousand won, that you have."

From then on Banji saved her pocket money, and also began to dream she was playing the piano every night. She even dreamed she was flying on a winged piano.

As she entered the elementary school, she came to know that many classmates were taking piano lessons. And she became diffident when they said, "Czerny," or "Beyer".

"Mom, please let me take piano lessons," she asked. But her mother couldn't answer then.

One day her mother drew a keyboard of a piano on a hard cover, put it on the desk, and fixed it with Scotch tape. She also colored Do, Re, Mi, Fa, So, La, Ti with the rainbow colors, red, orange, yellow, green, blue, indigo, and violet. Banji sang 're(d), ye(llow), bl(ue), re(d)' instead of 'Do, Mi, Sol, Do.'

"Mom, it doesn't make a sound because it's a paper piano."

"Think as if it were real, not paper, then it could make a sound really."

Banji played the paper piano as soon as she got up in the morning. She only knew Do, Re, Mi, Fa, So, La, Ti. But she practiced so hard that, gradually she could play some children's songs. When the paper keyboard wore out, her mother drew a new one and fixed it.

"Mom, a piano class opened next to Yungun's house. Sinae takes a lesson there."

When Banji became a second grader, a new piano class opened in her neighborhood. But her mother couldn't even conceive the idea of having her daughter take a lesson there. Her living conditions became worse because of the IMF. So she was even sadder than her daughter. She said to her daughter that she would let her go to the class in the case that their living conditions would be better.

Ding, Dong, Dang.

The sound of the piano from the class could be heard at Banji's house on sunny days. On such a day Banji was excited while her mother was nervous.

"Mom, that sound is beautiful, isn't it?"

Banji was happy to go to church on Sundays. When she went there early, she could sometimes touch the piano in the church. She touched it stealthily, standing beside the instructor of the choir who was playing the piano.

"Maybe you want to play it. Will you try to play it? Come on, push the keys."

The instructor would put Banji's small hands on the keyboard. But her hands suddenly became stiff and she wasn't able to push the keys properly.

In spring, Banji's village was filled with the fragrant tangerine flowers. Her parents came home late from their work in a big orchard and Banji was walking around near the piano class without having done her homework.

On a foggy evening, Banji listened to a beautiful sound from somewhere. She had never heard such a clear tone before. Unconsciously, she began to walk slowly in the direction the sound was coming from. She didn't know how far she had come nor where she was. Then she, who was moving slowly, suddenly screamed "Aak!" and there was a metallic clang at the same time.

"Ah! Aak! Mommy! Mommy! Ouch!…"

She was caught in a mouse trap. After crying and moaning, she was found unconscious with her left ankle almost cut. Because of the accident she went lame and had trouble listening. Later she became deaf. Her mother didn't draw the paper keyboard any more after ripping the one off the desk. She even changed the channel when she saw scenes piano playing on TV. But Banji still liked to listen to the sound of piano, next to the wall of the class. The worse her hearing became, the more closely she tried to listen. Having watched her, the teacher in the piano class sometimes took her to the piano and let her touch it. But her mother was angry about it, so the teacher didn't do that any more.

"Banji, why don't you pray! Jesus can hear you. He can do everything. And he will do something for you if it's right," The choir instructor said softly whenever she met Banji at church. Banji couldn't hear the bird's singing or the stream's murmuring any more.

"I really feel cramped about my hearing disability for hearing. I think the blind are much more tired than me."

She could understand people who were poorer and had harder lives than herself.

One day the instructor visited Banji's house.

"Mrs. Lee, Banji has a beautiful soul and she's very nice. Please let her play the piano. I'll teach her. I'm sure she'll do well. Of course I understand how you are hurt and sad. But I think you must let her do what she wants."

Thanks to her, Banji started learning to play the piano. When she was in the 5th grade, she became a very good player. Banji said she could hear nothing but the sound of the piano. But her mother was disappointed once again, hearing the doctor say; "She can't hear. In this case it's a kind of hallucination. Sometimes such an occasion arises. If she is absorbed entirely in something, she can feel a ringing in her ears. It's tinnitus."

Her mother thought Banji told a lie to play the piano, and that made her sad.

> A Piano Contest for Elementary Students through the Whole Province
> Sponsor: The Samda Daily News
> Date: September 9, 1999

The instructor who had taught her piano was excited, showing Banji the ad in the newspaper.

"Banji, you can do it, can't you? Now we don't have much time. Let's practice it."

The contest was two months from that day. The instructor chose 'Chopin's Etude' which Banji had practiced before, for the contest.

"Ma'am, it would be great if there weren't five staffs in a music book. As Mom taught me, I can say the name of notes even if I see rainbow-colored notes instead of black notes, although they are all mixed," said Banji while she practiced.

"How?"

"Do is red, Re is orange, Mi is yellow, and high Do is dark red, low Do is light red… then we can make notes by adding to them tails without staffs."

"That's a good idea. Then little children or people with lower I.Qs. would be able to read them easily." The teacher agreed with Banji.

It looked fantastic, but it seemed that she was destined to do something important, well, because she had had such a fantastic idea.

Watching her daughter, who was forgetting how to speak because of her hearing disability, Banji's mother was nervous that she could play the piano well in front of large audience. But Banji was so absorbed in practicing as to forget meals, and she was looking forward to the day.

At last the day came. Many people came into the Moonyeheogwan Theater. Banji was praying again and again while she waited for her turn.

"Please help me. Although I can't hear, please help me play well and make my parents and the teacher happy. Please help me."

After praying many times with her heart, she went on a stage and played 'Chopin's Etude' very well at first, without any trouble. And then her fingers which were hitting the keyboard very hard, came off the keyboard as if they were pulled by something.

A close look revealed circles colored with the rainbow colors. They looked like soap bubbles and also looked like tailed notes, around Banji's small body. These tailed notes flew above the audience and were gone.

"Oh! My! What a……!"

The impossible thing happened in the theater, and all in the theater started stir because of it. But the notes were dancing wavily as if they had nothing to do with it. Now Banji had finished playing and bowed modestly. Somebody clapped his hands and others also began to clap hands, standing up.

Banji's heart was hot like it was burning. Still the notes were dancing wavily as if the music had not ended.

Jae-Hyong Park

Meeting the Sun

The Introduction of the writer

Past president of Jeju Children's Literature Association, vice president of Jeju Writers' Association. Kyemong Children's Literature Award.
Publications: 〈Searching for Gumdoongee〉, 〈My Friend, Sahmrye〉, 〈Sad Songs of Dahrahngshi Hill〉
Address: 300-94, 3-Do 2-Dong, Jeju, Jejudo, Republic of Korea
Phone : 064)753-1288, 011-694-1266 / E-mail : pa1429@shinbiro.com

Meeting the Sun

by Jae-Hyong Park

The wind blew. Coming across the blue sea, the wind stroked my face and blew my hair again and again. I could see the isle of Gwantal far away beyond the waves on the horizon. I looked at it, as it stood alone in the sea. The wind touched my shoulder, but I couldn't stop my feeling of sadness.

Father didn't come back. The day before yesterday he went to the sea in the evening and never came back. He used to come into the garden smelling fishy and walking with long strides, wearing elastic boots. He usually brought some fish for the family meal. It felt like a lie that he was not coming.

Mother was crying as if father had died. She remembered father's saying that a fisherman could die anytime, and she was worried that those words caused bad luck. She went to the pier and the maritime police agency, walking tearfully with short, quick steps.

I felt sorry. I felt as if I had pushed father into the cold sea. It would be me, no one else, to blame if father couldn't come back. All my fault.

On that day our teacher scolded us for not being quiet during the classroom cleaning time. But we continued talking whenever our teacher couldn't see. Eun Jeong suggested going to Topdong to play.

"Hey, let's go ride bikes. We can see the ocean, too."

We all agreed to her proposal. I thought it would be funny to ride a bicycle or roller skate in the Topdong square. After finishing the cleaning we all started for Topdong. We walked to Topdong, passing by Dongmoon marketplace, along the fruit and clothes on display, then to the Dongmoon Rotary and toward the Sanji road. We all laughed and talked glibly like sparrows in the bamboo trees. Cold wind came over the sea but we didn't feel cold. We walked with a light step.

"Let's go looking at the fishing boats," Yoo Jin said when we passed by the fishery joint market.

"O.K."

Eun Jeong agreed and the other children turned toward the quay side. I didn't want to go the wharf where small fishing boats were packed densely. But I had to follow them, unwillingly. Then I met father there.

"Hey Sami, where are you going? Oh, your friends are here, too."

Father was taking a box of fish out of the boat, then saw me and shouted gladly.

"Well, well, to play······"

I was embarrassed meeting him in front of my friends, and couldn't speak any more.

"You, be good friends for my Sami, get along well," Father said with a bright smile and took some money out of his pocket and gave it to me.

"Sami, take this money and buy some bread and eat with your friends."

I wanted to run away because my friends would not like the smell of fish around my father's body. My father and mother always smelled fishy and mother used to call it the smell of the sea and didn't care. But I disliked the smell, worse than that of a rest room. I hesitated and didn't receive the money. Then Binna held out her hand.

"Thank you. We like eating."

Binna received the money as if she had come into an unexpected fortune.

"Thank you!"

Other friends said thanks, too.

"Have fun!"

Father smiled happily and walked to the fishery joint market with the box of fish on his shoulder. We went to the west pier through the side street. Then Binna held the money high with her thumb and index finger frowning.

"Oh, fishy smell! The money smells fishy. Sami's father smelled the same. My mother used to say money is dirty, I understand now."

Binna fanned herself with her hand in front of her nose and frowned as if the money was a dirty thing.

"You continue doing this?"

I was angry and looked at her, making a wry face.

"Why, anything wrong? Are you angry at me because I said the money smelled? Do you think I'm lying? Then smell the money! How terrible!"

Roughly Binna held out the money up to my nose.

"Why are you doing this? Nothing is wrong."

Jiyon tried to stop our quarreling. But I couldn't stop.

"You mean my father's money is dirty. Tell me then, why did you receive it? Why? Tell me!"

"What? He gave it so I got it. I didn't ask him for money. You didn't receive the money, so instead of you I got it. Here is the money. Get it. Dirty money!"

Binna threw the money to me as if it were trash. The money fell to the ground, then blew away on the wind. I didn't try to grab the money. I turned around crying and ran to our house. I heard friends' shouting. I didn't even look back.

"Did you enjoy yourself?"

In the evening father came back with some nut cookies for me and asked me affectionately. Father might buy the cookies at the penny candy store near the market with the fish-smelling money from his pocket.

"You are a really good father. Sami must be happy."

The woman at the store might flatter father handing him the bag of cookies. Father might be happy thinking of me, glad with the present, and walked smiling along the market road to home. The nut cookies had a savory odor, but I frowned.

"Why did you come to me in such a shabby clothes? I felt ashamed in front of my friends."

Unexpectedly my mouth made these reckless sentences. I didn't like the odor from my father, I didn't want my friends to meet my father in his working clothes, but I didn't think my father was shameful. But I already said he was a shame, as if I were an actress and had practiced those words.

"Oh, were you ashamed? I didn't know that."

Father looked surprised and embarrassed. Blushing, Father went out, coming back late at night. He was drunk.

"A shameful man, that's me."

Father talked to himself as if he were acting in a drunken and disorderly way. At once I realized it was because of me.

"Why are you a shameful man? You are the mainstay of our family. Don't say that in front of our children."

Mother reproved Father for acting like that. She thought he was drunk but I knew he wanted me to hear. I knew how badly I had behaved and regretted my words, but couldn't get out of the bed.

Father continued drinking for two days. He didn't go to the sea, only drank and sat with a sad face. Mother was angry at his drinking too much.

"What's wrong with you? New Year's Day is coming. We have to prepare the worship service for family ancestors and buy some new socks for children."

"O.K. I have to earn money. I am a bug only for money."

Mother was late from her business and father got ready to go out to the sea. I felt he was talking for me to hear. I couldn't apologize to him, only listen to his gravely walking steps. I thought his shoulders were weighed down.

Father didn't come back home. He should have come back in the morning but his boat, "Venus", didn't appear. The other boats all came back, cleaving the waves. They said there had been a sudden gust on the faraway sea, but every boat was all right. Father's boat never came back, as if it had forgotten to return. It was news that father's boat was missing; they announced that every newscast. Mother repeated coming and going between the pier and the police.

I was really sorry. Even though I didn't say it to Father, I was sorry. I felt it was pitch dark. What should I do if something had happened to father. In a state of anxiety, I couldn't sleep at night. When I closed my eyes father appeared with a sad look.

The sun was going down into the sea and the cloudy western sky became red.

'Where will Father be? Is he drifting about because of engine trouble, or floating on a plank in the sea?'

Looking at the evening sea I prayed father would be all right. I wanted to do something for father. I couldn't just wait until he came back. 'What can I do for him? How can I make him come back?'

Looking at the isle of Gwantal I tried to imagine father's face, tanned in the salt wind, and his whitening hair.

Without noticing it I shed big tears.

Looking at the sun for a long time I remembered a story in a book: If you prayed for something to the rising sun, your wish would come true.

'Can it be true? If I pray, Father will come back? Really? Yes, he would come back, that could be true.'

I wanted to believe the story. In the dark I walked droopingly back toward home. At the marketplace lights were bright and people were busy selling and buying things. No one looked sad. Mother's place was empty. She used to sell the fish father brought. Mother was not at home, either.

"You believe Father will come back, don't you," my brother Seung Bin asked me with a worried face.

"Of course. He will come back. Don't worry. Let's eat dinner."

I ate with him and did the dishes and try to read some books. But I could see no letters on the page. I was concentrating to hear father's boot-steps. Mother came back at midnight and went to bed without eating supper. I woke up early in the morning. Mother was sleeping. She might be tired, I guessed.

Opening the door, I went outside. It was chilly and I felt cold all around my body. I went to the main road through the side street lighted by street lamps. I was scared walking the road alone. I could see no one around. But I imagined father's face.

'I should pray for father's return.'

I hurried to Sara Hill and stepped on the stairs, looking at the stars in the sky. Praying in my mind, I climbed to the pavilion. From the pavilion I looked at the eastern sky. The morning star was shining above Wondan Hill. Before long the sun would come out of the horizon. The white sea waves were rushing into the beach.

I clasped my hands and turned to the east.

'Sami, don't worry. I will come back. I am busy with a big group of fish.'

I imagined hearing father's voice in the wind. 'That's true. Father will come back. Right.'

I prayed again and again, looking at the eastern sky. The sky was dim but brightening.

Young-Ju Jang

Seolmoondae-halmang

The Introduction of the writer
Secretary general of the Jeju Branch of P.E.N. Korea.
Korean Children's Literature Award, Korean Children's Story Writers' Award, Green Literature Award.
Publications: Several children's storybooks. 〈Storytelling〉, etc.
Address : 102 Deokjin Apts, 49-4 Donam-Dong, Jeju, Jejudo, Republic of Korea
E-mail : kp4075@hamail.net

Seolmoondae-halmang

by Young-Ju Jang

Once upon a time, older than the days long ago, when tigers smoked, there lived a person who was called Seolmoondae-halmang in Jeju Island. ('Halmang' means 'grandma' in Jeju dialect, so Seolmoondae is the grandma's name)

Do you know how big Seolmoondae-halmang's body was?

When she slept, for a comfortable sleep, Seolmoondae-halmang lay down with Mt. Halla as a pillow, putting one of her legs on Gwantal Island off-shore of Jeju City. When she did washing, she had to sit down on Mt. Halla to wash her clothes. Now can you imagine how big her body was?

When Seolmoondae-halmang got bored, she picked up stone blocks from the top of Mt. Halla and threw them into the sea one by one. They became islands, thus demonstrating she had incredibly strong power.

The huge, powerful woman Seolmoondae-halmang was wearing a skirt. Nobody knew who made it or how large it was.

One day she was making Mt. Halla, moving dust away in her skirt. The dust was leaking through holes in her skirt. At each place the dust dropped a volcanic hump was made, 360 humps total. The last place, where she put the rest of the dust down, became Mt. Halla.

After Seolmoondae-halmang finished making Mt. Halla, she sat down on its peak to rest. Then an edgy rock poked her buttocks. She got angry and pulled off the summit of Mt. Halla and flung it away. What about the hollow place on the top of Mt. Halla? It became Baekrokdam Lake. The edgy rock which was thrown away became Mt. Sanbang. That's why today the girth and depth of Baekrokdam Lake and the girth and hight of Sanbang are the same.

One day, Seolmoondae-halmang was sitting on Mt. Halla staring at the ocean. Then she had a desire to urinate. She pissed just where she sat down on the top of Mt. Halla. You may guess how strong the running urine was. It was strong and abundant enough that it caused a flood. People suffered disaster and one part of land was separated by the urine. Later, that cut-off land, they say, became Woo (Cow) Island.

There is a curious high rock at Seongsan Ilchoolbong hill which was used by Seolmoondae-halmang as an oil container for a lamp. First she lit a fire under the rock. But it was too short for a fire cup, so she added one more rock to the first rock used as an oil container for a lamp. Now it is called Deong-gyong-dole, a lamp stand stone.

Seolmoondae-halmang was huge and strong, even though she was a woman. She always wanted to wear underwear, so one day she gathered people to make a bet with them.

"Listen everybody, let's bet! If you make my underwear, I will build you a bridge to the mainland. Then you could go to the mainland on your own feet," she said.

But no one could answer quickly. They hesitated looking at each other before making a decision, because they couldn't guess how many bundles of silk would be needed to make it. They had no idea how big it should be, as you can probably guess.

"Anyway just let's bet, and try to find a solution as we go along," Seolmoondae-halmang suggested.

People wanted to come from and go to the mainland easily. At that time, passage was difficult, and sailing on a small boat from Jeju Island to the mainland was quite dangerous and inconvenient. Many people had bad accidents while they were sailing. So they made a decision to make underwear for Seolmoondae-halmang.

But they had a problem. There was not enough silk, even though people collected as much as they could. The reason was the size of the underwear. There had to be 100 bundles of silk to complete it. It was not easy to collect as much silk as that. (One bundle of silk is fifty rolls of silk).

So the people started working hard to get an enormous amount of silk. They bred silkworms and wove silk for a year without doing any other work. But, unfortunately, one bundle of silk was still lacking. They grew uneasy.

"We should talk with her and let her know the truth. Then let's ask for tolerance," someone said.

People went to visit Seolmoondae-halmang and explained their problem. Her answer was callous.

"You think about it. How could I wear such funny underwear which has a big hole in it? It would be ridiculous."

In fact, wearing torn underwear, as you may guess, was very embarrassing in the old days, too.

Despite the people begging her over and over, Seolmoondae-halmang never listened to them. She was playing with earth then she threw it away and gave up building a bridge. You can see the traces on the Jochun village coast and off-shore area. They are the remains of Seolmoondae-halmang's plan to build a bridge to the mainland.

If Seolmoondae-halmang's bridge had been completed at that time, there would have been lots of people driving between Jeju and Busan or Mokpo today. If people had worked much harder to prepare 100 bundles of silk, if they could have had only one more bundle of silk, we would have a highway to the main land now. Who knows?

One day, Seolmoondae-halmang suddenly disappeared. Where had she gone? It was midsummer. The weather was hot and much too sticky. There was not any shade to take shelter from the heat. Each time Seolmoondae-halmang took a step, she sweated a lot, as if it were raining. She tried to find water to take a bath and get away from the summer heat.

Seeking water, Seolmoondae-halmang arrived at the seaside near Mt. Halla.

"This is perfect; it should be cool. Shall I take a bath here?" she said to herself, looking around, and jumped into the water without thinking.

After entering the water Seolmoondae-halmang never got out. The depth of the water was enough to drown her. These days people still call the place Mooljangori (deep water).

Drama

Invocation Dance

Il-Hong Jang

Invocation Dance

The Introduction of the writer

Born in Jeju in 1950. Recommended and first recognized by 〈Modern Literature〉 in 1985. Awarded in the Spring Literature Contest by 〈Hahngook Daily Newspaper〉 Grand Prize in the Plays Contest by the Korean Ministry of Culture and Tourism. Korean Literature Award, Korean Playwrights Award, Monthly Literature Dongli Award.
Address : 102-1101 Huyndai Apts, Nohyung-Dong, Jeju, Jejudo, Republic of Korea / Phone : 010-3119-4353

Invocation Dance

by Il-Hong Jang

Dramatis Personae

Tansil
Mother
Gumnye
Juno
Drummer

⟨Stage⟩

On the right, there is a thatched-roof house with maru (a wooden-floored open space) with a room on each side. At the end of maru is a kitchen.

On the left is the gate, from which a stone wall goes around the house. In the yard stands a bead tree all alone.

With the curtain up, it's a summer dawn, Mother and Tansil being fast asleep on the maru.

Various common and hour-glass type drums, ceremonial swords, bells and colorful robes, etc. hung on the maru wall suggest that this is a shaman's house.

Mother: (She talks in sleep.) Rioters, rioters! Please, spare us! Our Pa has no faults. We're on the side of the mountain people! ⋯

Soldiers are coming, soldiers! Cops are coming! Oh, please, don't kill us! He, the father of my baby, is not a rioter. Please, don't kill him, please! (Sobs.)

Tansil: (Wakes up and shakes Mother.) Mom, mom.

Mother: (Opens her eyes.) What, what is it?

Tansil: A bad dream?

Mother: (Sitting up.) Dream? No, it's not a... That's right. It was a dream.

Tansil: You wept and sobbed loudly.

Mother: (Grinning.) Did I? I've had the same dream on the first day of the exorcist's rite.

Tansil: (As if intimidated.) Today again...are we having the rite?

Mother: You, fool! You don't know the Yeongdung Gran'ma's rite? (Hitting her own shoulders with fists.) Oh, my body, how exhausted! (Lying on her belly.) Please, tread on my back softly.

(Tansil treads on her back as told.)

Oh, good! How relieving! That's enough! (Sits up, massaging her own shoulders.) Did you hear the sound my bones made while you were treading them down?

Tansil: No.

Mother: My rib bones seem to be moving around on their own, chet! (Suddenly becomes serious.) Even if the sky shatters over our head, you should come with me to the rite today.

Tansil: I won't. (Moves toward the edge of the maru-floor.)

Mother: (Approaching Tansil.) Refusing your own mother will bring to you a lightening bolt out of the blue sky!

Tansil: (In a weak voice.) I can't help it, can I?

Mother: You are really obsessed with dirty spirits.

Tansil: (Showing little interest.) Why don't you rather tell me about your dream?

Mother: The dream? ⋯ It's very strange. There, a male shaman with a cowl suddenly appears from nowhere. He gives me a ritual sword and a bell and disappears. After a while, I see him beckoning to me on a steep hill. Following his desperate gestures, I try to climb the hill all night and wake before reaching him. Strangely enough, after the night of such a dream, we always have the ritual.

Tansil: There's nothing strange about it. Simply a bad dream about the rioters.

Mother: Rioters? (Nodding.) Maybe so. During the Third of April incident, my father died at the point of a rioter's bamboo pike, his intestines squeezed out. My first husband was shot by the government soldiers. When we found his body after two days, crows had already eaten his eyes and nose. Perhaps his was a milder case, for the gorge was filled with bodies with white skulls. (Shaking her head.) What a horrible scene it was! I can't help shuddering only to think of it.

Tansil: Your first husband?

Mother: Not your father, that man was⋯

Tansil: Why do you always avoid talking about my father?

Mother: No use talking about it. It's all in the past and gone.

Tansil: Oh, I remember. I had three family names. When I entered the primary school, I was Kim, and in the third grade I was Kang, and since the sixth grade I,ve been Pak after your surname. (Laughing sarcastically.) What a terribly blessed girl am I! (Stops laughing.) Whose daughter am I?

Mother: ······

Tansil: Which one was it?

Mother: Dead.

Tansil: (Abruptly sitting up.) A lie! You, a liar!

Mother: (Angrily.) What a way of talking to your mother! Watch your mouth!

Tansil: Don't treat me as a kid any more. All I want is the truth. Tell me the truth!

Mother: (Glaring at Tansil sharply.) All right. I'll tell you. Listen carefully. It was unusually cold that winter. November the nineteenth. Giving you birth, I was still lying in childbed when your pa, drunken, suddenly opened the door and shouted at me, "Which hooligan got you pregnant to bring this bastard!" (Crying.) Grasping my newborn baby, I went back to my mom's house that night through a snowstorm. Are you still curious to know who your father was?

Tansil: (Sarcastically.) Was that so? It was a hooligan that caused my birth!

Mother: He washed his hands twenty times a day. He followed me to the outhouse and kept watch of me to earn his peace of mind. That kind of a man he was. I could hardly breathe under his squeezing all the time. Without the two holes of my nostril, I couldn't get going.

Tansil: Don't talk about Father again.

Mother: To think of him even now, I get terrified and chills run on my back.

Tansil: I had a mysterious dream, too.

Mother: What was it?

Tansil: Performing the banishment releasing rite.

Mother: Banishment releasing? You?

Tansil: Ya.

Mother: Who's dead?

Tansil: A man.

Mother: What kind of a man?

Tansil: ….

Mother: You make me feel more curious.

Tansil: (As if talking in delirium.) Sun flower, cockscomb, dahlia, Indian lilac, morning glory, afternoon lady…… Ah, how happy I am!

Mother: What? What are you talking about? You gone crazy? You seem to need a rich course of obsession ritual performed for you.

Tansil: Was your father on the side of the government soldiers?

Mother: There were no your side and mine. We were on no sides.

Tansil: Wasn't he killed by the rebels?

Mother: Rioters or soldiers, they were all alike. They caught and killed us innocent villagers like frogs and locusts. In a neighboring village happened things like this. The soldiers gathered all the villagers in the school ground and suddenly shot at them. After the soldiers left, a man who survived the shooting crawled down to our village and asked for help. Because of an informer, he was caught and roped behind a jeep and pulled away, screaming for help. When the jeep made a stop, he was dead, his body torn like a rag, it was told.

Tansil: Such a terrible thing really happened?

Mother: (More passionately.) When soldiers swept through the village, there left only five with scrotums. The blood of the dead formed a brook and the tears of the survivors formed a river. The revengeful spirits of the dead hovered around the sky and they are still roaming around somewhere near the place. Tansil! Who could relieve them of the spite? Only mediums like us could do that.

Tansil: (Shaking her head.) I will never be a medium.

Mother: (Soothingly.) Hey, your grandma was one, too. We are a five-generation shamans' family. If one doesn't succeed the shamanism, our ancestors' spite would throw disasters on us. The way you came back home like a sick dog should be the sign of the anger of Samshin spirit, don't you know?

Tansil: ······

Mother: Recently you speak like one who lost her mind to a hallucination. All the hallucinations are bad goblins.

Tansil: I am a goblin, too, mom.

Mother: Are you crazy? A lecherous goblin must have possessed you! If we don't chase it away with a obsession rite, you won't enjoy your life to the full.

Tansil: I'd rather die than to live like this.

Mother: You spent your first ten months in my belly and don't you know anything about my mind yet?

Tansil: Do you anything about my mind?

Mother: ······

Tansil: Do you know what I dreamed of when I was a child? I wanted to be a nurse with a white cap on the head. I wanted to have an ordinary life. Mother: Our shaman ancestor will not let you alone. He will catch you and make you serve our god. No one can escape him. It's not me who gave birth to you. Samshin Gramma, our god of birth, blessed you as such. That's your fate.

Tansil: I shouldn't have come back. No, I shouldn't···

Mother: (Emphatically.) You are to come back!

Tansil: Mom, please! Please let me alone! I'll go back to the main land and do whatever I can. A servant, a sales girl, anything...

Mother: No, you won't! You made a narrow escape from the poisonous factory food and came home alive. You say you are going away again? Do you think you can beg for a cup of water with that thin body, not to mention a job?

Tansil: (Begs with both hands.) Mother! I'm begging you like this. Simply forget about a daughter of yours and let me go.

Mother: You bitch! Try for yourself. I'll follow you to the end of the earth and take you back, pulling you by the scruff of your neck. Last time I dragged you home, it was from the deck of the ferry Gaya. If I catch you once again this time, I'll have your loin seared with a hot iron so that you can no longer function as a bitch.

Tansil: (Fiercely shaking her head.) Never a shaman! I won't be one! If you force me to become one, I'll kill myself.

Mother: You, a cock sucker! You were going to die anyway! A trouble maker like you, you'd better be dead and gone! All right. If you want to be killed, I will kill you myself.

Mother, with a nylon string taken from the maru, binds Tansil's hands. Tansil resisted in vain. Mother brings in a sheet of white paper and a gourd dipper. As they do in the rite of spirit revival, she sprayed water from the gourd over Tansil's face and put the paper on it.

Tansil: (Hardly breathing.) Um, m, m.
Mother: Answer me! Are you going to be a medium or not? Give me your answer for the last time!

Tansil struggles and falls down over the edge of the maru. Mother, jumping down after her, sprays water and pastes another sheet of paper over her face.

Mother: You, a bitch! This will cure you of your stubbornness.
Tansil: Um, um, m, m⋯ (Trying to stand up, she faints and falls down.)
Mother: O, my baby is dying. (Peeling the paper away, she holds up Tansil's head.) Baby, wake up, oh, my baby!

Mother pours out water from the dipper over Tansil's face. Tansil slightly moves her head.

Mother: Oh, my baby. You are not dead. All right, my baby. I won't ask you to be a medium again. Please don't die! (Unbinds Tansil's hands and lays her on the maru.) Tansil, this is your mommy. Please open your eyes. Please. (She cries.)

Tansil: (With a deep breath, she sits up.)

Mother: Oh, my baby. You've come back!

Tansil: Did I fall asleep here? (She yawns.)

Mother: (Sobbing.) Mommy was wrong. Forgive me. I won't do it again.

Tansil: What, Mother?

Mother: Don't pretend you don't know anything, after you've terrified me so much.

Tansil: Pretend what? What are you talking about?

Mother: No, it's nothing. But do you really want to leave your mom and go far away?

Tansil: ……

Mother: (With a sob.) Tell me, my baby. I'll give what you wish. Our life is nothing but a few drops of dew on a taro leaf. No use fighting over small matters. That wouldn't let us live for ever. So, please tell me.

Tansil: (Very softly.) I want to go, mother. With a thatched house on a hill on the shore, I want to spend a long, long day, diving and whistling out my breath like my friend, Gilnyeo. There will be seasonal produces from the sea on the table for the children; turban shells, abalones, sea slugs, fresh octopus, sea-weeds, ⋯ The fresh seasonal products of the sea will be spread on the table. When the sun, a big fire ball, went down over the horizon, I will mend the socks of my children under the light of an oil lamp. When my husband sales back to the port with a boatful of fish, I will run down to the wharf, calling out the name of the father of my children. But when I am gone, how would you live on, Mom?

Mother: (Holding Tansil's hands.) Tansil, you don't have to worry about me. I am still young.

Tansil: Is fifty-two young?

Mother: Happy or unhappy, it's my own fate. Whatever happens, I could support myself, don't you think? When I finish the rite for Yeongdung Grandma, I'll give you some money for the trip. Go wherever you want to go. Yes, it's better than dying. Wherever you may go, try to keep well. What I care most is about your being well, and healthy. (Turning to the other side, she washes her tears.)

Tansil: ......

Mother: (Sighs.) I am fifty-two now and in a short while, I will go and see the flower garden in the western sky. How can I bear any grudge against our life? I cannot ask for more than be buried where my umbilical cord was burned.

Tansil: Don,t say anything like that. You must live a long, long life.

Mother: I have lived all my life depending on you, my only child. It's all for you that I have endured the disdainful treatments and hardship of every kind.

Tansil: I know, mother. Whenever I walked to the factory before dawn, and walked back to the place with a friend under the stars, how I longed to see the wrinkled face of yours!

Mother: My only flesh and blood··· While you were away, the pillow under my head was soaked through and through. (In a tone of a traditional air.) There's smoke from coal burning. No smoke whatever from heart burning. In the brook flows water from rotten tree stumps on the hill. In my eyes flows water from rotten intestines··· My first man was killed during the disturbance. Next one left me for his morbid suspicion. Last one was burned to death on a New Year's eve after a drunkard's crazy misdemeanor. When people rushed to save him, the rascal was burnt dark like a piece of charcoal. My mom, still alive then, said a shaman should have a twisted life. When I heard that, I left everything to become a shaman.

Tansil: I remember, Mom. I watched our house burn from under the eaves of the neighboring house. It was a horrible night. The dark body of my father who always tormented me, the burnt remains of my pencil case and mommy's dress and my favorite brown blouse⋯ What I cared most was my diary lost in the fire.

Mother: On the way back from that rascal's burial, I made my mind again and again to bury everything, all the past days, in the deep well of my heart. Forget everything, every injury, and someday there will be a new flesh budding from the old.

Tansil: Mom, you said you were going to a rite for Yeongdung Gramma, didn't you?

Mother: (Looking up the sky.) Oh, my forgetfulness! It's already noon. I must hurry. Go inside and fetch yourself something to eat and take a nap.

Tansil: Yeah, I will.

Mother hurriedly goes into the room and takes out the bundle
of shaman's robe and tools.

Mother: I will be back with lots of cakes and fruits.
Tansil: All right, Mom.

Mother goes out. Tansil lays herself on the maru. After a while, Gumnye cautiously walks in.

Gumnye: Tansil! (No answer.) Anybody home?
Tansil: (Holding up her head.) Who is it? Oh, it's Gumnye, isn't it? Well, what's up?
Gumnye: Nothing… Just to kill my time. Where's your mother?
Tansil: She's gone to perform a rite on the shore.
Gumnye: I know. The Yeongdung rite was going to be held.
Tansil: (Sitting up on the edge of the maru.) Please sit down. Everybody must be busy with works in the field. How could you find time to leave it?
Gumnye: (Sits down.) My parents don't know I am here. There is something I want to ask of you.
Tansil: Something to ask of me?
Gumnye: Yes.
Tansil: What about?
Gumnye: Well… You went to work at a factory in Seoul, didn't you?
Tansil: Is that a news?
Gumnye: Where's the factory? What do they produce?
Tansil: Why do you want to know?
Gumnye: Just curious.
Tansil: It's on the Cheonggyecheon. A clothing factory. Leather and fur.
Gumnye: How much do you make a month?
Tansil: Well, it depends. Newcomers get one hundred thousand. A skilled hand may get more than two hundred thousand.

Gumnye: I'd like to work in the factory. What do you think?

Tansil: (Staring at Gumnye for sometime.) Gumnye, don't do that. It will be a disaster.

Gumnye: Why do you say so?

Tansil: (Softly.) There is no place like home.

Gumnye: (Irritated a little.) Do you think I don't know that? I'm simply sick of working in the field. After paying for fertilizer, insecticides, working hands, seeds and everything, there is nothing left for us. You know my brother is quite a bright boy. He got in the high school this year, but we have to take him out of school because we cannot pay his tuition fee. My parents has no ability to support their kid's schooling. (Emphatically.) I will make money for my brother's schooling by working in the factory. My brother should not repeat the fate I have suffered.

Tansil: Do you know what Seoul is really like?

Gumnye: Certainly not a dungeon of a man-devouring tiger? You yourself have been there.

Tansil: If you want to have your body and mind seriously hurt, it exactly is the place.

Gumnye: I will never complain if my brother grows up proudly upon my ruin.

Tansil: You, fool! The damage is only upon you. Who would understand you as much as you deserve?

Gumnye: I don't care if no one understands me.

Tansil: Food from the factory working is not for everybody. It's nothing like working on the farm. I worked fourteen hours a day for three years with my hands all swelled up, and what do you think I've got? Nothing but a rent room with five hundred thousand seed money and this exhausted body of mine. The room where I suffered three winters was part of a shed in a slum area on a hill, and every winter I was almost killed by toxic gas from coal burning. That's not all. Part of my hearing is gone because of the noises in the shop. I was diagnosed as developing tuberculosis because the dust in the place damaged my lungs. (Disdainfully.) Do you still want to go to the hell?

Gumnye: (Intimidated.) But you yourself have been to the hell, haven't you?

Tansil: That's why I am trying to stop you.

Gumnye: We will see. By all means, I will go. I will send home all my monthly pay for my brother's schooling.

Tansil: Monthly pay? Yes, there is something like monthly salary. If you pay back the advance amount, rent, food, and the meager amount of savings, you are left with nothing. I couldn't manage to buy a skirt on sale, let alone eating out. Whenever in the market I sat before a small dish of imitation sausages, dead tired after a night shift, I couldn't stop crying. Do you really want to go?

Gumnye: (Nods gravely.)

Tansil: When?

Gumnye: Right away. Tomorrow.

Tansil: If you go, go with a hard mind. Never fall into a tender relationship.

Gumnye: There won't be anything like that. I made up my mind firmly.

Tansil: Once you leave home, even with your determination, you feel lonely sometimes, and become weak-minded.

Gumnye: Tansil. Did you have a boyfriend in Seoul?

Tansil: (Blushing.) Me? No···

Gumnye: Ha ha. There is no secret between us, is there, Tansil? Tell me about it.

Tansil: ······

Gumnye: There was a guy who betrayed you. Isn't that right? That's why you never go out and see people after you came back.

Tansil: (Hesitantly.) Yes, that sort of a thing. Besides, my ill health...

Gumnye: What sort of a thing? Can't you tell me more?

Tansil: That's enough. Don't ask for more. (In a depressed voice.) I will not be able to function as a healthy grownup any more.

Gumnye: Yes, I heard the village people say you've become a cripple from working in the factory. I see you've become thin and your face worn out.

Tansil: A cripple? Oh, this headache! I have to lie down. (Lies down on the edge of the maru. The drum sound of the exorcist's rite from afar.)

Gumnye: Well. I'll see you, then.

Tansil: (Waving her hands.) Ao, the sound, that sound...

Gumnye: What sound? I hear nothing. (Speeding up of the rhythmic sound of the exorcist ritual.)

Tansil: (Covering her years.) Ah, ah, ah!

Gumnye: (Bewildered.) Why? What's wrong?

Tansil: (Twisting her body with foam on the lips.) Ah, augh!

Gumnye: (In a great bewilderment.) What should I do?

As she tries to grasp Tansil's arms, she was thrown away on the ground. Gumenye squats there, watching Tansil's fit. As the ritual sound calms down, Tansil, stretching herself languidly on the floor. breathing heavily.

Gumnye: (Approaches Tansil.) Tansil, are you all right? You sweat like raining. I must go and tell your mother what happened. Tansil, wait a little. I will bring mom.

Gumnye goes out hurriedly. Lights fade out except for the two spots in the center of the stage. Juno comes in on the left spot.

Juno: Sorry to bother you since you must be busy. I only want to return the handkerchief. The blood on your handkerchief I couldn't clean out. So I bought a new one. I was really grateful yesterday. It was the first time in my life that I felt such a warm hand. When I was a child, my mom stopped my nostrils with small balls of cotton whenever my nose bled and softly tapped my head by the nape. You treated me exactly as my mom did. With handkerchief instead of cotton balls. (Taking out a handkerchief.) Only a token of my thanks.

Tansil: (Coming in on the right spot.) Thank you. (She takes it.) You don't have to feel grateful. Didn't you help me when I got injured.

Juno: Yes, I did. You got a sewing machine needle stuck on the back of your hand. It's a light case. I know a guy working for an electronics factory who had his shoulder blade cut out because of his injury in a conveyor belt accident. I saw many who got their hands amputated in the press work. How is your hand?

Tansil: (Hiding her hand.) All cured, with five stitches.

Juno: You fell asleep sitting at the sewing machine.

Tansil: Yes. I heard the sound of an exorcist ritual.

Juno: A ritual?

Tansil: (A little embarrassed.) No… Nothing. Nothing at all.

Juno: When you get sleepy, why don't you sing a song? They say you have your favorite song.

Tansil: A favorite song?

Juno: I-eo Island.

Tansil: (Smiling.) I-eo Do Sa-na.

Juno: Yes. That's right. I-eo Do Sa-na. It's all known around the cutting section. You sing the song very well.

Tansil: The spitful woman divers of Jejudo sing the song wrenching their bitter hearts.

Juno: Well, let me hear it.

Tansil: (Pretends a stern expression.) No, I won't. I am not a singer.

Juno: Ha, ha! Unfortunately I am not blessed with a nice folk song. You look tired. Things are very tough?

Tansil: The shipping date approaching, pressure gets heavier. Anyway I must work late hours to make up for the raised rent and unpaid savings.

Juno: So, we are not human with warm blood. We are only machines working endlessly at a turn of a switch.

Tansil: My friend Gyeonghi sold herself to a drinking place, saying what's the meaning of a life like that.

Juno: She had a nice body and pretty face. So something to sell. That way she could make an easier life.

Tansil: When the shipping is done, the president said, there will be a bonus pay. Juno: Don't feel grateful at such nice words. Isn't our president a church elder by title? Invited by the president to give a preaching once a month, what can the minister talk about except "You never steal!", "Keep commandments!", and such. They are simply afraid of having factory tools stolen by the workers, that's all. (Becomes more passionately.) Rats! To us workers, cold and hungry, they only extend inhuman body-searches and wages much below the living cost. What do they offer to their church and charity? Fifty million for church renovation, one hundred million for certain social cause… Yes, it's to give back God's to God, and Caesar's to Caesar, right?

Tansil: I got a note the other day.

Juno: What note?

Tansil: It said I should write down my name if I want to join the strike.

Juno: So?

Tansil: I didn't put my name.

Juno: Why?

Tansil: I was afraid.

Juno: We need courage. Each of us is weak like a grass leaf, but when we stand up all together, we can be very strong. A plantain grows under a carriage wheel and a dandelion blooms even when it's trodden by a horse.

Tansil: I don't know difficult theories. I'm only an ignorant girl from an island. I don't suppose I can join the strike.

Juno: What do you say? Is the rumor true then?

Tansil: What does it say?

Juno: No, no. Er.. To tell you the truth, I'm going to quit.

Tansil: What do you mean? Quit?

Juno: They will fire me. I got their notice today.

Tansil: ⋯

Juno: Don't ask me why.

Tansil: I know their reason.

Juno: You know it?

Tansil: At the fellow workers' sit-in the other day, Sukja, my roommate, was one of the leaders. When she had disappeared, they called me to their office. There the production line director and the cutting section chief asked me where Sukja was. I answered I didn't know. Then they said something about you.

Juno: About me?

Tansil: Yes. They asked me if I knew you very well. I said you were only one of the fellow workers. "No more contact!" they said. They said you are a dangerous person, a radical student under the guise of a laborer.

Juno: (Angrily.) Bastards! I worked hard for the company, harder than anyone else. Sometimes with bleeding nose, I worked more than their money asked for. Tansil: When I didn't join the strike, the workers called me a spy. I know they think I betrayed my co-workers. You too think so, don't you?

Juno: Stop it. Now I have to leave anyway.

Tansil: I found out at the beginning that you were not the kind of a person who works in a like this.

Juno: Found out?

Tansil: (Looking at Juno's hand.) Your hand — small and white. Prettier than a girl's hand.

Juno: (Hesitantly.) Well, I will confess everything. I was pinpointed as the major plotter of the last strike. So they fired me. I will never forget about you, a girl like an unspoiled flower in the field, in this dirty and corrupt world. Good bye! (Exit.)

Tansil: Oh, Juno! Juno!

Tansil follows Juno with her eyes. Spots fade out and the lights resume. Mother and Gumnye come out hurriedly.

Mother: My baby! What's the matter? What's happening?

Tansil: (Lying languidly as before.) I'm all right.

Gumnye: Oh, God! I don't understand this! I thought Tansil was hit by a sinister star!

Mother: (Touches Tansil's forehead.) What a heat! A burning fire! What can we do? We must send for a doctor. Don't move, Tansil. Don't!

Tansil: (Trying to sit up.) Don't go, Mother. I'll be all right, if you stay by me.

Mother: But we must do something. Let me put a cold towel on your head. (Goes into the kitchen.)

Gumnye: Tansil⋯ Are you really all right?

Tansil: (With a forced smile.) Yeah.

Gumnye: The fit. You got it from your working in Seoul, right?

Tansil: ...

Gumnye: Tansil, I am scared. What should I do with this business of going to Seoul? (Mother brings a towel and a basin of water.) I think I must go. Take care, Tansil. Good bye. (Goes out.)

Mother: Good bye. Thank you for what you've done.

Tansil: (Hanging on Mother's arm.) Mom. Don't go anywhere. Stay with me!

Mother: Yes, yes. Don't worry! (Brings a wooden pillow on the maru.) Stay calm. Close your eyes and try to sleep. (Tansil lies down. Mother puts the towel on Tansil's forehead.) Finishing the beginning ceremonyl, we were conducting the invocation ceremony for the Dragon King when Gumnye came up in short breath and told me that you fell and fainted. Immeadiately I ran home without telling anything even to the head shaman. Er···, according to Gumnye, you had an affair with a man in Seoul. Is it true?

Tansil: ···

Mother: Is it? Is it true that after drinking every drop of honey out of you, a guy had thrown you away?

Tansil: No, Mom.

Mother: Are you telling me the truth? That guy had left a bitter spite in your heart, didn't he? That son of a bitch will suffer a great ill fortune, I assure you. Didn't I tell you the story during the disturbance? Do you know who the informer of the man who, having crawled out of the mound the dead, blood soaked, begged for life but was put to death? It was my first husband. He struggled for his own life doing anything and everything, but someone falsely accused him of having a connection with rioters and he was arrested and killed. If somebody causes others to weep with tears, he himself is doomed to cry with blood. If someone hits a nail into someone else's bosom, he will surely have a spear put through his own bosom. Surely he will.

Tansil: I am not abandoned.

Mother: Then, what?

Tansil: (Slowly sits up.) I saw his dead body.

Mother: (Surprised.) What do you say?

Tansil: The body stretched long with eyes open and tongue protruded. (Trembles.)

Mother: Hanged himself?

Tansil: I got a letter from the man, who had quit the job at our factory, saying that he wanted to see me. I searched the slum area on a hill to get to his place. After I saw the dead body, I felt dizzy and extremely weak. When I sit at the sewing machine, the machine turns into his face and the noise into his crying. (Trembles and crouches.) The dead body appeared in my dream every night. With a scream I woke to find I was all soaked with sweat.

Mother: What did I tell you? You are possessed with a spirit of a goblin.

Tansil: In the dream last night, I performed the rite of releasing his exile. Next day, you hear the drum sounds of the rite all day long. Whenever I hear the sound, I must perform the ritual dance as in the dream, but since I don't know how to dance, my limbs get twisted and I can hardly breathe.

Mother: I suppose you are doomed to be a shaman before the eighteen thousand invoked gods and to devote yourself to the three gods governing child birth. No one can escape one's fate.

(A drummer, a square woman in her forties, comes in.)

Drummer: (In a sullen voice.) What are you doing here, lady? It's time for the Old Man's play after the meeting the Dragon King. and you are leisurely spending your time with a grown up daughter?

Mother: Tansil suddenly fell ill. I don't know what to do right now. I know I must go, but with this?

Drummer: (As if reproaching.) You don't have to handle a daughter as big as a horse so softly. In the old days, she is old enough to have produced a couple of little ones, and yet, do you think she still needs milk during the ritual performance?

Mother: (Angry but controlling herself.) It's not like that. There are some reasons...

Drummer: Our lady full of such energy when young. Now you get old and cannot perform a ritual in one sweep. Anyway, we must go quick. Head shaman is very furious. You know him well. When he gets angry, he even chews water.

Mother: What should I do? My baby is ill with heat like an oven.

Tansil: Mom, don't worry about me.

Drummer: See? Let,s go quick. A drummer like me has only some drums to hit.

Without a lady like you, the Old Man play should crumble. Am I not right? Mother: Tansil, I will peek in the ritual for a short while and be back soon. Get inside and lie yourself down.

Tansil: It's cool out here.

Mother: Try to be patient even if it hurts, you know?

Tansil: (Weakly) Yes.

Drummer: (To Tansil.) Where do you feel the hurt? I have Painstop with me. Let me give you some.

Tansil: No, thank you.

Drummer: (Taking out some tablets.) Try it. It's the best cure for headaches.

Mother: (Coarsely.) Don't shake a fan at a house on fire. Come on!

Drummer: What you say? Do my drugs call the wrath of the earth gods? It's out of my kindness. You should at least understand that, shouldn't you?

Mother: Take them for yourself for your own good!

Drummer: Forget it if you don't like it. They say eunuchs may sometimes decline a governorship. You are sickening and nauseous...

Mother: If we are so sickening to you, why don't you become a shaman yourself?

Drummer: (Blushing.) What do you say? You really are a haughty person. Don't be so proud of yourself. Are there any select ones for becoming shamans? Don't you know the saying that a dog at a school may recite poems after three years? I myself learned a lot by watching over the shoulder, as I followed the ritual party, hitting the drums, for several years. I can perform the part of the old man in the Old Man play. Don't elate your spirit too high with our kind applause. Do you think the rituals couldn't go on without you? Not so at all!

Mother: If so, go on and try to perform my part.

Drummer: Of course, I can. May I try?

Mother: (Shows distrust with snuffles.)

Drummer: You don't believe me? Don't despise a person for no reason. Well, open your small eyes as wide as you open your legs for men and watch carefully.

Mother: Stop silly talking and do the play.

Drummer: (Pretends to put a pipe in the mouth and sways her body.) Ha, ha, ha! "I'm one of the sons of Minister Huh who lives in the eateries quarter on the hill of Namsam. I heard that my seventh and youngest brother is here in the Jeju island to look around the Halla mountain. So I have come here to see him. Once on the top of the Halla, I look around and hear the sound of a gong. There is a sweet fragrance all around. When I advance, someone invites me in. So, here I am. Ha, ha, ha! (Pretends to hold a pipe in one hand and walk unsteadily.)

Mother: (Staring at her coldly.) Is this the Old Man play or the Cripple Dance?

Drummer: (Doesn't know how to answer.)

Mother: (Gravely.) A king of a country and a shaman of a village are designated by the god in heaven. There are certain things a man can do and can't do. You must keep that in mind.

Drummer: Well, things get more interesting. You take yourself as designated by gods, but it's a mistake.

Mother: I don't want to have a quarrel with you any more, so let's hurry. (Goes out.)

Drummer: Well, as you wish. (Takes out the drug again.) Tansil, take three tabs of this and sleep well. This Painstop is the best medicine for headache, toothache and the monthly ache, you know.

Tansil: Thank you, Aunt Jocheon!

Drummer: Don't mention it. Because of the fiery character of your mother, we have quarrels quite often. But we share between us candies that are already in the mouth. We are such friends, you know.

Tansil: I know that. Mother sometimes···

Drummer: I know it, too, that your mother is not of an ordinary kind. Usually she is soft and quiet. Once on the stage with the bell and ritual sword in her hands, her eyes shine differently. Her verbosity and exorcising ability is well known to everybody in this area. Your grand mother was more famous, they say. Older people still talk about her that there has been no greater shaman after her. It's peculiar to your family. Perhaps, you owe it to earnest worshipping of gods or to having ancestors' tombs at the right place... (Suddenly.) What am I doing now? I must go, Tansil. (Goes out.)

A short interval. Sounds from the ritual ring from afar. Tansil tries to stop her ears, but the sounds get louder and louder. She rolls on the floor, twisting her limbs and body. Suddenly she became stiff, as if electrified, and stands up slowly in the form of a bird ready to fly. Through her stretched arms comes down a mysterious light and her face glows with delight and energy. All of a sudden, she puts on shaman's cap and the robe and takes up the bell and the sword. She jumps down on the ground and begins to dance to the ringing ritual sound.

Tansil: (Shaking her sword.)
> Spirits of ill fortune!
> This is evil spirit.
> This is evil goblin.
> Which one is sinister?

Unable to go to the other world,
Unable to return to this world, either.
You must be an evil spirit!
Take a blow of this famous sword!
It is not a sword to expel people.
It is one to expel evil spirits.
Like a lightening bolt onto the wide court,
Like a thunder bolt onto the narrow court,
Let us resolve it, coming in and going out.
Far away, far away, Hush!

Waving her robe fiercely, her dance gets more heated. Mother with a bundle comes in. In her bewilderment, she stops still with her mouth open wide. At last she shouts.

Mother: Finally, god came down upon my baby! My baby is possessed with god!

The sound of the gong and cymbals rise. Mother, begging and bowing in all directions, dances with Tansil. When the surf-like sound dies down, the mother and daughter wakes from the delirium.

Tansil: (Runs into her mother's bosom.) Mom!

Mother: (Tapping on Tansil's back.) Excellent, my girl! Now you are possessed with god. You are a fine daughter of a shaman. You are now the god-designated shaman!

Tansil: Mom! For him, I wanted to perform the ritual for releasing from exile. I liked him so much. We had to separate without even exchanging a word... (Crying.) Mother!

Mother: (With tears in her eyes.) Oh, my poor baby! My dearest!

>A spot light on Mother's face with a smile on her lips and tears in her eyes.

>The curtain comes down.

Essay

A Fly-Swatter
The Star-Pouring Night
The Tiny Life In the Orchid Pot

Tae-Gook Kang

A Fly-Swatter

The Introduction of the writer

Member of the Korean Writers' Association, board member of Modern Essays. Professor Emeritus at Jeju National University
Publications : 〈Pieces of Scribbling〉, 〈Pieces of Memories〉, 〈How Dare You?〉, 〈Essays or Novels〉. etc.
Address : 77-9 Donam-Dong, Jeju, Jejudo, Republic of Korea
Phone : 064) 758-8817

A Fly-Swatter

by Tae-Gook Kang

I was practicing Zen meditation in a temple which I had begun to go to when I was a college student. Sitting toward the wall with legs crossed, I lowered my eyes at an angle of 45 degrees.

It was just after lunch, and at such an angle my eyes closed naturally. Nodding and nodding, I was immersed in a sweet sleep. I heard birds singing and smelled the scent of flowers, then all the women I had met in the past danced merrily around me, making a circle. I was about to get out of the circle when someone touched me on the waist. At that moment I woke up.

It was a sign that I should be slapped and correct my posture. The monk on duty, walking silently among the Zen practicers, helping them, saw me.

Joining my hands I inclined my head to avoid my ear being hurt while being slapped. Through my right shoulder flew the slap. The slapping sound broke the silence and then my dream. It was a dream within a dream.

My wife was staring around with a fly-swatter in her hand. She seemed to be trying to find and catch a fly. I felt something on my shoulder and found a flattened fly. On the wall behind me was a bloody mark. The slapping in the dream was, I thought, the sound of the fly-swatter.

My wife was repeating her motion of striking flies in the air. She could be considered clumsy or vulgar. Looking at my simple wife I had a wriggling desire to rearrange my dream.

I was born in Japan. Around the end of the Pacific War, my grandfather took me in his arms and crossed the Pacific, battling B-29 fighters. He believed that to rescue and protect the eldest grandson was his mission.

After graduating from middle school in Jeju, I crossed the Pacific again to study near my parents in Japan. But my parents died and my uncle, a successful businessman, supported me to attend university.

I was interested in Zen meditation then, and practiced it at Yongpyong Temple in Hokui, staying sometimes a month or a year. Those experiences gave me much energy.

I lost my grandparents and uncles in these years. I thought of going back to hometown after their deaths.

Practicing Zen meditation at the temple, I considered my subject of going back home or not. I heard the sweet sounds of birds, streams, and wind in the tree branches. Sometimes they sounded like melancholy whisperings of my ancestors.

Around the late 1960s there was no electricity, running water, or gas in Jeju island villages. Jeju island was 50 or 100 years behind Tokyo in culture.

However I decided to come back to Jeju to take care of the memorial services for my ancestors and to mow the grass on their graves.

The walls and the ceiling, stained with smoking soot of my ancestors, the kitchen where my grandmother, with tears in her eyes caused by the smoke, used to cook rice with burning barley straw, and sparrows chirping in their nest under the eaves of the grass-roofed house, all welcomed me.

Relatives got together almost everyday to select a bride for the oldest grandson of the main family. Among the girls in the district of the province they selected a bridal candidate according to the unique rules of our family.

Prolific pedigree, many children, delicious kimchi, bean paste, soy sauce, good working in the field and at sea···the bridal candidate's family should have those things. Any acupuncturist, fortuneteller, exorcist, or mental disorder···the family of future bride should not have those.

They never considered how pretty or graceful the girl was, or her intelligence or educational background. My view of womanhood, cultivated in the city was totally ignored.

They announced to me that a bride had been picked. They used old words as if they were choosing a bride for a prince in an old palace. I felt confused. As I guessed, the girl was plain and unsophisticated, an original Jeju island woman. I could do nothing but get married to her. She gave birth to two boys and two girls. She made delicious food and all my family was strong and healthy.

Although my wife often forgot things, she never forgot the memorial service days for my ancestors. She made friends easily and became a central figure among relatives. Supported firmly by relatives, she seemed to dominate and manage me. I was always someone from another country and needed to be watched. If she took her eyes off me I might do something beyond her imagination, she believed.

She was good at working both in the field and the sea and helped me overcome many difficulties as a life partner. However, she never read any of my writing. Usually she tried to read the works of her husband but fell into a sound sleep. These days I read some passages of my writing to her and by her reaction I measure them; for example I try to find out if she feels sad or laughs at the right parts and decide on their quality. Sometimes I wonder, if I read this or that to her, what face she will make. And I hope she will be stimulated and begin to read various books. Gauguin, Chopin, Mendelssohn, Händel, Natalie Wood, Clint Eastwood, Choonwon Gwang Soo Lee, Professor Gwang Soo Mah, Bernard Show, Descartes, Kant, Schopenhauer ⋯ They are useless for my wife because they are not rice, cake nor anything to eat. They are fair but empty phrases and a lullaby for her. She is as strong as a fly-swatter because she gets no intellectual disturbance. Compared to her I am weak, because philosophy, literature, music and all miscellaneous articles including conscientiousness bother me.

The silences between us are deep. Loneliness comes from the closed circuit of conversation and I roam. Sometimes I imagine myself as a hero in a movie, who, drifting on at sea, arrives on an island. Then, caught by a native girl, he tries to escape but never succeeds. Sometimes I struggle with myself, embellishing my situation.

So, to my wife, I'm a suspicious husband. She holds her ground undauntedly, straightening and cleaning silently, slowly like a cow or bear. With her fly-swatter she is driving away great modern women, flying around me like flies in my memory of youth. I can see my portrait, thin and weary, wandering about temples, Haeinsa, Bumoesa, Naksansa. It might be renunciation or a broader outlook I was seeking through penance. When I suggest going out to eat or drink some tea my wife rejects it, saying it is much better and cheaper buying food with that money and cooking and eating at home. Usually I am disappointed but accept it, thinking she is good and frugal. She is a girl from island, grown in sweat and soil in the farm village. For me, grown up like an orphan, she offers a kind of stability.

Looking at her with my eyes half-woken from my spring dream, I feel she is waving with a fly-swatter as if dancing a Buddhist dance. Without showing the slightest sign of sorrow for having to wake me from my happy dream, she does her job. Her innocent face is quiet and lucid, although wrinkled.

Trying to understand her and be well, I have lived or decayed for 30 years. Sometimes the years are not classified into a life or dreams…

Last winter our oldest daughter, 27 years old, got married.

Ga-Young Kim

The Star-Pouring Night

The Introduction of the writer
President of Jeju Essay Association. Korean Writers' Awards, Grand Prize.
Publications: 〈When a Women Loves a Man〉, 〈Women with Good Luck with Men〉, etc.
Address : 1001 Jaehyung Park Ville, 914-1 Nohyung-Dong, Jeju, Jejudo, Republic of Korea / Phone : 064) 745-2101, 018-693-6512

The Star-Pouring Night

by Ga-Young Kim

I went to Hamduk beach with a broken heart. I was hurt because my lover changed his mind about me. It was around the end of summer. The sea was terribly calm. Fresh wind was blowing from over the ocean announcing the end of summer. I pulled the ring from my finger and threw it into the sea with all my strength, and wept, a little.

I was born in a seaside village, and since my childhood almost always enjoyed summer near the ocean. But after throwing the ring into the sea I felt as if I had become an orphan.

From that day on the sea water only looked cold to me. No more swimming days for me. When I felt I couldn't stand the hot weather I dipped only my hands and feet in the seawater. Every time I did that I could feel on my toes a kind of warmth still remaining in the water. And, closing my eyes, it seemed to me I could feel free; the troubles in my mind— betrayal (I could forgive the most difficult things), untruth, sadness, and even anxiety- disappeared, erased from inside me.

Whenever I felt oppressed, I used to go to Hamduk beach. And there I sometimes remembered the sad memories of my ring, my broken heart, and my unfaithful ex-lover.

Last summer, a hot wind was blowing at Hamduk beach, even at night. The wind was hotter than human body temperature. In spite of the steaming heat, some young men and women, who never knew fatigue, were enjoying themselves, playing the guitar and dancing. Some of them were running into and out of the water, again and again, like flying fish. The scene was really fantastic. If I had been young, I could have run into the water, swimming splendidly to the melody of my friends' guitar and then come out. I looked up the sky while I was thinking. In the night sky over Hamduk beach, numerous stars, like pins stuck in a pile of black velvet, were making a river. Watching the sky I felt absorbed into that river. I walked on the beach. Suddenly a passion aroused me. I felt like soaking my body in the dark sea. It was an uncontrollable desire.

Fortunately there was no moon. There was no one there at the end of the beach. Taking off only my sandals, I walked into the sea with my clothes on. Silently sat I in the water, waist-deep. At that moment, the moon came out of the clouds and I found the sea was glittering like a giant glow-worm. Once I saw bioluminescence, and the sea was bigger and brighter bioluminescence. I was happy in that glowing sea. It felt like the sea was hugging me. No. I was not only happy, but also lonely. I wanted to cry for the beauty of the sea. I was really sorry I had no one to share such wonderful scenery with.

Then I realized I was not alone. There was a man close to me. Lost in my thinking, I had not been aware when he came. He was also wearing his clothes. In the moonlight I couldn't know how old he was or what he looked like. I was a little scared. It seemed certain he was not a native Jeju Islander.

"Until now I have never seen so many and so beautiful jewels as these," I said to him, rather muttered. He answered after thinking for a while. "If you want, I'll give them all to you. Those are my gifts."

I laughed and said thanks to him. I had had no experience of receiving any jewelry from any man until then. But that night, I received a great many jewels from a stranger. No other woman in the world received more jewels than I. I was about to say such a thing to him, but he was already swimming away.

At last, I recovered from my wound I had gotten 26 years ago because of my lover's infidelity. Then I could afford to remember how I threw my ring away without sorrow. I was able to keep it as a beautiful recollection. That night, at Hamduk beach.

Myung-Chul Cho

The Tiny Life In the Orchid Pot

The Introduction of the writer

First recognized in 〈Literary Trends〉 (Essay). Board member of the Korean Essayists' Association and the Korean Literature Association.
Publications : 〈Wife's Smile, Woongnyeo's Smile〉, 〈Traffic Lights and Dolharbahng〉, 〈Going Wind and Coming Light〉, etc.
Address : 701 Seobahn Apts, 132-44 1-Do 2-Dong, Jeju, Jejudo, Republic of Korea / Phone : 064) 757-3535, 011-665-7656

The Tiny Life in the Orchid Pot

by Myong-Chul Cho

I like orchids. I've been an orchid lover for long time. So, I'd rather say I love orchids. But I feel a little bit guilty to say that these days. Because, last winter, I failed in helping my suffering orchids. One of my teachers who taught me in elementary school gave me an orchid pot. It was a rare Jeju orchid which bloomed in the winter. I've kept that pot and enjoyed looking it everyday. It is already 30 years I've taken care of that orchid.

It buds out at the beginning of spring and blooms when autumn leaves fall. Its petals looks like cranes flying off an aged pine tree. Great fragrance also makes me feel joy of life. When I learned that it was a top-rate kind of orchid, called 'Jungbang', pleasure spread through my heart.

Unfortunately, I had to take the plant to the orchid hospital this spring. I felt anxious about its health. I was worried whether it would come to naught though I've taken care of it and cherished the plant so long.

I moved to an apartment 2 years ago; after all my children left, the house looked too big and so empty. My orchids might have had difficulty to adjust to a new environment, and their health was getting worse from then on. It looked hard for them to be high in the air of the 7th floor. Last winter, even those which survived frost damage got sick.

From late spring to early autumn I used to leave my orchid pots in the shade under the tree in my old garden when I lived in the house. Then, my precious orchids conversed with fair sunlight and wind in daytime. At night, they whispered with the moon and stars. And late autumn, I used to put them near the southern window of the living room to get warm sunlight. Their leaves kept green and good looking. They were green animation diffusing fragrance through the universe.

But I guess the new environment in apartment is different from that of house. I left the orchids along the southern balcony next to my study to get them sunlight during the winter. I watered them twice a month and kept the doors closed to protect them from cold air.

But that kind of care was a failure. I was shocked when I opened the door to see if they were fine one month later.

Some leaves of the Jeju winter orchid had already withered in midwinter. I thought they were dead and that cutting them would be better for the rest of the leaves. And after watering the orchids I closed the door again, without knowing the cold air sneaked in at night.

Only one month later, I found out my orchids were suffering seriously because of what I had done for them. I picked the dead ones out and tried to refresh some weak ones by soaking them in the tepid water. But the wounds seemed too deep for them to recover and smile again.

When spring came to Sara Hill, I took some orchid pots to the hospital to cure their serious frost damage. I carried the other pots to the northen balcony, which seemed a better place for them at that time. After arranging them newly I could take care of them right next to me, though a lot of the sunlight didn't come through. I gave them "Natural Mineral 22" every three or four days, waiting for their new buds. I had a stressful time again because there came out no buds until the end of spring.

By the beginning of summer new orchid leaves sprouted. I exulted over them after the long wait. Suddenly I remembered the words of Mencius: "All lives can grow up only through human harmony even though the sky and the earth give good conditions."

All creatures are begotten through harmony. All beings must obey nature; against the sky and the earth only death will come. Being harmonious according to universal law is eternal. The harmony of the orchids and I is that of mankind and nature, a combination of objects and self.

What force makes the plant sprout isolated in the high apartment building? Some handfuls of soil in the pot, water, wind, sunlight and my love made a balance, a reconciliation between nature and human being.

"Although all things in the universe look to exist apart they are related intrinsically," the Avatamska Sutra says.

Also a far-sighted leader, Haewall said: "Nature is a living personality and our parent."

All in the universe is one, and can only be born through the harmony of heaven and earth. All creatures come from the harmony, including huge elephants, whales, flies, minnows, great forests in Africa, and insignificant weeds. Who cannot give a deep bow in reverence to this grand truth?

Those who think to be endowed with supremacy have used science as a vehicle to dominate the world and desolate the earth. Now they fly a flag to conquer the universe. Every country is trying hard to follow them. They are accelerating universal destruction. It's a discord of human beings with the earth, the universe.

These haughty human beings even try to invent life and birth. Such horrible things as deciphering of the human genome, and manipulation of DNA and human reproduction take place. These are the defiance of human beings to the authority of heaven and earth, and will bring the chaotic genesis again.

I look at the limitless sky, the sea coming in contact with the sky, the mountains sitting up straight, they are silent.

The heaven and earth! The root and the center of mysterious life. I'm willing to lower my head to admire the unity of life.

At last I can hear the laughing sound of my orchids. The tiny smile of new leaves. I perceive they share the power of life with me. Now I feel the world of the Avatamska Sutra where all the creatures are connected. The ecstasy of being alive in life's harmony spreads.

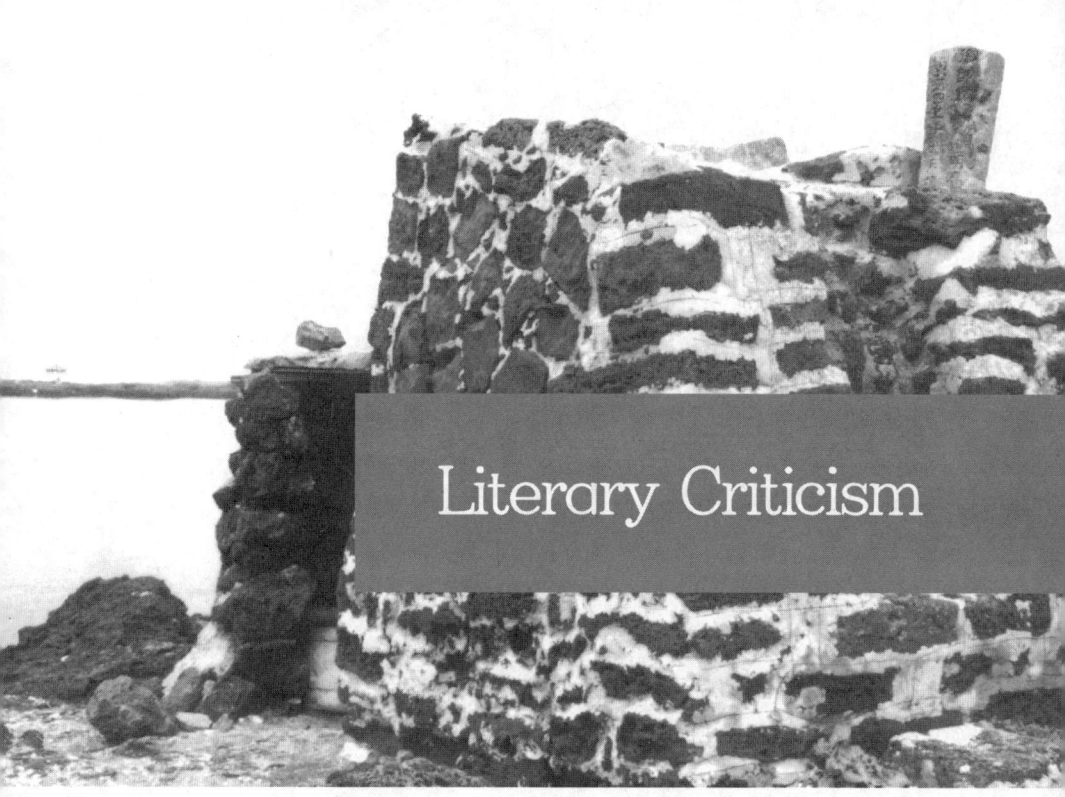

Literary Criticism

Narrative : The Heritage of the Ceremony
for Water and Imagination

Seung-Haeng Shin

Narrative : The Heritage of the Ceremony for Water and Imagination

The Introduction of the writer

Member of the Korean Writers' Association, board member of the Korean Literary Critics' Association, Professor at Jeju College of Technology.
Publications : 〈Whistles of Women Divers〉, 〈Moon-phoong-ji〉, 〈Encounter of Language and Literature〉
Address : 101 Hyangsahn Apts, 296-6 Yeong-Dong, Jeju, Jejudo, Republic of Korea / Phone : 064) 746-2544, 011-9664-2544

Narrative: The Heritage of the Ceremony for Water and Imagination
— Shamanism and Jeju Literature

by Seung-Haeng Shin

1. Introduction

Water is the origin of life and at the same time it is the thing which makes us have fear and veneration. According to Genesis, God ruled man through Noah. The world flooded for 150 days, so the history of human beings was succeeded by Noah's Ark. It is connected with the fear of water that the Tunguses prayed in front of Lake Baikal, which is the deepest lake in the world and is known as the origin of shamanism. Why did they pray in front of water? It is the essential fear of being conscious of life.

Korean narrative is also based on the fear of water. As the tales in the age of Three Kingdoms changed and developed novels in the age of Yi Dynasty, Jeju Literature is based on such tales. And the tales became the source of creation. In the tales there were both shamanism and taboos. Water made life and it had always been connected to our lives as the symbol of providence.

In literature the images of water, shown in various ways, are the source of emotion. So the river often appears as an essential image of life and death connected with time and tide, the lake is beautified as an image of memories and continuous thoughts, the rain yearning or sorrow, the fog or dew self-examination, and the sea fear or waiting. Therefore it may be possible expressing the circumstance like following diagram.

$$\frac{\text{living and dying} + \text{water and life}}{(\text{ the space of figuration })} = \text{coming into conflicting structure}$$

In this point of view, the power of water is essence of existence tuned by primitive and spiritual imagination of water. This is the very Animism and the essence of literature. Then what relation is there between water and taboo in shamanism?

2. Shamanism and the Identity of Water

In shamanism in Jeju, water is the origin of folk beliefs both directly and indirectly. Also, we can find it a taboo. Because they tried to discover the symbol of original meaning by taking baths and cleaning altars with water before ceremonies.

For example, a housewife takes water from a spring at daybreak and puts a bowl of the water in a soy jar in the backyard to pray for her family's health and long lives to the goddess of kitchen. In a joint ceremony for the town, the priest puts three bowls of water on an altar, pouring out his soul after taking a bath and controlling his mind. A shaman also puts a bowl of water on his altar as soon as he gets up, before he starts his daily work.

For reference, there are vestiges of taboo and water in many islands; a spring for the rite in Pungdo, an isolated island in Gyeonggi province, and the one in Deockjukdo, in Soyado, in Wido, in Whangdo, Seosan Chungnam and in many other islands. —excerpt from pages 123-138 in The Symbol of the Original Meaning of Water by Teagon Kim—

According to Alan Dundes, such an original meaning of water appears in North American Indian's tales. —reference from The Structure and the Meaning of A Tutelar Deity in Jeju by Jugun Jang—

The examples from these tales is;

A) The sentence, "A monster imprisoned the water of the whole world," catches our attention for the object of proof.

B) This sentence "A hero killed the monster and released the water" has the same meaning.

Here we can notice the fact that water has much effect on the base of shamanism.

$$\text{In case A)}, \quad \frac{\text{monster} + \text{water}}{\text{(the essence of fear)}} = \text{water is the origin of life(fear)}$$

$$\text{In case B)}, \quad \frac{\text{hero} + \text{water}}{\quad} = \text{water is the absolute being of the}$$

right to live (desire for ruling)

    (the essence of the desire for ruling)

  Water looks ordinary, but it exists as a restored space which shows us the dark and light before life and death. And it symbolizes the role of time. The constant fact is that an old boatman, Charon, comes and goes to the time of life and death, that is, to this world and the next world, through the river. We can find many kinds of shamanism and ceremonies for water in Jeju. One of them is that Seolmoondae Halmang appeared from the sea. Another is the stone statue called 'water mom'. The stone is 75 cm in height and is in the camellia woods. The woods are near Daedong spring, which is at 13, Yi Do 2dong Jeju City. They think the stone keeps the spring from getting dry and they worship the stone. And there is another 'water mom' taking care of a spring in Yongdam, Jeju City. —(Korean Shamanism Picture Record, p.197 by Taegon Kim, 1982)—

  Around Yongyun a tale has been transmitted orally; there was a ceremony praying for rain, an old man came there by chance, he stopped and ordered them to hold five rolls of silk high, and then he wrote the chinese character '龍', meaning a dragon, on the silk, the letter suddenly became a real dragon and flew into the sky and the dragon made raindrops, so the long drought ended. Because the relation with water symbolizes the recurrence and the life like that, water has been a great influence on our daily life, emotion, and literature.

3. Water and the Aesthetics of Shamanism

When we see the works on shamanism and taboos in Jeju literature, we can find lots of taboos and wisdom described in harmony. Especially, The Story of Weeds written by O Sungchan, is the novel composed and quoted from the Jeju legend Seo Gyijin Byunintae (by Yongjun Hyun, Jeju Legend, 1967) with a modern sense. Byunintae, who was wicked and would told lies, raped Jobangjang's wife while they were crossing Halla Mountain and threatened her with the affair and extorted money from her. A Swift Horse's Dream (1983) and Kimnyung Sagul Exorcism, written by Gileon Hyun, in which the legend was verified through the snake and the service of exorcism which are the basis of the legend are also adaptations from Jeju legend. The drama Never Look Back (1996) written by Yongjun Kang is an adaptation from the legend about the king snake and its cave, too. The story is: The hero died because he had broken the taboo, 'After killing the snake, never look back.' We can take a look at the activities of a shaman who takes the soul of the dead out of Wangsari Sea. Now I am going to consider it concretely with The Island in the Wind written by Giyoung Hyun.

His works are The Bird Singing in a Remote Region, The Island in the Wind , Suni's Uncle, and so on. His novel, as if it were a service of exorcism itself, drew many shamans in it. This novel, 'The Island in the Wind' whose background is the women divers' resistance to Japan in January 1932, is about daily lives and wishes of the women divers who live in Hado and Sewha, North Province, Jeju. On the isolated island, the women divers were lonely, poor, and suffering under tyranny of the Japanese imperialism. They struggled to cover their rough and tumble of life through shamanism and taboos, and expressed their sorrow or unfair treatment to the sea.

> When the women divers ran to east and west and in a row, the higher-level women divers went into the water with their bare feet and threw handfuls of millet into the sea. "We sow the seeds of millet, please give us good harvest. We sow the seeds of conches and abalones, please give us lots of conches and abalones. Please make us, the women divers in Sewhari, live comfortably and happily.
>
> After the divers who sowed the seeds of millet moved backward, two hundred of divers threw lumps of rice wrapped in white paper toward the sea with all their might.
>
> excerpt from The Island in the Wind

The activity of a shaman moving around the altar with a bowl of water and floating small lumps of charcoal and red peppers on the water in bowl is another example of their faith in water. Moreover their prayers for being out of poverty can be regarded as their religion in water.

> Doa put five bowls of steaming rice cooked right now in the basket, put the basket on the bow with Gumchun's help, and prostrated herself before it. Other women divers bowed toward the bow with their hands together. Doa's clear voice praying to the dragon king could be heard. "Blue dragon in the east, White dragon in the west, Red dragon in the south, Black dragon in the north, Yellow dragon in the center, we prepared a plain dinner but poured our soul into it. Please, let us, the women divers of Sewhari, cross the sea safely. Other women divers bowed again, praying with low voices.
>
> excerpt from The Island in the Wind

Water was the object of worship and one of ardent appeal. The relation between water and ceremony began from the sea, river or spring generally. Especially, the dragon god was the prop and stay of mentality as the symbol of the faith in water. The example is;

> "Uncle, why are the waves rough when the wind is calm on the Sasu sea?" asked a woman diver.
> "Well, even though we don't know about the sea a thousand fathoms deep, maybe, it's because of the swift current flowing in the ravine in the deep sea. I think it's the same reason as the neck of a rapids has a swift current.
> "No", Doa, who has been sulky, retorted sharply, "in a shallow stream plays a bird but in the deep water plays a dragon. Because the king dragon takes a deep breath in the sea, there's big wave. There must be a palace of the king dragon in the sea a thousand fathoms deep······it was in eight fathoms-deep water where I saw a group of red coral was waving with the current like the woods leaning with the wind. My heart sank into my boots when I thought I had come too far in this deep sea. I heard there were souls of dead women divers in the beautiful coral woods······ Maybe is it the entrance of the way to the palace of the dragon king?
>
> excerpt from The Island in the Wind

It was the imagination of water. It was the fear of life that they could not give up even though they were in distress for their livelihood. That made group emotion, and led them to own their daily lives jointly. Such consciousness of joint ownership made the feeling of togetherness and belief.

The exorcism rite performed by the sea accompanied the words to repose the departed souls of their husbands who died by accident in the sea. With enchanted words the shaman called many gods who were ruling the next world. He made them happy with dance and song in rhythm to a drum, and then he explained the pitiful circumstance and the poor soul departed three days ago, and prayed for them to enter the next world peacefully. And he reposed all of the mortifying souls that couldn't go to the next world and were hovering around a shady and damp place in the dark.

> I know how you were in distress, and thank you, thank you. Thank you for bringing my dead body and burying it in my hometown. My eighteen-year-old wife, don't cry anymore. I don't have any lingering regret or anything to complain about. It was my fate to die young. I was out of luck to be alive. So who can I be bitter against?⋯ sobbing quietly, Jeongsim cried out loudly at last, and the viewers shed tears, too.
>
> excerpt from The Island in the Wind

Like this, the shaman did not only give a hint on the base of personal and group emotion but also showed the course of how individual and group conflict happened. It was a process to reveal the conflict of time which hadn't become public in a restrained society. Through the history of Jeju the writers worked out their bad feelings they had conceived because they couldn't say what they wanted to say. The background of The Island in the Wind is Sewha and Hado in Jeju. The writer described a woman who lived under Japanese imperialism and her daily life and circumstances. He described her miserable life in her natural environment, the island. Also he described the women divers' resistance to Japan rising gradually, and their struggling for the right to live. That was their protest for the truth as the people of Jeju. There are many folk songs in this work. We must not fail to notice that the songs release them from depression.

The tutelar deity was helpless. Yeoouk couldn't forget the tears flowing silently down her father's cheek, swollen like a ball, when he was dying. The bitter world in which a fisherman couldn't help selling his boat and he had to be a manual laborer. The motorboat of the Japanese swept the bottom of the sea with its dragnet······

> Some birds sing at night, too
> Other birds sing in the daytime, too
> This bird, that bird, the bird like me
> You sing all day and night like me
>
> excerpt from The Island in the Wind

In shamanism the tragedy was not intended to promote antagonism or conflict, but was intended to expect the effect of drama by describing the spirit of that time really and psychologically.

> A) We are poor women divers living in Jeju Do
>   All the whole world knows our miserable lives
>   On a rainy day, on a snowy day, even on a windy day
>   We are troubled with the waves of the sea
>
> B) "Yes, we won a victory over this fight. Being imprisoned doesn't mean defeat. The enemies can imprison our body but they cannot shut up our mind."
>   "Of course. It's a long fight, there was a fight before, and the fight will go on."
>   "That's right, we are like the toad which intended to be eaten by the snake to bear its babies. As the toad is dying inside the snake, it spouts poison and kills the snake. And then its babies are born in it and

grow eating their mother's dead body and the dead snake."

excerpt from The Island in the Wind

In case A, the writer described the lives of people on Jeju Island, especially poor women divers who struggled for life with the strong sea waves. Their difficult condition was beyond their control. So the central figures in the novel died or ran away. But in case B, they would like to make a new world by breaking down the structure of their lives. So it's not a tragedy. Both the death of hero of Suni's Uncle and the death of hero of The Bird Singing in a Remote Region are the course of acheiving catharsis.

After all. it is not for the dead but for the living to work off a grudge through the shaman. It's for the people in Jeju living in the present age. Like this, Jeju narrative brings the present age and the shamanism.

4. Conclusion

I said that water, after all, is the origin of life and the object of fear. Man is the main object of ceremony by the shaman. So literature is related to water as a taboo. In literature the imagination of water appears variously as the symbol of spiritual essence.

Water and Life + Water and Fear = The Catharsis through Shaman

The writer Hyun Giyoung described shamanism as the ceremony for the living and a kind of catharsis in his novel. In other words he would like to give the readers pleasure by relieving the sorrow and sighs of people on Jeju

Island. He unfolded the period of suffering with the background of the sea to repose lots of dead people who had suffered under tyranny of Japanese imperialism.

His novel The Island in the Wind illuminates the perseverance and life of people living on an island through the sea and the women divers that appeared because of the circumstances of suffering. The relationship of the water and the ceremony is worthy like that. And we can also grope for the phase and the identity of narrative in many ways.

제주펜무크 ❶

제주섬의 바람

■ 영어번역 강방영 외

Je
Ju

푸른사상

발간사

오 성 찬 (제주 PEN 회장)

　국제펜클럽 한국본부 제주지역위원회(약칭 제주 PEN) 회원들이 오래 소망하던 영어로 번역된 회원 작품집이 발간되는 것을 매우 기쁘게 생각한다. 이 작품집은 글로벌 시대를 맞이하여 '제주 소재 문학작품'을 널리 내외에 소개하기 위한 첫 시도로 이루어졌다.
　그 동안 제주에서는 일부 작가들이 영어, 혹은 일어로 시와 소설, 혹은 전설을 번역하여 발표한 적이 있으며, 집단적으로는 1996년에 일본 와세다대학 조선어문연구소 소장으로 재직하던 한국문학 통의 문학평론가 오오무라 마스오 교수가 〈탐라 이야기—제주도 문학선〉을 일어로 번역해서 일본에서 출판한 바가 있다. 이 작업은 오로지 오오무라 교수 개인의 의지에 의한 것이었지만, 이 작품집이 아마도 제주문학을 외국어로 번역, 소개한 최초의 작품집이 될 터이다. 글로벌 시대라고 하고, 제주가 국제자유도시를 표방하고 있으나, 사실 제주의 문학은 아직 세계를 향해서는 걸음마 단계라고 하는 것이 바른 말일 것이다. 이런 시점에 제주 PEN 회원들 작품을 시, 소설, 아동문학, 수필, 평론까지 전 분야를 망라하여 영어로 번역하고, 세상에 내놓게 되는 이 기회는 가슴 설레게 하는 바가 있다.
　그러나 한편 부끄럽기도 하다. 이제 겨우 첫 걸음이라니. 이번을 계기로 앞으로 10호, 100호, 제주의 문학작품들이 세계 각국어로 번역되어 세상에 내놓아지고, 마침내는 세계 문학의 반열에 이르기까지 꾸준한 노력들이 있어지기를 기약해 본다. 이 일을 위해 여기 저기 자본을 찾아다니며 수고한 임원들과, 선선히 예산을 허락해준 제주도와 제주시 당국에 고마운 뜻을 전한다. 또 번역이 지난한 작업인 줄 알면서도 선뜻 맡아서 수준 높은 번역을 완성해준 강방영 한라대학 교수와 그 팀에게도 진심으로 감사를 드린다. 게다가 이 일은 처음부터 장일홍, 김승립, 장영주 등 출판을 위한 소위원들이 맡아서 추진했음을 밝혀둔다.

2004년 12월

차례

발간사 • 237

■ 시·시조

- **양중해** 243
    산마루에서 • 244   수평선 • 246
- **강통원** 249
    제주도濟州島 Ⅰ • 250   한라산漢拏山의 눈꽃 Ⅰ • 252
- **김승립** 254
    문門에 대하여 • 255   섬 • 257
- **김양수** 258
    너는 누구더냐 • 259   망실亡失 • 261
- **김용길** 263
    작심作心 • 264   제주 억새꽃 울음 • 265
- **나기철** 268
    비원悲願 • 269   회억回憶 • 270
- **문충성** 271
    수평선 • 272   새 • 273
- **문태길** 274
    종 • 275   진달래 • 276
- **양전형** 277
    아내 • 278   우도봉 연가 • 279
- **오영호** 281
    억새꽃 들판에서 • 282   일몰 앞에서 • 283

차례

- 윤봉택 ··· 284
    바람 부는 날엔 • 285   바람 6 • 286
- 정인수 ··· 288
    해녀海女 • 289   억새꽃 • 290
- 한기팔 ··· 291
    별의 방목放牧 • 292   거기서 알 수 없는 • 293

■ 소 설

- 최현식 ··· 297
    샐비어 • 298
- 고시홍 ··· 328
    계명戒命의 도시 • 329
- 오성찬 ··· 354
    버려지는 사람들 • 355

■ 아동문학

- 김영기 ··· 379
    등대 • 380   한라산 2 • 381
- 김종두 ··· 382
    마라도 • 383   한라산 • 385
- 강순복 ··· 386
    종이피아노 • 387

차례

- 박재형 395
  해맞이 • 396
- 장영주 404
  설문대할망 • 405

■ 희곡

- 장일홍 411
  강신무降神舞 • 412

■ 수필

- 강태국 441
  파리채 • 442
- 김가영 447
  별 쏟아지던 밤 • 448
- 조명철 451
  난분 속의 작은 생명 • 452

■ 문학평론

- 신승행 459
  서사문학은 물의 제의祭儀와 상상력想像力의 유산 • 461

시 · 시조

산마루에서 • 수평선
제주도濟州島 I • 한라산漢拏山의 눈꽃 I
문門에 대하여 • 섬
너는 누구더냐 • 망실亡失
작심作心 • 제주 억새꽃 울음
비원悲願 • 회억回憶
수평선 • 새
종 • 진달래
아내 • 우도봉 연가
억새꽃 들판에서 • 일몰 앞에서
바람 부는 날엔 • 바람
해녀海女 • 억새꽃
별의 방목放牧 • 거기서 알 수 없는

양중해

산마루에서
수평선

필자 소개

《사상계》를 통해 데뷔.
한국문협 제주도지부장과 한국예총 제주도지부장 역임. 한국문
화원연합회 제주도지부장, 국제펜클럽 한국본부 이사(현)
시집 『파도』 『한라별곡』 『수평선』

산마루에서 외 1편

양중해

1
흰 구름이 쉬다가
떠난
산마루.
오늘은 내가
흰구름으로 쉬고 있다.

아름다운 추억으로
되돌아보는
강물이며 산봉우리며
다시 다다를
푸른 숲과 산봉우리들…

그리워 소리 지르면
메아리로만 울려오던 먼 산
오늘은 내가
그 산마루에 앉아
메아리로 소리 질러 본다.

일만 시름 잊고, 죽음처럼
한잠 자고도 싶지만
바람이 부는 소리
구름들이 몰려오는 소리
나는 다시 떠나야 한다.

다음은
어느 산마루에서 쉬랴?
어느 산마루에 누워서
오늘의 이 산마루를
그리움으로나 불러 보랴?

수평선

제주도 사람들은
수평선 안에서 산다.

까마득한 옛날부터
한라산의 발치라면 어디에라도 터를 잡고
수평선을 등지면 한라산
한라산을 등지면 수평선
그 누구도
길고 짧은 한 평생을
수평선에 갇히어
수평선 안에서 살다가
수평선 안에서 삶을 마친다.

제주도 사람들은
수평선 밖 어디쯤에
이어도가 있다고 믿어왔으나
다녀온 사람은 아무도 없다.

수평선 안이 답답하면
이어도를 찾아 배를 띄워 보지만

노를 저어 나가다 보면
앞으로 나갔던 만큼씩
다시 밖으로 물러서 버리는 수평선
제주도 사람들은
그 누구도
수평선을 한 번도 건너보지 못하고
이어도에도 가보지 못하였다.

제주도에서는 해도 수평선에서 뜨고
달도 수평선에서 뜨고
해도 달도
수평선으로 진다.
구름도 수평선에서 일어나
수평선 안에서만 떠밀려 다니다가
수평선에서 사라진다.

제주도의 수평선은
저렇게 아름답고
저렇게 조용하게 보이지만
수평선에서는, 지금도

거센 파도가 일고 있다.
제주도 사람들의
기쁨과 눈물
삶의 맥박이
쉬임 없이 고동치고 있는 수평선.

수평선은
제주도 사람들의 숙명이다.
선택이 주어지지 않는
한정된 우주이다.

강통원

제주도濟州島 I
한라산漢拏山의 눈꽃 I

필자 소개

제주대학교 영어영문학과 졸업, 명예문학박사. 1977년 《시문학》으로 등단.
한국예총 제주도지부장과 한국문협 제주도지부장 역임. 한국현대시협 중앙
위원. 한국시문학회 지도위원., 제주대학교 명예교수(현)
시집 「무적霧笛」, 「상류와 하류」「Cheju island enlalia flower」

제주도濟州島 I 외 1편

강통원

불이 탄다, 불이 탄다,
훨훨훨 불이 탄다.
환상인가, 나의 환시幻視인가,
어느 신神의 분노인가 신의 저주인가,
멸망의 불길인가,
창조의 불길인가,
무슨 신화神話 전설의 불길
생명의 불길이
저렇게 맹렬히 타고 있는 것인가.
한정없이 치솟는 불길
불타는 제주도濟州島
개벽의 천지도 저렇게 타고 있었는가,
어디서 불씨가 날아왔는가,
언제 여기까지 불씨가 날아들었는가.
개벽 전야前夜의 아득한 시공
아마 그것은 50억 년쯤 되는 것일까.
깨지고 터지며 날아오르며 가량없이 타오르며
얼마나 전율적인 불꽃축제였는가.
캄캄한 지맥地脈으로부터
거대한 산맥처럼 다시 솟구쳐 오르며

불길은 바다를 태우고
천지 분간도 없이
천지에 가득
황홀한 불의 축제祝祭를 다시 벌여 놓고
신神은 저렇게 환희의 축배를 들고 있는 것인가.
가량할 길 없는 전사前史의 불길
다시 한번 바다가 찢어지고
땅이 쪼개지고
산山이 부서지며 산이 사라지고
초원도 사라지고
제주도는 어디로 사라져 가고 있는가.
천지에 흩날리는 분분한 잿가루
천지를 뒤흔들며 포효하는
불구름 속으로부터
한라산처럼 쌓여 오르는
잿더미로부터
다시 생명의 싹이 트고
생명의 숨결과 몸짓이 꿈틀거리며
제주의 전야는
저렇게 틔어 오고 있는 것인가.
불이 탄다, 불이 탄다.

한라산漢拏山의 눈꽃 I
― 상류와 하류 · 29

나무숲에 잎이 지고
오랜 겨울잠의 언저리에
하얀 눈꽃이 피어
숲의 꿈을 덮고 있다.
누구의 손길이 꽃씨를 뿌렸는가.
찬바람에 불려 오는
이 꽃들은
꽃씨를 심지 않아도
피어나는 꽃인가 보다.
꽃이 피어도
열매를 맺지 않는 꽃인가 보다.
어느 손길이 꽃밭을 가꾸는가.
나비라든가
벌이라든가
그런 것들은 꽃밭을 잃어버리고
나비라든가
벌이라든가
그런 것들도 지금은
먼 겨울잠의 꿈길을 헤매고 있다.

여기는 오로지
헐벗은 산새의
하염없는 사랑이 있고
꿈이 있을 뿐.
어느 날인가
싸늘한 꿈 속에서
눈부신 햇살을 보고
햇빛 쏟아지는 산비탈에
망아지 울음 소리를 들으면
산새의 시린 날갯죽지와
얼어붙은 숲의 손목이
따뜻하게 풀리는
봄의 길목으로 나서게 되리라.

김승립

문門에 대하여
섬

필자 소개

시인.
제주시 이도2동 402-11, 064) 753-3185, 019-9101-3185
시집 『등외품等外品』

문門에 대하여 외 1편

김승립

오, 열리지 않는 문
서로 낯설어 바라볼 때
우리는 행복했느니

악수와 포옹에 길들어
빠르게 영혼을 바꾸고
얼굴 치장한 사랑은
얼마나 무잡한 것이랴

닫힌 문 앞에서
너머 그리움 심어두고
안타까움의 나무 가꿀 때

키오르는 나무 위로
바람 불고 아프게 비가 친다 해도
나무 밑 잠의 숨결은
꽃불을 밝혔느니

이제 우리 문을 잃고
서서 우네

오래된 낯섬 이미 없어져
데면데면한 얼굴로
우리 그렇게 서 있네

더욱 낯설어 막막하게
막막하게

섬

　　　1
불편한 잠 끝에
묻어나는
순 한국산 설움아

오늘 뜨락에 비 듣는다

　　　2
무엇으로 눈뜨리
그대 겨드랑이에 무성히 핀
가화假花들,
한 시절 비늘 잃고 그대
유영遊泳치 못함으로
잠드는 바다
잠드는 푸르청청
물빛

김양수

너는 누구더냐
망실亡失

필자 소개
1990년 《심상》지 신인상 등단. 한국시인협회, 심상시인회 회원.
시집 「바람도 휴식이 그리울 것이다」 「어머니 당신이 있기에 절망도
희망입니다」 「목금 타는 그늘에서」

너는 누구더냐 외 1편

김양수

본시 너와 나
빈 가지에 돋는 나뭇잎같은
아니면 물과 불처럼,
그도 아니면 강물에 어리는
구름이었던가
관계의 거리를 잴 수 없음이
하늘의 무게만 안타깝기만 한데

너는 말문을 빗장 질러 좋겠다.

본시 너와 나는 무엇이었더냐
혹
빛과 그늘처럼
그게 아니면 수의囚衣를 매는 단추에
그 구멍이나 아니었던가
네 쓸쓸해진 뒷모습에 내리는
햇살의 광도를 헤아릴 길 없어
가슴 저리다.

세상을 다 준다고 다시 오지 않음을
아는데
너는 누구더냐

명패名牌없는 세상에서 너를 만나면
그때는 알까 몰라
네 검은 동공에 떠돌던 낡은 얼굴 하나
어둠의 등걸에 걸어 두느니
그 날이 오면
너와 나 참매미의 목젖으로 살아나
한 시절을 목놓아
울음 울어도 좋으리.

망실亡失

무엇이었을까
우리가 가졌다고 믿었던 것들은
어느 것들이었던가,
바람을 가두지 못하는
그물처럼
구멍 난 가슴을 흔드는
숲의 몸부림만 커지고 있으니

알았을까,
우리가 간직했던 것들이
가을 낙엽을 태우는 연기처럼
소슬하기만 하다는 것을
짐작이나 했을까,
바위보다 무거운 별리의 끝에서
지울 것조차 찾을 수 없으니

가고 말 일이라면,
비 날씨를 예감하듯
버릴 수 있을 줄 알았다면

그림자 마저 지워야하는 허탈은 없을 걸,
무소만 같았던
너를 가둘만한 우리,
폭포로 지는
내 눈물 가둬 둘만한
연못 하나를 준비 못했으니,

빈손인 채,
야위어 가는 그리움을 더위잡음조차
빈손이어서
어둠보다 더 깊은
환청幻聽에 목을 놓고 있으니
이 세상에 남을 망실亡失도
너의 것으로 돌려주고 싶구나

김용길

작심 作心
제주 억새꽃 울음

필자 소개
제주도문학상(예술부문)과 서귀포시민문화상 수상.
한국문협 서귀포지부장 역임.
시집 『바다와 섬의 이중주』
대한민국 제주도 서귀포시 서귀동 118 정방빌라 206
064) 762-4943, 011-694-9229

작심作心 외 1편

김용길

그대 외로움의 강안江岸에서는
풀꽃의 이름들을 읽지 않으리
이별처럼 푸른 별들의 이름을 부르지 않으리
그대 고운 유년幼年의 사랑 이야기
빈 이름표 팔랑거리는 새들의 노래를 부르지 않으리.

사람 냄새 나는 곳에서는
고통과 연민의 흥건한 눈물빛 뵈지 않으리
오랜 날 살아온 진실의 텃밭
허울과 빈 껍데기 씨앗을 뿌리지 않으리.

이제는 그대 이름을 가슴에 안으리
용서와 화해의 땅
손때묻은 세월의 문고리를 떼지 않으리
묻히운 채로 그대 외로움의 묘지에서는
새 비명을 세우지 않으리.

제주 억새꽃 울음

    1
제주섬 어디서든
억새꽃 핀다
들길 자갈밭에서든
시벌건 오름에서든
하얗게 하얗게 피어나서
바람처럼 운다

휘저으면 휘젓는 대로
밟히면 밟히는 대로
흔들리다 쓰러져 울고
쓰러지다 일어서 운다.

    2
들길에서는 새가 되어 운다
오름길 가시덤불 숲길에서는
어미 잃은 노루새끼처럼 운다

목이 말라 운다
마른 계곡 사이

햇살 타는 메아리
산그늘 어둠이 내리면
머리 산발하고
달빛으로 운다.

3
파도처럼 운다
밀려와 부서지는
벼랑 위의 꿈

제주섬 둘레둘레
울음의 파도
흰 띠 두른 채
먼 길 떠나는
영혼의 새
부유浮遊하는 갈매기 되어 운다.

4
가슴으로 운다
울고 울다 가벼워진

빈 몸
나비같은 풀씨들은

폴폴날아
어디로든 날아
부딪는대로 닿는대로
소리없이 주저앉아 운다

실낱같은 뿌리 한 가닥
가는 인연의 생명줄
내릴 수만 있다면
어디서든 억새꽃 피어나서 울리라.

나기철

비원悲願
회억回憶

필자 소개

1953년 서울 출생. 제주대 국문학과 졸업.
1987년 《시문학》으로 등단. 〈깨어있음의 시〉 동인.
시집 「섬들의 오랜 꿈」 「남양여인숙」

비원悲願 외 1편

나기철

나는 죽어 사라악紗羅岳에 들르리.
별도악別刀岳 사이 어디쯤
먼 물결소리 모으리.
사랑을 돌보리.
나는 죽어서도 거리에 나오리.
무덤을 깨고 밤 열한시
그 베겟모 머리카락을 땋으리.
산국山菊 한 광주리 놓고 오리.

회억回憶

'나', 북두칠성, 저녁수평선, 감기, 묘지명墓碑銘, 라보엠,
갈대밭, 생일, 소풍, '종鐘' 천함, '파란꽃', 바보……바보.

수평선에 쌓이는 저녁 싸락눈.

싸락눈에 덮이는
연민의
남빛
목청……

문충성

수평선
새

필자 소개

제주시 출생. 한국외국어대학원 불어과 졸업. 문학박사.
《문학과 지성》을 통해 등단.
시집 『제주바다』 『내 손금에서 자라는 무지개』 『섬에서 부른 마지막 노래』 등. 문학연구서 『프랑스의 상징주의 시와 한국의 현대시』

수평선 외 1편

문충성

얼마나 많은 수평선이 있나 이 세상
나의 목숨 둘레
하나로 둘러싸여 언제나
새로운 그리움에 떨게 하는 것
어느 날 바다에서
나는 찾았다 고기를 낚다
인간이 사는 땅을 자애의 손길로 재우고 있는 수평선을
인간들이 켜 논
불빛을 안은 채 산을 이루고 바람 속을
내달려와 수평선은
나의 목숨 둘레에 하얀 금을 그어놓았다
폭풍우가 수평선을 어둠 속에 지워놓는다 해도
어둠을 삭이고 새벽을 잠 깨우며
눈먼 태양을 나의 가슴에 떠올려
바다 물결을 노래하게 한다

새

푸르름 푸르름 속으로 숱한 새들이 날아가고 있었다
숱한 새들이 푸르름의 빙하 속을 날고 있었다

새들은 차가운 바람 그
가없는 넓이에 밀리고 있었다 나는
자꾸만 새들을 날려보내고

푸르름 속을 떠도는 새들이여 이제껏 맨발
붙일 한 뼘 땅도 마련하지 못했느냐 돌아오너라 차라리
지친 날갯죽지 접고 나의 새들이여
그러나 내 품은 빈 가죽뿐

너희들 울음 속 난청難聽의 땅 그 속으로
내 그림자는 사위어들고 푸르름 속으로
푸르름을 날아오르던 새들이
자꾸만 떨어지고 있었다 한입씩 내 울음을 베어 물고

문태길

종
진달래

필자 소개
한국문협 제주지회장 역임. 제주시민상 수상.
시집 『마라도 등대』 외

종 외 1편

문태길

언제나 내 목소린
하늘을 마음껏 날아

구름과 만나면
미소지으며 스쳐가고

돌풍을
만나는 날엔
더욱 크게 부서지리라.

울다가 지치면
시냇물에 목 축이고

길 잃은 사람들이
제 갈길 찾을 때까지

울리고
또 울리리라
번뇌의 언덕을 향해.

진달래

우리들 사랑이
영원하기 위해서는

화사한 이 뜨락도
그냥 두고 가야 한다.

간절한
안개 저편에
피어날 꿈을 향해

가슴을 적시는 건
봄비만이 아닐텐데

자꾸만 솜털처럼
흩날리며 가는 이여

그리움
무너진 자리
자욱마다 피어나리.

양전형

아내
우도봉 연가

필자 소개
한라산문학 동인. 열린문학상, 한국자유시인상 수상.
시집 『나는 둘이다』 『길에 사는 민들레』 『사랑은 소리가 나지
않는다』 등.

아내 외 1편

양전형

아내는 키가 작아
내게 매달릴 땐 뒷발을 들지만요
오일장 인파 속에서는
보일 듯 말 듯 하지만요
들앉는 자리가 어찌나 넓은지
매무새가 얼마나 당찬지
집안 구석구석
아이들 가슴 빈 틈마다
내 어설픈 날밤질 방황길마다
꽉꽉 찹지요.
정말,
초하루의 약속 하나 가득 키워
온 세상에 뿌리는 보름달 같구요
설한풍에도 꼿꼿이 피어나
향기 나고 청초한 수선화 같아요.

우도봉 연가

항구에 물들었다 뱃고동 친다
잠시 머물렀던 사람들 떠날 시간
간밤의 가엾던 꿈 털어내며 하나 둘 일어선다

갈 사람 가고 남을 사람 남아라
섬은 한 번도 어느 누구를 붙들지 않았다
섬에서는 누구나 이별을 한다
섬에 남는 것들은 모두 기다림이며
기다림이 커지면 꽃이 된다

파도 드세거나
짙은 해무에 가려진 새벽일수록
갯메꽃은 입 더 크게 벌린다
천년 전 떠난 그대 돌아오는 길 잃을까
무적은 새끼 잃은 어미소처럼 부르짖고
바다 향해 핀 갯메꽃 목젖이 점점 붉어 간다

내가 아는 오랜 이름 하나여
무적 소리 찾아 이 등대 아래로 오라

섬에 있으면 다 아름다운 것
섬에 남으면 누구든 피어 나는 것
우리 또한 이 섬에 어떤 꽃송이가 되어

오영호

억새꽃 들판에서
일몰 앞에서

필자 소개

제주시조문학회 회장 역임.
한국시조시인협회 이사, 제주펜클럽 부지부장(현)
시집 『풀잎 만한 이유』. 한국시조비평문학상 수상.

억새꽃 들판에서 외 1편

오영호

봄 햇살 말아 쥐고 누리 밝힌 쪽빛 바람
그 옛날 청무靑蕪 덮던 세월의 날개 위로
오늘은 은빛 말씀이 도란도란 열린다.

낮과 밤 빈손 들고 선 나무들 묵시 속에
흰머리 서걱이는 소리 시공을 짜르더니
푸드득 장끼 한 마리 삶의 매듭 풀고 있나.

일몰 앞에서

서귀포 보목리 늦가을 저녁 바닷가
졸고 있는 문섬까지 불러 놓은 시인 몇이
썰물에 빠져나가는 시어들을 낚고 있다
햇덩이, 새섬 섶섬 그 너머 수평선 위
서서히 떨어지는 장엄한 순간 앞에
시인들 가슴을 닫고 숨소리도 멎었다
그 때, 하혈下血 번진 바다가 하는 말씀
초심初心으로 돌아가라 초심으로 돌아가라
허영의 검정 옷을 벗고 태우고 살라 한다.

윤봉택

바람 부는 날엔
바람 6

필자 소개

서귀포시 출생.
월간 《문예사조》 신인상. 시 「바람 부는 섬」 외 당선.
시집 『농부에게도 그리움이 있다』 『이름 없는 풀꽃이 어디 있으랴』

바람 부는 날엔 외 1편

윤 봉 택

바람 부는 날엔 그 섬이 그립다.
사람아,
그리워하는 것이
죄가 된다면
사람을 그리워하는 것이
죄가 된다면
그리운 사람 찾아 떠나는 것이
죄가 된다면
차라리 그 죄를 짓고 살아가자.

기다리지 않아도
사랑의 안개가 되어
유년의 강물로 멱을 감기는
아픈 그대여
이대로 흐르다 보면
다시 그 섬에서 만날 수 있을지,

시간은 먼 기억의 잔잔한
기슭에서 투명한 물보라를 날리는데,
오늘처럼 바람 부는 날엔
그 섬이 있는 바다가 그립다.

바람 6

땅이여
너를 팔고 다시 버리고
바람의 씨앗을 심는구나
잡초도 꽃피울 수 없는, 해초인 듯
바람인 듯 뿌리 내린 섬
이 아침상 위에 네 식구 마주앉아
손자놈 흘린 밥알 주우시며
먼 길 떠나신 어머니
일어서다 지친 삶의 옹이에서
젖은 가슴 흔드는 제주바람
오늘 다시 불어 연체된 어둠을 날린다
더 낮은 곳 더
따스한 곳을 위하여
이 겨울 깊은 눈은 나리고
눈이 쌓이지 않아 슬픈 마을에
한 집 건너 한 마을 지나는
각혈 소리
하이얀 눈뜨면 오늘 아침은 설날인데
유자꽃잎 지듯 지는 듯 파도 타는 슬픔이여

압류된 닻이여
왜 섬을 떠나지 못하느냐
바람이여

정인수

해녀海女
억새꽃

필자 소개
1974년 《한국문학》 신인상 당선. 제주도문화상 수상.
시집 「삼다도」

해녀海女 외 1편

정인수

해녀는
물 속에서만 눈을 뜨고 입을 연다.

남몰래 옷을 벗어
모든 것을 내맡겨도

오히려 못 믿을 곳은
휘파람
저
너머
세상.

억새꽃

찌든 아내의 눈두덩을 보다 못해
억새꽃 한아름 꺾어다가
오지 동이에 꽂아 놓았다.

할머님이 물려주신
마음 비운 지 오랜 오지 동이
아가리가 커서 궁상맞더니만
인제야 임자를 만났구나

맹물만으론 채울 수 없는
허기진 세상에서 억새꽃을 만나
한아름 통째로 받아놓고 보니
푸짐하고 넉넉도 하다

거실이 삽시에 환해지는구나,
찌든 아내의 눈두덩에
주름이 펴지는구나, 옳거니!

한기팔

별의 방목放牧
거기서 알 수 없는

필자 소개
1975년 《심상》으로 등단.
한국문협 제주도지부장, 한국문협 서귀포지부장 역임.
제주도문화상, 서귀포시민상, 제주문학상 수상.
시집 『말과 침묵 사이』 외 5권.

별의 방목放牧 외 1편

한기팔

영혼이 따뜻한 사람은
언제나 창가에
별을 두고 산다.
옛 유목민의 후예처럼
하늘의 거대한 풀밭에
별을 방목放牧한다
우리의 영혼은 외로우나
밤마다 별과 더불어
자신의 살아온 한 생을 이야기한다.
산마루에 걸린 구름은
나의 목동牧童이다.
연못가에 나와 앉으면
물가를 찾아온 양떼들처럼
별들을 몰고 내려와
첨벙거리다 간다.

거기서 알 수 없는

1

고개를 넘으면
쪽빛 바다
거기서 알 수 없는
바람이 불지

그리운 사람
먼 목소리
거기서 알 수 없는
눈은 내리지

2

돌아오다 생각하니
문득 푸른 바다를 잊어
이 작은 떨림의
눈물이 되게 하는
바다

그대의 귓속말

소설

샐비어
계명戒命의 도시
버려지는 사람들

 최현식

샐비어

필자 소개

1924년 11월 28일(음력) 함경남도 홍원 출생.
1957년 조선일보 신춘문예에 소설 「노루」 당선.
한국문협, 국제펜클럽, 한국소설가협회, 한국문협 제주지회 회원(현)
소설집 『홍상紅裳』 『흑묘일기黑猫日記』 『먼 산山』 등.

샐비어

최현식

"…이걸 언아가 잘라놨니? 차돌아!"

강한 액센트의 함경도 사투리에 나는 눈을 떴다. 꽃밭을 향해 도어는 열어 놓은 채로였고, 매미의 울음소리가 흐리멍덩한 머릿속에 잡힌다. 분명히 어머니의 목소리였는데…, 그리고 으레껏 되받쳐지게 마련인 차돌이의 "모르쿠다. 나 안 그랬수다." 제주 사투리도 들리지 않는다. 잠들 때보다 한결 약해진 것 같은 꽃밭 위의 햇볕인데 샐비어의 푸진 주홍朱紅 가에서 서성거리고 있던 흰나비 한 마리가 빠른 지그재그로 담을 넘어 푸르름 속으로 사라졌다. '꿈이었군… 전후에 사연이 없는 목소리뿐인 기묘한 꿈….' 나는 나비의 비상을 마지막까지 지켜 보다가 책상 위의 손목 시계로 눈길을 돌렸다. 십분 전 다섯시. 어머니를 부축하고 병원을 나선 것이 두시경, 소주병을 사들고 집에 돌아와 조금 과하다시피 마시며 이럭저럭 세시쯤에나 잠들었을 터이니 넉넉 두 시간은 잔 셈이다. 나는 심한 갈증을 깨닫고 글라스에다 주전자의 냉수를 채워 마셨다. 갈증은 누그러졌지만 가슴속의 고동은 마찬가지였다.

　K병원. 어머니는 진찰을 마치고 대기실의 소파에 돌아왔다.
　입과 눈짓으로 몹시 목안이 말라든다고 말했다. 나는 간호원에게 엽차를 부탁하고 진찰실에 들어갔다. "독감입니다. 그런데…" K원장은 말을 잇지 못하고 얼마동안을 머뭇거리다가 "통증을 말씀 안 하시던가요?" 물었다. "말씀하신 적이 없습니다만…." 나는 대답하고 봄부터 소화가 좋지 않았으며 탈모증이 있기 시작했음을 말해 주었다. "좀더 세밀히 진찰해 봐야 알 일이겠지만 위암인 것 같습니다." "위암이오?" 책상 위에서 선풍기가 바람을 뿜어 돌리고 있었다. 나는 손수건을 꺼내 이마의 땀을 훔쳤다. "윗부분인데, 손에 잡힐 정도로 나타나는군요." "손에 잡혀요?" "그래서 통증 말씀을…." "전혀요…." "다행스러운 일입니다만… 환자가 알게 되어서는…." "네, 엑스레이를 찍어 보면 어떨까요?" "환자에게 고통을 드리게 되겠지만 찍어는 봐야지요. 간경화 같은 것으로도 생각해 볼 수 있을 것입니다만, 처방은 같은 것이 될겝니다. 감기부터 다스린 연후에 다시 진찰해 보기로 합시다." "위암이 확실하다면 얼마만큼 견디어 낼 수 있을까요?" "나이가 나이니까… 6개월 정도로 보면 되겠지요." "6개월…." 나는 입밖에 말을 내지 못하고 진찰실을 나섰다. 어머니는 수술실에서 주사를 맞고 있었다. "독감이랍니다 3,4일 치료를 받으시면…" 내 말을 어머니는 "음…" 하는 눈짓으로 받고, 우리는 병원을 나섰다. 나는 막바로 다른 병원을 찾아볼까 했으나 어머니에게 안겨줄 부담을 생각하고 그만두었다. 집에 돌아와 어머니를 누워있게 하고는 현관 밖으로 아내를 불러내어 진단 이야기를 해주고 속심을 부탁했다. "정월부터 가슴이 답답하시다면서 계속 활명수를…." 아내는 얼굴에 띤 울기를 가라앉히지 못한다. "아직은 확실한 것이 아니니까 간병이나 잘 해드리고 있어요." 나는 말해 주고 소주병을 비우기 시작했다. 석 잔, 다섯 잔, 천천히 자작하면서 공자가어 孔子家語에 이런 가르침이 있었노라고 동계動悸의 자신을 타일렀다.
'군자君子는 재앙이 와도 두려워하지 않으며 복이 와도 기뻐하지 않는다.'

샐비어의 주홍 속에, 어느새 한 마리의 흰나비가 다시 와 있었다. 조금 전에 담 너머로 사라졌던 그 놈인지도 모른다. 꽃에 앉을 생각을 않고는 분주히 너울거리다가 아까의 그 길을 똑같은 지그재그로 사라졌다.

"나비에게도 길이 있어요. 일정하게 찾아다니는 길이 있습니다." 작년 여름에 한라산에 올랐다. 기도를 위한 등반이었다.

토요일 오후에 차로 어리목 산장山莊까지 가서 밤을 새우고는 이튿날 아침에 저수지 쪽으로 올라 정상에서 점심, 개미등 쪽으로 내리는 1박 2일의 코스였다.

산장의 주인 S씨에게 동행을 부탁하여 조금 이르다시피 길을 잡았다. 밤새 꾸물거리던 비 날씨는 출발 무렵에 안개로 바뀌더니 해발 1천미터에서 개기 시작했다. 마침내 활짝 열려진 창공. 제주 휘파람새 소리의 산수국山水菊 길목. 륙색의 등은 땀으로 젖는다.

"한 십분 더 가면 기가 막히는 광경을 만나게 됩니다." 단 하나의 산을 놓고 150번도 더 올랐다는 S씨. 우쭐거리는 말투이다. "뭐인데요?" 나는 가쁜 숨결의 걸음을 멈추어 보였다. "미리 말해 버리면 흥이 식어 버리니까요." S씨는 입가의 미소를 거두지 않고 곧장 앞장을 선다.

마침내, 그 기가 막히는 광경 앞에서 걸음을 멈추었다. 오른편에 밋밋하니 내리뻗은 비탈을 황색을 주조로 하는 꽃들이 온통 뒤덮었다. "야하아." 나는 부지중 환성을 꺼냈다. 꽃보다도 나비의 무리에 놀란 것이었다. "야하아." 거듭 꺼내는데, 초록빛 실뱀 한 마리가 빗물방울로 반짝이는 꽃잎들 위를 깔면서 날 듯이 직선으로 달렸다. 놀란 것은 나뿐이었다. 나비들 그대로 춤추고 있었고, 꽃들은 반짝이고, 곁의 S씨는 여전한 미소였다. "독산가요?" "아니에요. 이름은 모릅니다만 독이 없는 …" 하는 S씨에게 나는 담배를 권한다.

꽃 꽃 꽃 / 나비 나비 나비/ 잎새의 일곱 빛깔의/ 햇물 무지개/ 다치지 말라/ 포효하는 화사花蛇….

나는 스스로를 잊어버리는 홍조에 묻혀서 이런 서투른 즉흥을 잡다가 "지금 여기가 해발 얼마쯤이지요?" 하고 S씨에게 눈길을 돌렸다.

"천… 600쯤…."

이제 365미터를 오르면 백록담白鹿潭, 나는 마지막 피치를 다짐하며 벗어 놨던 류색을 챙겨 드는데, S씨는 '나비의 길'에 관한 지식을 가르쳐 주었다. 그리고는 거미의 생태도 관찰해 보면 재미가 있다고 덧붙였다. 나비를 무희라고 한다면 거미는 집시라고 말할 수 있을 것이다. 일정한 서식처가 없다. 이 산의 것도 수백 종류를 헤아리게 될 것인데 그 중에서도 다리가 긴 놈들은 풀밭 위를 놀랄 만큼 빠른 걸음으로 다니면서 나비의 길목에다 그물을 놓는다. 탄탄한 그물을.

우리는 꽃벌판에서 떠났다.

구상나무·암고란岩高蘭 벌판을 지나 정상 턱에 다다랐다.

나는 걸음을 멈추고 자잘한 꽃들의 잔디 위에 무릎을 꿇었다.

가슴에 두 손을 모아 봉우리 위의 짙푸른 하늘을 향해 기도의 자세를 가다듬었다. 무아경의 몇 분. 천천히 일어섰다.

"무슨 축원입니까?" 등 뒤에서 S씨의 장난기 목소리. "맞추어 보십시오." 나는 싱그레 눈웃음을 돌린다. "남과 북의 평화통일 아닙니까?" "그런 김빠진 것… 맞추어 보세요. 술 한잔 내지요." "허허…." S씨는 웃음을 날리고 한동안 마주 쳐다보다가 "아들을 얻게 해주십사 하는…." 나는 기도의 주제를 밝혔다. "아아따, 대신문사의 국장답지 않게요." S씨는 정색을 해보인다. "요즘에, 대가 어디 있어요."

"하하하…." 함께 큰웃음을 터뜨리고, 나는 어머니의 기도

―어머니는 네 번째 손녀 이름을 차돌이라 지어 주자고 우기셨다. 옛날 가까운 문중의 조부뻘 되는 누구네가 이 이름 다음에 아들을 얻었다면서. 그러나 이런 명명도 허사였다. 울고 있는 며느리에게 "젊은 나이에 또 낳으면 되지비…" 달래면서도 우직한 시어머니는 가슴속의 어둠을 밖에 내보이지 않았다. 그 '또 낳으면'의 해산이 이달 중이다―를 대신했노라고 말했다. 그리고는 정상까지의 이십여 분 동안, 산에 대한 나의 믿음은 이런 옛일 때문일 것이라고 덧붙였다.

―고향에 해발 약 200미터의 산이 있다. 야산이긴 하지만 명산으로 생각된다. 북에서 거리의 전체를 품고 앉았는데 그 모양이 날개를 펴고 앉은 학 같다 해서 학두봉이라고 한다.

봄 한철의 진달래 철쭉은 우리나라 어느 산에서도 흔히 볼 수 있는 멋일 터이지만, 일찍이 노송의 숲속에다 향교鄕校를 앉히고는 많은 일꾼들을 길러 냈었고, 개화 후에는 두 개의 보통학교가 이 산기슭에 세워졌다. 내가 몇 살 때부터 시작된 일인지는 생각나지 않지만 해마다 어머니는 이 산에 제를 드렸다. 뻐꾸기 철이니까 5월초가 될 것이다. 새벽에 놋솥에다 정성들여 마련한 이밥을 머리 위에 이고 10리 길의 산에 오른다. 해가 올라, 열시쯤 되어서 철쭉꽃을 한아름 안고 내려온다. 꽃은 생기가 남아 있었다. 나는 받아서 얼른 꽃병을 만들었다. 그리고는 어머니와 함께 젯밥의 조반을 먹는데 하얀 이밥이 그렇게 맛있을 수가 없었다. 보통학교 2학년 때로 기억된다. 하루는 방과 후에 벗들과 어울려 뒷산에 진달래 꺾으러 올랐다. 절벽을 타다가 발을 빗딛고 미끄러 떨어졌는데 두어 발 아래의 소나무 밑그루가 추락을 막아

주었다. 벗들이 몰려와 허리띠를 이어서 끌어 올려 주었다. 이 일을 당한 후로는 진달래의 뒷산에 다시 오르지 않았다. 해마다 어머니가 꺾어오는 철쭉을 받아 품고는 죽을 뻔했던 절벽의 추억으로 등골에 소름을 돋치곤 했었다. 40년이 지난 지금까지도 그 소나무의 무성한 가지와 튼실한 밑그루의 자태가 선하다.

아들을… 기도를 명심하고 오른 백록담. 잇달아 손녀 다섯을 받은 어머니의 안타까움은 저 호수만큼이나 깊은 것이리라. 나는 조심스레 이마의 땀을 훔쳤다.

산에서 내려온 사흘 후였다. 그날밤 나는 얼근하게 취해서 집에 들어왔다. 현관에 들어서는데 어머니가 황급히 나와 맞으면서 눈짓으로 거동을 조심하라고 말했다. 나는 어머니 방에서 새어나오는 앓음소리로 사연을 직감하고 잠잠히 바깥채의 내 방에 건너와 잠자리에 들었다. 이내 곯아떨어졌다.

"아애비. 야아, 아애비!"

목소리에 나는 눈을 떴다. 흐리멍덩한 의식에서나마 음성이 어머니의 것임을 알아차리고 머리를 소리 쪽으로 일으켜 가다듬었다.

"네에…."

"야아, 아애비. 아들입매." 약간 떨리고 있는 듯한 나직한 음성. 조용히 문이 닫혔다.

"몇 시예요?" 나는 좀더 머리를 일으켜 세워 물었다.

"한시 좀 넘어서…." 문 밖에서 급한 듯한 목소리. 그리고는 잰 발걸음소리가 현관께로 멀어져 갔다.

어머니의 걸음소리가 꺼지자 "앙앙앙…." 무거운 고요를 오직 하나의 울음소리가 적셔 냈다.

나는 얼마동안 입가에 미소를 머금고 있다가 다시 잠길에 들었다.

이튿날 아침, 어머니는 귀한 자식은 이름을 상스럽게 지어 주어야 되는 법이라면서 '개똥이'를 제의했다.

"좋을 것 같군요." 나는 동의해 주고 일터로 나섰다. 바로 7월 4일 열시. '나 평양 다녀왔습니다'의 그날이었다. 동료들은 모두 다방에 몰려 나가서 텔레비전을 보고 있었다. 남북공동성명. 온거리가 당장 북행열차의 기적소리가 울려 퍼질 것 같은 기대와 흥분으로 들떠 있던 그날, 종일 나는 마음을 가다듬지 못하고 지냈다. 동료들의 축복을 거리낌없는 히죽거림으로 받아주고 하며, 손에 일이 잡히질 않아 들락날락 서성거렸다. 경박함을 조심해야지, 하면서도 안 되었다―조국의 평화통일, 양편 수뇌들 사이에서는 이미 서울·평양 사이를 오가며 믿음직스러운 악수가 나누어졌고, 공동선언문을 놓고 축배가 교환되었다는 어마어마한 사실, 그런 감격 때문일까 하고 자신을 생각해 보았다. 아니었다. 큰일과 작은일을 분별 못하는 소인이라고 자꾸 마음을 고쳐 잡아보려 해도 안 되었다― "야아, 아애비. 아들입매." 어머니의 그 떨리는 듯한 음성과 분주한 발걸음, 개똥이의 탄생, 이른바 작은 나의 일을 뇌리에서 지워버릴 도리가 없었다.

…샐비어의 꽃밭에는 어둠이 들기 시작했다. 매미는 여전히 울어대고 이따금 길목 놀이터에서 조무래기들의 환성이 고요를 적셔 놓곤 했다. 뒤꼍에서 그릇소리가 들려오는 것이 아내가 개똥이를 업고 저녁밥을 짓고 있는 모양이었다. 나는 일어나 어머니 방으로 건너갔다.

어머니는 누워 있었다.

"좀 어떠세요?"

"어지럽지만, 머리는 덜 아픈 것 같아… 여기가 이렇게 답답하니…."

어머니는 가슴 한 중앙을 만져 보였다.

"며칠 치료를 받으시면…."

나는 어머니 머리맡에 다가앉았다 이마를 짚어 보았다. 열이 처진 것 같은 느낌이다.
 "잡숫고 싶으신 것은 없습니까?'
 "통 입맛이 없으니…."
 어머니는 미간을 찌푸려 보였다.
 —잘 견디시면 6개월….
 나는 어머니 얼굴에서 시선을 뗐다. 가슴(어머니가 만져 보이는 그 자리)에 묵직한 것이 들앉으면서 숨이 가빠지는 느낌이었다.
 —참으로 모르고 있기만 못한 일….
 나는 턱을 쓰다듬으며 여섯 달이라는 시공을 헤아려 보았다. 8월, 9월, 10월…임종. 눈을 뜨고 앉아 지켜 볼 수 없는 부대낌일까. 아니고 잠들듯이 조용히 숨을 거두는 그런 하나님의 부르심이었으면 얼마나…아버지는 숨을 거두기 며칠 전부터 기나긴 가을밤을 새우기가 힘이 들어 어머니에게 안락사를 호소했었다는데….
 나는 임종이라는 것을 지켜 본 일이 없다. 아버지 때에는 고향에서 100리 떨어진 시골 국민학교에서 교편을 잡고 있었다. 전보로 아들을 부르자는 어머니의 부탁을 아버지는 끝내 막았다는 것이었다—교사가 제 아비의 임종 때문에 앞당겨 교단을 비워서야 되겠느냐고. 음력 9월이었으니까 북국에서는 깊은 가을이었다. 고향에서 전갈이 달려오기 전날밤 나는 큰 구렁이가 방안에 들어온 꿈을 꾸고는 아버지의 임종을 예감했었다. 열아홉 살의 상주, 시신 앞에 꿇어앉아 처음으로 곡이라는 것을 배웠는데, 음절이 어쩌나 빨랐던지 뒤에서 지켜 보고 있던 어느 아주머니가 천천히 하라고 타일러 주었다. 입관 때에는 목놓아 울었다. 아버지 5년 전에 할머니, 엄동설한의 동짓달이었다. 그보다 5년 전인 한여름에 할아버지의 장사가 있었다. 9일장이었던가, 아무튼 여러 날을 국수와 돼지고기와 죽과 만장의 웅성거림이었다. 곡소리의 간간을 희미한 촛불가에서 떠돌고 있던 모기의 울음소리, 앵 앵… 가늘면서도 날카로운 그 소리가 이상하게도 뇌리에서 지워지질 않는다. 할아버지의 훨씬 이전에 단 하나의 누이동생을 잃었는데, 해마다 한식 추석 아침에 공동묘지의 그 작은 무덤 앞에다 어머니가 사과 한 알을 묻어 주곤 하던 기억밖에는 생각나는 것이 없다. 아버지 후로 서른한 해. 해방이 있던 해에 어머니와 둘이 남으로 넘어오게 되었으니, 그동안에 있었을 혈육들의 많은 타계들을 목도할 길이 없게 되었다. 외갓집의 할아버지는 돌아가셨을 게고, 아랫마을 새집의 할머니는, 큰고모는, 만약 살아 있다면 나이가… 간혹 어머니와의 대화에서 생사가 점쳐지고, 그럴 적마다 나는 어머니의 얼굴에서 단절의 외로움을 쉽게 읽어내곤 했었다.

나는 어머니 얼굴에 눈길을 돌렸다. 어머니는 가슴에 두 손을 모아 얹어 놓고 잠길에 들어 있었다.

　　아아
　　생명은 영원 속에 태어나고
　　영원 속에서 죽어간다.
　　그저 그것뿐이라고 하는 것은
　　인간의 유일唯一의 영광이며
　　생물의 유일의 애수이다.

나는 어느 일본 시인의 '묵시록'默示錄이라는 시의 구절을 생각하다 말고는 일어나 조용히 문을 닫고 어머니 방에서 물러 섰다.

세 군데의 병원을 찾아다니는 동안 한 달이 지났다. 세 군데 모두가 같은 진단이었다. 끝내 엑스레이만은 피했다. 뻔한 결과일 터이니 고통을 주는 일밖에는 안 된다는 생각에서였다.
 어머니는 감기가 나은 후로는 빨래도 돌보고 뜨락을 거닐면서 꽃나무들도 만져 주게 되었다. 그러나 그런 손붙임은 원래가 자상하고 한가히 앉아 있기를 싫어하는 성깔에서의 새벽 한때의 일일 뿐 낮 종일은 누워 있어야만 했다.
 어느날 나는 어머니의 초상화를 부탁해 보자는 생각에서 C화백을 집에 청하여 박주를 나누었다. 낼까말까 망설이다가 꺼낸 청이었는데 C씨는 쾌히 맡아 주었다. 그래서 앨범 속의 어머니 사진 중 석 장을 골라 내었다. 한 장은 50대의 흑백 독사진이었고, 다른 두 장은 작년 봄 서귀포 구경 때 차돌이와 함께 찍은 칼라였다. 석 장을 종합하여 60대의 모습을 십호 정도에다 담아 보기로 하였다.
 "물감은 프랑스 것을 쓰지요."
 취기 때문인지 기염을 보여 주는 C씨에게,
 "아이고, 과분해서요."
 나는 진심으로 감사해 마지않는다.
 "제작에 한 달 정도는… 큰 기댈랑 마십시오."
 하고 C씨는 어머니의 병세를 물었다.
 나는 그런 정도의 날짜라면 걱정할 형편은 아니라고 대답해 주었다, 그리고는 굳이 사양하는 C에게 한란寒蘭 분 하나를 선사했다.
 "이걸… 너무 과하지 않습니까."
 한길에 나와서도 거북해 하는 C씨. 나는 택시를 잡아서 난분을 넣어 주었다.
 ─이 그림의 일도 어머니가 눈치채서는….
 나는 방에 돌아와 앨범을 챙겨 거두면서 마음속으로 다짐했다.

이미 며칠 사이에 예민해진 어머니의 마음자리를 깨닫게 된 때문이다.
며칠 전, 정말 뜻밖의 일이었다. 집의 다섯 평 가량 되는 꽃밭은 어머니 손으로 가꾸어진 것이다. 집을 마련한 후, 아홉 해 동안 나는 사들이기만 했었을 뿐 손을 씻으면 그것으로 끝나 버렸고, 뒷일은 어머니가 도맡아 왔었다. 흙을 빻아 심고 물을 주고 거름을 장만하고, 심지어는 농약을 뿌려 주는 일까지도 어머니의 소관사로 되어 있다. 어떤 때 아내가 민망스럽다고 나를 꾸짖으면 어머니는 "놔두라고 해요. 벽에다 못도 박을 줄 모르는 사람보구…" 하며 두둔해 주고는 전혀 괘념하질 않는다. 어머니의 원예, 배운 것은 아닐 터인데 꽃밭의 목련꽃·치자·산다화, 뒷곁의 밀감나무 할 것 없이 모두 칠칠하니 잘 커가고 있다. 나의 어릴 때 기억으로는 어머니가 좋아하는 꽃은 채송화(장독대가에 가득했던)라고 생각했다. 그러던 것이 서울에서의 한때는 나팔꽃으로 바뀌었고, 제주에 내려와서는 샐비어가 되었다. 지난 10년 동안, 어머니가 깨꽃이라고 하는 이 꽃은 어느 해를 거르지 않고 집의 앞마당을 푸진 주홍으로 물들여 왔다. 어머니의 말을 빌면 샐비어는 청신한 꽃빛깔뿐만이 아니고, 먼저 핀 것은 지면서도 수없이 새로운 피움으로 넉넉히 석 달을 건재하는 그 생기는 달리 비길 데가 없을 것이라고.
이 샐비어 곁에다 올봄에 서귀포에서 백목련(3년생) 두 그루를 얻어다 심었다. 뿌리가 좋아 쉽게 활착을 보게 되었는데 그만 하나의 밑그루를 쥐가 갉아 놨다. 어머니는 못된 놈이라고 분을 참지 못해 하면서 막바로 철사망을 구해다가 다시 침범을 못하게 밑그루를 싸주었다, 그러나 타격이 심했던 모양이어서 이른 여름에 들면서부터 시들시들 마르기 시작하더니 어머니의 와병 무렵에는 서너 개의 잎만을 남기는 절망을 보여 주었다.

며칠 전, 어머니는 이 앓고 있는 목련을 뽑아서 치워 버리면 싶다고 나에게 말한 것이다. 전에는 가망이 없다고 생각되는 나무를 내가 뽑아 버리자고 하면 새해 봄까지 기다려 보자고 말리던 어머니, 아직은 잎을 지니고 있어 어쩌면 소생을 생각해 볼 수 있는 것을 치워 버리면 싶다고 한다. 나는 뭉클하는 가슴속을 의식하고는 한참을 어머니의 표정을 살펴보며 망설이다가 뽑아 버리기로 마음을 잡았다. 일은 어렵지 않았다. 두어 마디로 부러뜨려 뒤켠에 갖다 버리고 돌아왔다.

"시원하다."

마루에서 샐비어께에 눈길을 붓고 앉아 있던 어머니는 입가에 상그레 웃음을 담았다.

나는 어머니 곁에 나란히 앉았다. 동향 마루. 구름이 머흘거리는 하늘은 모색이 짙어가고 있었다.

"구경을 다니자구 했었는데… 일본두 가보구 미국두 가보구…."

어머니는 전후가 없이 이런 말을 꺼냈다.

"여행이라니요?"

"아아니, 그저…."

어머니는 입가의 웃음을 감춘다. 부질없는 생각이었다고 스스로를 뉘우쳐 보는 것이겠다.

"아마도 어머니만큼 구경을 많이 한 사람도 많지 않을 겝니다."

"그래…."

어머니는 다시 미소를 짓는다.

"자, 이북에서는 함흥·원산·평양, 나오셔서 서울·목포·제주, 제일 남쪽이라는 서귀포까지 구경하시구, 비행기도 몇 번 타보시구요… 이제 병 나으시면 부산으로 경주 쪽만 구경하시면 팔도강산 안 가보신 데가 없는 셈이지요. 외국에야 아무나 쉽게…."

"그래 그래, 비행기두 타보구…?"
어머니는 활기를 띠는 목소리로 맞장구였다.
"어머니, 나 일곱 살까지 젖 먹었다지요?"
나는 화제를 바꿀 요량으로 응석기의 말투로 물었다.
"참 잘두 매달려 붙어서… 마지막엔 젖이 쓰다구 하면서…."
어머니는 말을 끊었다가,
"어떻게 보챘던지 누구 한 사람 들쳐 업고 밖에 나가야 모두들 밥상을 받아 놓구 앉을 생각을 했지비."
덧붙이며 묻지 않은 이야기로 신바람을 내는 것이었다.

나의 기억으로는 얼마나 보채었는지, 또 일곱 살까지 먹은 젖이 어떤 맛이었는지 전혀 막막한 이야기다. 다만 한 가지 생생히 기억하고 있는 어머니 얼굴이 있다. 잿속의 마지막 불티처럼 꺼질 듯 가물거리다가 되살아나곤 하는 이상한 기억.

…화창한 봄날 한낮. 나는 동구 밖 가로수 길가에 있었다. 아카시아 꽃이 한창이었다. 쭈그리고 앉아 신작로께를 지켜 보고 있었다. 어머니가 오지 않을까 하고. 집에서 지쳐 울다가 마중을 나온 거겠다. 그 햇빛이 가득한 길을 홀연히 어머니가 나타났다. 따뜻한 햇볕과 무엇인가를 머리에 이고 있는 어머니의 얼굴뿐, 신작로의 어디에서 어떤 걸음걸이로 왔는지, 그런 전후 순서는 생각나지 않는다. 검은 머리카락, 둥그스름한 얼굴에 활짝 잡는 웃음이 성큼 다가와 내 손을 잡았다는 기억뿐이다.

나는 간혹 이 이상한 기억의 이야기를 꺼내면 어머니는 네가 다섯 살(어머니가 스물아홉 살이었으니까) 때였었다고 한다. 젖을 먹었다는 일곱 살의 기억은 못하고…무슨 착각이 아니냐고 되물으면, 어머니는 머리에 이고 있던 것이 손재봉틀이었으니 틀림이 없다는 것이다.

이 기억속의 어머니 얼굴, 손을 잡히고 쳐다보던 그 높이가 어머니와 나 사이에 가장 자연스러운 위치일 것이라고, 그후의 많은 일월을 두고 나는 이따금 문득 상기해 보곤 한다. 그리고 그런 추억은 위태로운 고비의 나에게 안정을 일깨워 주어 일어서게 했는지도 모른다.

어머니의 손재봉틀. 큰집은 해사海事로 많던 가산을 망쳐 버리고 세간을 난 우리 세 식구는 아버지의 술로 밑창이 빠져 어머니는 삯바느질을 결심한 것이다. 연후 십수 년을 어머니는 손재봉틀에 매달리는 고생이었고. 아버지는 마흔 살에 결국 술로 하여 세상을 떠난 것이다.

꽃밭의 샐비어는 볼품없이 퇴색해 버리고, 그 곁에서 흠뻑 물기를 머금은 국화가 봉오리를 지었다.

일요일마다 교회의 분들이 찾아와서 성경을 놓고, 어머니를 위한 기도를 드려 주었다. 기도가 있는 날의 어머니는 약간 생기를 돌이키는 것 같았다. 아이들의 밥상에도 어울려 보고 '할머니'의 '할'을 발음해 내는 개똥이를 무릎에 품고 마냥 대견스럽다는 표정으로 숟가락질을 가르쳐 주기도 한다.

그러나 그런 생기는 아침 한때의 일일 뿐, 안색으로 보나 수면이 고르지 못한 것으로 보아 악화를 쉽게 짐작할 수 있었다.

어느날 어머니의 초상화가 왔다.

"뜻하지 않았던 여행으로 약속이 늦어… 죄송합니다."

C씨가 끌러 놓은 그림을 놓고 나는 한눈에 걸작이라고 사의를 표했다. 눈·귀·입매, 환한 반백의 60대 모습이었다.

C씨와 나는 소주상을 놓고 앉았다. 나는 잔을 비우며 책상 위에 놓은 그림의 어머니 얼굴을 지켜보며 하다가 문득 아버지 사진이 초라함을 깨달았다. 설·추석, 음력 9월 열이렛날(아버지의 기일), 이렇게 일년

에 세 번만 온 식구 앞에 모습을 보이곤 하는 아버지의 흰 두루마기의 흑백사진을 책상 위의 '어머니'와 동석 시키자고 생각해 보았다. '격이 말이 아니군.' 머리를 젓다 말고는 C씨에게 잔을 돌렸다.

아버지의 사진. 서른다섯 아니면 여섯 살 때의 모습일 것이다.

이런 기억이 생각난다. "사진을 찾아오라." 아버지의 분부. 나는 거리의 S사진관으로 단숨에 달려 올라갔다. 사진관 주인은 아버지의 술친구임을 나는 알고 있었다. 사진대는 이미 술자리에서 마무리가 되어 있었는지 나는 빈손으로 찾으러 나선 것 같은 기억이다. 한 가지 이제도 잊혀지질 않는 것은 사진관 주인 곁에서 아버지의 사진을 물끄러미 (시력이 좋지 않음인지) 눈여겨보고 있던 한 초로의 사나이가 "여인인가요?" 하고 혼잣말로 중얼거린 일이다. 사진관 주인의 그 훤칠한 키와 길쭉한 얼굴 윤곽은 어렴풋이 생각나는데 초로의 사나이가 어떤 얼굴이었는지는 전혀 잡히질 않는다. 그러나 "여인인가요?"의 여인만은 이상하게 분명히 기억된다. 여인? 무슨 뜻일까. 변변치 못한 생김새라는 말일까. 잘생겼다는 말일까. 나는 헐떡거리면서 집에 돌아와 아버지에게 사진을 건네고는 '여인'의 이야기를 꺼냈다. 조심스레 아버지의 표정을 지켜 보는데 아버지는 입가에 빙그레 웃음을 띠면서 여인은 여자를 말하는 것이라고. 여인?… 나도 덩달아 웃다가 바깥의 놀이터로 나갔다. 벗들과 어울리기 시작했지만 자꾸 어색해지는 가슴속을 억제할 도리가 없었다. 여자 같다면 변변치 못할 수 있다는 말이 될 것이다. 맞는 말일는지도 모른다. 나는 좀체로 놀이에 신바람이 나질 않았다.

여자 닮았다는 아버지. 어쩌다가 사업을 벌이면 인부들에게 노임을 너무 후하게 주어서 번번이 실패하게 마련이었다는 어머니의 이야기를 빌 것 없이 친구들이 권하는 술잔을 적당한 선에서 거절하지 못하여 끝내는 중독으로 타계했다는 사실만으로도 아버지의 여인성女人性

은 짐작이 된다.

　내가 찾아온 그 명함판 사진이 어떤 과정을 통해 대판으로 확대 되어 젯상에 올려지게 되었는지는 얼른 생각이 나지 않는다.

　어머니 품속에 간직되어(해방 전 북에서의 사진은 이 한 장 뿐이다) 38선을 넘어 왔었고, 그로부터 20년쯤 지나서 제주시의 어느 사진관에서 확대되었을 것일 게라는 짐작인 것이다. 그리고 이 확대는 우리들의 제주 정착定着과 거의 그 시기를 같이하는 것이라는 생각이다.

　"자, 듭시다."

　나는 C씨에게 권하고 아내를 불러 작은 병 하나를 더 청했다.

　새 병의 술을 반쯤 비우면서 한참 동안 난蘭 가꾸기 이야기를 나누다가 나는 '아버지 사진이 있는데…' 말을 꺼낼 뻔한 스스로를 아프게 뉘우쳤다. 잔을 단숨에 비워 C씨에게 돌리고 어색한 심정을 얼버무렸다. 그리고는 헝클어지는 가슴을 가다듬어 생각을 고쳐잡았다. 삼십대의 아버지는 그 젊음으로, 흰 두루마기의 사진으로 두고 접하면 그것으로써 족한 일일 것이다. 그림으로 바꾸어 보아도, 어머니의 반백으로 고쳐볼 수 없는 것, 도리어 더 구겨 버리는 일이 될 것이다. 한 가지 부족한 데가 있다면 어머니의 것보다 작고 틀이 초라하다는 일일 것이다 동석을 위해서 틀을 갈고 같은 크기로 확대해야지.

　한 가을에 들어, 어느 일요일 해질 무렵의 일이었다. 예배 보러온 교회의 분들을 배웅하고 마루에 앉은 어머니는 조금 생기를 띠는 것 같은 눈매로 꽃밭을 지켜보고 있었다.

　나는 난분에 물을 주고 있었다.

　"아애비, 저 깨꽃 치워 버립새, 다 시들었는데…."

　깐깐하다고 생각되는 어머니 목소리에 나는 일손을 멈추고 꽃밭으로 시선을 돌렸다. 반쯤 핀 국화 곁의 샐비어는 끝에다 아직도 몇 잎의 꽃을 지니고 있었다.

"더 놔둡시다. 씨나 받아두고 치워야지요."

"씨? 받아두었습매."

"언제요?"

"벌써지…."

―어디다 두었지요?

나는 입 밖에 말을 내지 않았다. 실수를 할 뻔했다고 자신을 뉘우쳤다.

어머니는 나의 동요를 눈치챘는지, 한동안 침묵을 짓고 있다가,

"봉지에 싸서 작은방 애들 책상 위 선반에다 매달아 두었습매."

하고 나직이 말했다.

나는 뜨거운 것이 가슴을 헤집고 밀려듦을 깨닫고 부지중 긴 한숨을 몰아 쉬었다.

"차돌이더러 국화를 다치지 말라구 욕해둡새."

어머니의 목소리가 다시 깔깔해졌다.

"예, 호되게 욕해 놓겠어요."

나는 대답하고 꺼낼 뻔한 고소를 참았다. 며칠 전의 일이 생각났기 때문이었다.

마당에 찢어 놓은 국화 꽃봉오리 두 개가 떨어져 있었다.

그것을 주워서 쓰레기 통에 버린 어머니는 차돌이를 불러 들였다. "요년이, 초란이같이 싱숭생숭한 장난을…." 눈을 부릅떠 꾸짖었다.

"개똥이가 꺾어 달래서…." 차돌이는 태연스레 엇섰다.

전 같으면 "모르쿠다. 나 앙 그랬수다."로 도망쳐 버렸을 터인데 개똥이를 들고 나선 것이다. ― '할머니가 자기를 닮아서 눈치도 빠르고

부지런할 게라는 개똥이', 그 한치도 물러설수 없는 편애를 차돌이는 잘 알고 있다. 아니나다를까. 어머니는 "개똥이가…" 낮추는 음성이었다.

　나는 난분을 방안에 옮겨 놓고 마루에 가서 어머니 곁에 앉았다.
　"국화가 피는 것이 늦습니다."
　나는 담배를 피워 물고 혼잣말로 어머니의 시선을 살폈다.
　"날씨가 이렇게 따뜻한데… 추워야 빨리 피지."
　어머니는 국화께에 눈길을 잡고 있는 채 말했다.
　추워야 빨리 피는 국화. 정말 그럴까… 나는 생각해 보았다.
　아니지, 따뜻해야겠지. 추워야지, 어머니 말이 맞을 것 같아. 아니지, 착각일 거야.
　나는 답을 못 맺는 자신이 우스워 속으로 웃고 있는데,
　"이 9월달을 넘기면 한 3년 더 앉아질 것 같은데…."
　어머니는 혼잣말을 중얼거렸다.
　"어머님두… 무슨 말씀을…."
　"아닙매. 아애비는 모릅매."
하고 어머니는 음력 9월에는 아버지 뿐만 아니고 집안의 많은 사람들이 이 세상을 떠났다면서 이름을 들어 헤아려 보이는 것이었다.
　"이제 다 되어 가는군요."
　나는 화제를 바꿀 생각으로 K호텔(열 아홉층의 작업장)을 손짓해 가리켰다.
　"음."
　어머니는 응대하고 시선을 들었다.
　동쪽 시계를 온통 차지하고 있는 거대한 물건에서는 작업이 한창이었다. 작렬하는 산소의 불꽃. 철근을 다루는 듯한 강렬한 금속성이 들

려온다.

 K호텔. 어머니는 잘못된 일이라고 곧잘 노기가 서리는 눈길로 쳐다보면서 못마땅해 하는 것이었다.

 올봄에 제주시 한복판 제일 높은 자리에 19층 건물이 세워지기 시작했다. 일본의 어느 재벌과의 합자라는 말도 들리는 K호텔의 실체가 이렇게 어마어마한 건물일 줄을 미처 생각(시민들)하지 못했다. 10층, 15층… 점차 그 거구를 드러내면서 한라산을 무색케 하는 높이에 시민들은 장소가 잘못 택해졌음을 말하기 시작했다. 변두리에 나가서 세워졌더라면 하는 불만들이었다.

 어느날 어머니는 저게(K호텔) 뭐냐고 묻기에 나는 호텔이라는 물건이라고 대답해 주었다. 호텔이 뭐냐기에 여관이라고 했더니 "밥집이군"하고 가벼운 코웃음을 꺼내 보였다.

 "호텔이랬지? 흥!"

 어머니는 어느날의 그 코웃음을 다시 꺼냈다.

 "19층짜리 호텔을 지어 돈을 벌어 들인다는데 나쁘십니까?"

 나는 어머니의 고소를 지켜 보고 있다가 떠보는 말투로 물었다.

 "돈을 벌어? 얼마나 번다는데?"

 "각재기(갈퀴)루 마구 긁어들이듯 번답디다."

 "흠, 각재기루?"

 어머니는 내 표현이 우습다는 것이겠다. 어금니를 맞무는 듯한 표정이 되더니,

 "돈이믄 단가?"

하고 중얼거리다가,

 "저 꼭대기서 내려다보믄 우리집 마당두 보이겠지? 이렇게 앉아 있는 것두…."

힘을 주어 말했다.

"예, 내려다 보일 겝니다."

"내려다보여, 응!"

"보이믄 어떻습니까. 외국 사람들 끌어들여 돈을 벌어야지요."

"돈이믄 다라… 외국 사람들 끌어들여… 배부른 돼지가 되믄 좋겠군."

어머니는 눈시울에 잔주름을 잡는데, 노기가 틀림없다고 나는 생각했다.

"유식한 말씀 다 하십니다."

나는 벙긋 웃어 보였다.

"배부른 돼지래서?"

"네."

나는 소리를 내어 웃었다.

어머니도 입가에 미소를 담아 보이다가 추운기가 느껴진다면서 방 안에 들어갔다.

나는 그대로 앉아서 담배를 빨고 있었다.

어머니는 무학無學이다. 이력을 적는다면 1900년 7월 1일생(음력), 스무 살에 출가, 오누이를 낳았고, 50고개에 들어서면서 기독교인이 되었다. 성경은 한 구절도 읽어내지 못하지만 독실하다는 점에서는 마음 놓고 자랑할 수 있을 것이다. 1900년은 이른바 20세기의 첫머리, 그러니까 네 번의 전쟁을 겪은 셈이 된다.

노일露日, 1·2차 세계대전, 6·25.

그 6·25를 겪고 있는 동안 어머니는 이름을 고쳐쓰기 시작했다. '李會孫'을 '金順'으로 바꾸었다. 이 개명은 1·4 후퇴 후 어머니와 내가 만 4년 동안을 헤어져 있는 사이의 일이었다.

"어머니, 이름을 고치셨군요." 개명을 알고 놀라 보였더니 어머니는 "어쩌다 그렇게 되었지." 숨숨하니 받아넘길 뿐 새 이름이 좋아보이느냐, 어쩌냐고 더 이야기가 없었다. '금순이'. 나는 한때 피난 부산에서 유행한 '영도다리 난간 위에 초승달만 외로이 떴네….' 가락에 나오는 '그 음순아…'가 머리에 떠오르므로 조금 쑥스러운 기분이었으나, 그래도 '曾孫'보다는 상급이라고 생각되었다. 부르기에 어감이 부드럽고, 한자로 쓰게 되는 경우에도 맵시가 있어 보이고, 아무튼 '이금순'은 어머니가 기독교에 몸을 담게 되면서부터일 것이다. 어머니의 연보 봉투로 그런 짐작인 것이다. "똑똑한 글씨로 곱게 한 줄 적어달라"고 어머니가 봉투를 내놓으면, 나는 아무리 바쁜 일 중이더라도 우선하여 봉투를 받아 펜을 들어야 했었다. 내가 신춘문예에 당선되었을 때, 제대했을 때, 성란이 입학, 차돌이 탄생, 개똥이 등등… 뭐이라고 씁니까? 물으면, 잘 알고 있으면서 번번이 어째서 묻느냐고 못마땅해 한다. 그래서 '감사합니다'를 제목으로 놓고는 조금 낮추어서 '이금순'을 써서 넘겨 주면, 간직해 두었던 깨끗한 지폐 일봉―封을 꾸려서 아이들의 손이 미치지 못할 높은 곳에 두었다가 품고 나서는 것이다.

하느님에 대한 믿음. 내가 늘 자랑해서 부끄럽지 않다고 생각하는 어머니의 덕德은 이 질박한 신앙이 그 바탕이 되는 것 같다. 덕이라는 말이 나왔으니 말이지만, 어머니의 덕성은 내가 알고 있는 이 세상의 어느 영웅 위인에 못지않은 것이리라는 생각이다. 조금 거추장스러운 표현이 되는 것 같지만, 해방 후의 많은 애국지사 집권자들보다는 세상사를 생각하는 안목이 못하지 않으리라.

어머니의 어록語錄, 더욱 어리석은 자존自尊이 되는 것 같지만, '과욕은 금물이다.'를 비롯하여 내가 익혀 잊지 못하고 있는 몇 가지가 있다.

'공짜를 탐내지 말라. 그것에는 반드시 말썽이 뒤따르기 마련이다.' 어머니는 이 교훈을 늘 명심하고 있으면서도 평생 두 번 부끄러운 일을 당했노라고 얼굴을 붉히곤 하는 에피소드가 있다.

1946년, 내가 서울로 넘어오고 고향에 단신으로 남은 어머니는 마을의 친구들과 어울려 평양 장사를 다녔다. 혹심한 식량난, 고향의 해산물을 가지고 가서 곡식이나 고무신 따위 필수품으로 바꾸어 오는 왕래였다. 몇 차례 재미를 봐오다가 그만 알몸이 되어 장사를 놓게 되었다. 물건을 팔아 쥔 돈을 품고 노점가를 거닐다가 골목길에 양복감을 놓고 앉은 쑤왈탕판(어머니의 표현을 빌면)에 걸려든 것이었다. 허름한 옷차림의 사나이(양복감을 놓고 앉은)는 팔지 않겠노라고 마구 손을 내어젓는데, 둘레에 모여선 객들이 너나 할 것 없이 몇 마씩을 사가지고 물러가기에 덮어놓고 다섯 마를 샀다는 것이다. 여인숙에 돌아와서 펼쳐 놓고 보니 한마라던 물건이 책상보 한 장도 안되는 날림이 아닌가. 그만 눈앞이 캄캄해서 허둥지둥 그 골목길을 찾아가 보았으나 깨끗이 종적을 감추어 버린 파장, 그제서야 정신이 들면서 전후 사정이 잡히더라는 것이다.

어머니가 잊지 못하는 두 번째의 쑤왈탕판은 환도 무렵의 서울에서였다. 1·4 후퇴 때 어머니는 서울에 남야 있었다. 동대문시장에 쌀가게(노점)를 놓고 돈을 조금 쥐게 되었다. 어느 이른 봄날 해질 무렵, 가게를 파하고 빠른 걸음으로 원서동의 단간방을 향해 창경원 서편 고갯길을 올라가고 있었다. 골목길에서 깨끗한 옷차림의 젊은 여자가 나타나 불러 세우더라고. 나이는 스물댓 쯤으로 보였고, 이쁘장하게 생긴 얼굴이 나쁜 인상은 아니었다.

"아주머니, 피엑스(PX)에서 나온 고급 화장분인데 헐값으로 나누어 드릴 테니 살 생각이 없느냐?"고 방긋 웃어대며, 피엑스는 미군부대를 말하는 것이고, 분은 틀림없는 고급 미제, 도매가격도 안 되는 헐값이니 곱절은 누구의 돈을 받을지 모르게 될 것이니…이런 말들을 단숨에 늘어놓고는 앞가슴 품속에서 분통을 꺼내 살짜기 열어서 냄새를 맡아보라고 내미는데, 그 향기가 그렇게 좋아 보일 수 없더라는 것이다 "가봅시다." 물건이 있다는 곳으로 따라나섰다. 지니고 있던 돈을 몽땅 털어놓고 한아름의 화장분을 보자기에 쌌다. 집에 와서 보니 통속의 것은 밀가루였다.

평양 때의 일이 생각나서 찾아나서지는 않았다. "반반하게 생긴 년이…" 천만 뜻밖이었다고 하면서, 어머니는 이 일 이후로는 어떤 경우일지라도 길에서 걸음을 멈추지 않기로 결심했다고.

어록에 속하는 이야기를 한 가지만 더 점철해 두어야 하겠다.

어머니는 이 삽화揷話를 여러 번 되풀이하여 음미한 것으로 나는 기억한다.

앞에서도 약간 비쳤지만, 6·25 그해 10월 그믐에 나는 이른바 제이국민병의 몸으로 서울을 떠났다. 내가 떠난 뒤에 어머니는 성북동 셋방에서 원서동의 친척집으로 이사하도록 되어 있었다.

친척집의 가족 전부가 피난을 나서고 칠십 난 할머니만이 남게 되어 함께 의지하고 지내는 것이 좋으리라는 생각에서였다. 이사를 하자 어머니는 쌀장사를 시작했다. 김치도 담그어 넣은 채였고, 마당에 우물이 있으니 물 걱정도 없고, 쌀만 가지면 연명은 될 것이라는 계산이었다.

그 정월의 서울은 폐허라 해도 과언이 아닐 만큼 텅 비어 있었다. 눈이 쌓여도 길 쓸 사람이 없었다. 인적이 드문 백설의 거리에 중공군과 북한군이 들어왔다. 상수도가 망가져 있었기 때문에 그들은 우물이 있는 집을 찾아 허둥거렸다. 그런 판국에 이 원서동 집이 안전할 리가 없었다. 북한군 다섯이 여군 둘을 거느리고 점거했다. 어머니네는 안채와 사랑방을 내주고 문간방을 맡았다. 여군들은 주로 취사를 맡고 있었다. 백설의 한겨울을 보내고 2월 그믐에 접어들면서 한강을 사이에 두는 치열한 공방전이 벌어졌다. 쏴아, 쾅, 쏴아 쾅. 강을 건너오는 듯한 포탄이 창경원 북쪽의 산언저리 일대를 밤낮없이 때려 부수었다. 제대로 치료를 받지 못한 부상자들을 아무렇게나 모아 싣고 달리는 마차 행렬, 길목에 벌어진 누더기 옷들. 패전이 뚜렷했다.

그런 어느날, 그들은 집안의 장롱을 뒤지더니, 속에서 흰 천만을 골라내어 저만큼씩 나누어 배낭에 꾸려 넣었다. 밤이 깊어서였다. 여군 둘이는 문간방의 어머니네를 찾아왔다.

"이걸 잡숩새." 고향이 청진이라는 아가씨가 쇠고깃국이라면서 창문을 열었다. 처음 보는 선물이 아니었다. 몇 차례 베풀어진 온정. 받는 편이 언제나 이쪽이 되기는 하지만. "고맙습매. 좀 올라옵새." 안에서 같은 함경도 사투리가 권했다.

"예." 좁은 방안에 네 사람이 모여 앉았다. 촛불이 밝혀져 있었다.

"그동안 신세 많이 졌습매." 청진아가씨가 말을 꺼냈다. "신세라니요?" 어머니가 놀라 보였다. "내일 아침에 떠나게 되었습매." 아가씨는 주저하지 않고 후퇴를 말했다. 그리고는 장롱 속의 흰 천들은 미안하게 되었는데, 눈속의 싸움에서 위장용으로 쓰일 것이니 용서해 주면 싶다고 덧붙였다.

"아주마이, 우리하구 같이 가지 않겠습매." 얼마 간의 침묵 후에 아가씨는 어머니에게 북행을 권했다.

"단 두 몸인 아들이 남으로 내려갔는데 생사도 모르는 내가 어떻게…" 어머니 말에 아가씨는 더 입문을 열지 않고, 멍한 표정이 되더니 마침내 눈물을 떨구기 시작했다.

이튿날 그들은 흰 천을 꾸려 담은 배낭을 걸머 메고 분주히 떠났다. "그렇게 슬피 울 수가…." 어머니는 이야기 때마다 목이 메는지 목소리가 젖었다. 닭똥 같은 눈물을 뚝뚝 떨구면서, 전번 여름 후퇴 때에도 두만강 건너까지 수숫가루로 허기진 몸을 끌며 발다리가 퉁퉁 부었댔는데, 어떻게 또 저 눈길을 나서겠느냐고….

환도 후, 원서동 집은 식구들이 되돌아오고 어머니는 그대로 문간방에 머물러 있었다. 군복의 나는 그 방에서 어머니를 만났다. 인편에 서로 기별은 오가고 있었지만 4년만의 상봉이었다. 그 전날 아가씨가 울고 떠났다는 자리에서 이번에는 어머니가 내 손을 잡고 눈물로 뺨을 적셨다.

음력 9월 열이렛날은 아버지의 기일. 제사를 놓고 나와 아내 사이에 실랑이가 있었다. 나는 차리느라고 웅성거리게 되면 어머니에게 충격이 클 것이니 올해만은 거르자고 했다. 아내는 이웃에서 모두들 알고 있는 일인데 그냥 넘길 수 있겠느냐는 것이었다. 그래서 어머니 의향을 물어 보기로 했다 어머니는 동네의 가까운 이웃들만 청하기로 하고 간단히 치르면 싶다는 의견이었다.

그날 어머니는 활기를 띠는 음성으로 제사일에 백지나 다름없는 나에게 술잔은 이렇게 올리고 과실은 이렇게 하면서 다른 때와는 달리 유달리 마음을 썼다.

"교인답지 않게요…."

나의 농 섞는 말에,

"아버진 교인이 아니었으니까… 그러나 이담에 내 때에는 절대로…."

어머니는 정색을 해보였다.

이튿날 나는 출근이 늦음을 일터에 알리고 늦잠을 자고 있었다.

아내가 깨우는 소리에 눈을 떴다.

어머니가 설사하고 토하는데 빨리 의사를 불러야 하겠다는 것이었다.

나는 파자마바람에 뛰쳐나갔다.

어머니는 신음하고 있었다. 또 뒷간에 가야겠다고 몸을 일으켰다. 아내가 부축한다.

나는 뒷간까지 가실 것 없이 마루에서 요강을 쓰시도록 하라고 아내에게 말했다.

어머니는 대뜸 눈시울에 노기를 띠어 건네면서 아직 그런 몰골은 되지 않았노라는 말을 입속으로 더듬거렸다.

나는 요강을 강요하고는 K원장에게 전화를 걸었다. 대충 병세를 말하고 왕진을 부탁했다.

십분쯤 지나서 K원장은 간호원에게 링겔을 쥐여서 나타났다.

진맥, 혈압, 가슴의 덩어리를 만져보고 두 대의 주사를 놓게 한 다음에 링겔. 그리고는 K원장과 나는 어머니 방을 나왔다.

"참, 기적이군요. 아직도 거동을 하시다니…"

하고 K원장은 평소의 참을성인지는 몰라도 대단한 투병이라고 경탄해 보였다.

아내가 커피를 가져 왔다.

나는 K원장에게 권하고,

"앞으로 얼마 동안이나…"

목소리를 낮추어 물었다.

"아마 이번이 고비가 될는지 모르지요. 혈압이 낮군요. 아무튼 먼길 출타 안하는 게 좋을 겝니다."

"통증 없이도…."

"암이라고 통증이 있는 것은 아니니까요. 전혀 없는 수도 있지요."

"오시게 해서… 죄송합니다."

"천만에요…."

링겔 뒤처리는 아내가 맡기로 하고 K원장과 간호원은 떠났다.

어머니가 잠길에 들어 있는 동안 나는 전화국을 불러 어머니방의 전화기를 내 방으로 옮겨 놨다. 짐짓 어머니가 신경을 쓰게 될 것 같아서 옮겨 놓자고 했었는데, 어머니가 못마땅해 하는 눈치였기에 미루고 있었던 일이다.

이튿날 어머니는 약간 생기를 돌이켰다. 마침 일요일이어서 나는 종일을 텔레비전을 낮게 틀어 놓고 어머니 머리맡을 지켰다.

"좀, 어떻습니까."

"음… 좀 괜찮아…."

어머니는 목이 마르다고 물을 청한다. 나는 주전자의 엽차를 컵에 따라서 숟가락으로 입안을 적셔 주기 시작했다 한 모금 두 모금, 나는 손이 떨렸다—작은 체구이긴 하지만 다부졌던 몸매의 어느 한구석도 제 모습이 아니구나. 큼직하고 복스럽던 귓볼도 쪼그라 붙어 찾아볼 수 없게 되었고, 오똑한 콧날만은 얼굴이 반으로 줄었기 때문에 살아 있어 보이는 것이겠고, 인후께에서 탁 탁 뛰고 있는 혈관.

나는 흐트러지려는 의식을 가다듬어,

"그만 드릴까요?"

물었다.

"음…."

어머니는 눈짓으로 말하고,

"이 가슴을 열어서 삭 씻어버릴 수 없을까?"

내 얼굴을 지켜보았다.

"무슨 말씀이세요."

나는 입술을 깨물고 있다가 말했다.

"의사마다 시원히 말해주지 않으니…."

어머니는 혼잣말을 중얼거리고 조용히 눈을 감았다.

"또 전쟁을 하구 있다지?"

어머니의 음성에 나는 다시 머리맡으로 다가앉았다.

"네, 먼 데서입니다. 젊은 사람들이 많이 죽어가고 있어요."

"젊은 사람들이? 우리나라 사람들은 안 가 있지 애?"

"네, 안 가 있습니다. 이스라엘과 애급이라는 나라인데, 아주 먼 데서입니다"

"음…물…."

어머니는 다시 물을 청했다.

'젊은 사람들이 많이 죽어가고 있어요.' 부지중 꺼낸 말이지만, 다분히 어떤 저의를 품고 있었다. '젊은이들의 죽음'이 어머니에게 위안이 될 성싶다는 그런 타산에서였다.

나는 아버지 때에도 이와 비슷한 대화를 가진 일이 있었다. 아버지는 임종 다섯 달 전부터 불치를 알고 있었다. 사망진단서에는 인후결핵으로 되어 있었지만 여러 가지 병을 겸하고 있었다. 위하수에다, 술로 하여 간도 말이 아니게 나빠 있었을 것이다. 2차대전이 한창인 때였다. 어느날 나는 누워 있는 아버지에게 지금 싸움터에서 많은 젊은이들이 죽어가고 있다고 말했다. 아버지는 내 말뜻을 이해하였음인지 "응…" 하고 입가에 싱그레 웃음을 지어 보였다―나이 사십으로 가는 목숨, 이십대의 청춘들의 죽음에 비하면 참으로 행복스러운 일이지… 조금도 슬프지 않다.

그때 아버지는 웃음을 머금어 주었는데 지금 어머니는 '우리나라 사람들은 안 가 있겠지?'로 받았다. 위안을 위해서라는 내 의중이 빗나간 것이 되었다면 나로서는 조금 섭섭한 이야기가 될 수 밖에 없지만, 어쩌면 어머니는 스스로의 몸을 넘어서서 이웃들, 말하자면 크고 넓은 '나라'라는 것을 염려하고 있는 것일는지도 모른다.
 나는 다시 어머니 입술로 물을 가져 가면서 참을 수 없는 동계로 손이 떨렸다.

 국화가 활짝 폈다. 한라산정에는 첫눈이 내렸는데 꽃밭에는 작은 노랑나비들이 다녀가곤 한다.
 "이걸 언아가 잘라 놨니? 차돌아!" 얼마를 안 있어, 저 꽃밭 언저리에서 이런 어머니의 목소리도 듣지 못하게 될 것이다.
 나는 국화를 놓고 생각했다.
 새해 봄 샐비어의 씨는 누구 손에서 뿌려질까. 아내가 아니면 내손이 되겠지. 봉지의 씨앗은 아이들의 책상 위 선반에 매달려 있다고 알려 주었지. 뿌려 놓기만 하면 어머니 때의 것처럼 푸짐한 주홍으로 온 마당을 비춰 주겠지.
 샐비어는 해가 바뀌면서 다시 생각해 볼 일이고, 이해 안에 맞이하게 될 어머니의 임종은 어떻게 하지. 어떤 촌로村老가 이세상의 온갖 죽음과 탄생은 간조干潮 때라고 했으니, 어머니의 임종도 제주바다의 물이 빠져나갈 때가 되겠지. 야밤중이나 새벽에… '어머니, 어머니…' 몇 번 불러 보고, 조용히 내려 쓰다듬어 눈을 감게 하고, 아이들이 일어나 웅성거리고, 시신을 모시고 향불. 아. 한꺼번에 무너져 앉는 질서. 그러나 허둥거리지는 말아야지. 영전에다 큼직한 아가리의 국화꽃병을 놓을 것을 명심하고 장례의 절차는 교회의 분들에게 의논해서 하고, 비석에다는 성경 한 구절을 넣어야지. 어떤 성구가 적당할까. '살아서 나를 믿는자는 영원히 죽지 않으리라' '너희는 근심하겠으나 너희 근심이 도리어 기쁨이 되리라' '흙으로 돌아갈지어다' 어쩐지 마음에 차질 않는군. 그럼 어떻게 하지.

국화꽃 언저리에 작은 노랑나비가 와서 하늘거리고 있었다.
그렇지, K시인의 이런 묘지송墓地頌이 있었지.

그대들은 이 세상을 마치고 작은 제일祭日 하나를 남겼을 뿐
옛날은 이 세상에 없고, 그대들이 옛날을 이루고 있다.

어쩌다, 잘못인지 노랑나비가 낮게 날아가며
이 가을 한 무덤 위에서 자꾸만 저 하늘에 뒤가 있다고 일러준다.

고시홍

계명戒命의 도시

필자 소개

1972년 제주대학 국어국문학과 졸업. 《월간문학》 신인상 데뷔.
한국소설가협회, 제주학연구소 등 회원, 제주시교육청 장학사(현).
탐라문화상 수상.
소설집 『대통령의 손수건』 『계명의 도시』 외

계명戒命의 도시

고시홍

 심한 갈증과 전화벨 소리에 눈을 떴다. 입 안이 종이컵처럼 건조했다. 나는 눈을 지르감은 채 수화기를 집어들었다.
 "여보오세요……."
 딸그락! 하는 소리에 이어 쇳가루 같은 금속음이 귓잔등을 때렸다. 한마디 대꾸도 없이 일방적으로 차단당했다. 두 번째였다. 잘못 걸려온 전화인 듯했다. 아침 댓바람부터 전화가 걸려올 만한 일이 없었다. 거듭되는 전화벨과 갈증에 의해 눈을 뜬 나는 이불 속에 파묻혀 있던 몸을 끌어냈다. 마른침을 긁어내어 목젖을 축였다. 썩은 개숫물 냄새가 자꾸만 구토증을 일으켰다.
 기억에 남아 있는 것은, 누군가의 부축을 받으며 박지용 사장 집을 빠져 나오던 장면뿐이다. 턱을 받치고 수도 꼭지를 비틀었다. 명치 끝에 고였던 미열이 수돗물에 씻겨 나갔다.
 "술하고 원수진 일 있어요? 쉰 문턱에 들어선 양반이, 나이값 좀 하세요."

"내 걱정은 말고, 과부 연습이나 잘해 두라구."
나는 불퉁스레 내뱉었다.
"저 독살맞을 입. 저승 사자도 이빨만은 빼내놓고 데려가겠수!"
아내는, 말이 씨가 된다는 말을 흘리며 어머니 방으로 들어갔다.
어머니 방은 비어 있었다. 오늘도 시골로 내려간 모양이었다. 잠자리는 그냥 깔려 있었다. 베갯모에 달라붙어 있던 한 오라기의 회백색 머리카락이 내 시선을 붙들었다. 방안으로 들어서자 역한 냄새가 비위를 건드렸다.
"저건 뭐요?"
나는 머리맡에 놓여 있는 사발을 턱으로 가리켰다.
"무슨 원한이 그리 많은지, 원……."
걸레질을 끝낸 아내가 마늘과 양파 조각이 뒤섞여 있는 사발을 들고 나갔다. 호텔 건물로 벼랑을 이룬 사이로 한라산 등성이가 들어왔다.
나는 반쯤 열려 있던 창문을 활짝 열어제쳤다. 불꽃에 휩싸여 있던 고향 마을이 지워졌다. 눈이 부셨다. 제발 집에 불일랑 지르지 말아 줍서……. 워커에 짓눌린 어머니의 젖은 육성이 총성을 삼켰다. 마늘 냄새는 차츰 송장 썩는 냄새로 바뀌었다. 고향 사람들은 마늘을, 악취를 제거하는 소독약 대용으로 썼었다. 무더운 계절에 장사를 지내는 날이면, 상여꾼들은 하나같이 마늘을 알사탕마냥 입 안에 넣은 채 상여 노래를 부르곤 했었다.
"식사하시란 말 안 들리세욧."
"밥 생각은 없으니 마실 거나 있음 좀 줘요."
"이 가는 덴 약도 의사도 없다는데 어떡하죠."
요즘에 와서 더욱 심하다고 했다.
"그래, 저걸 먹으니 효력이 좀 있대?"

"먹는 게 아니라 그냥 머리맡에 두고 냄새만 나게 하는 모양이에요."

나는 씁쓸한 미소를 닦아내며 거울 앞에 섰다. 다시 전화벨이 울렸다.

넥타이 매듭을 짓던 손놀림을 잠시 멈췄다. 전화를 받는 아내의 모습이 거울에 비쳤다.

나는 계속 송수화기에서 새어 나오는 목소리에 귀를 기울였다.

……

그럴 필욘 없고, 내 말만 그냥 전해요. 양한구와 박줏잔깨나 같이 나눴던 사람이어서 하는 말인데, 몸조심하라고 해요. 우리 나란 어디까지나 반공국가란 말요. 그렇게 얘기하면 알 거요.

나는 자물쇠 채우는 금속음을 뒤로 하고 방을 나왔다. 지난 밤, 박 사장네 집 건넌방에서 흘러나오던 육성들이 자동차 경적 속에 파묻혔다. 박 사장, 괜한 짓거리 허지 말게, 몸 다쳐. 자손 없이 내버려진 골총(廢塚)을 건드려서 득될 것 없어……

"무슨 일예요, 여보."

아내가 현관문을 열고 뒤따라 나왔다.

"당신은 몰라도 될 일야."

나는 아내의 겁먹은 얼굴을 외면한 채 짐짓 미소를 지었다.

"뭐라구요? 옆에 서서 전화 내용 다 들었으면서……."

"걱정할 거 없대두."

나는 어처구니없다는 듯한 아내의 표정을 훔쳐 보며 대문간으로 향했다.

"한 이삼 년 더 있다가 사표를 내겠다는 사람 집안에 붙들어 매놓고 또 무슨 일을 저질렀는지……."

그런저런 각오는 하고 착수한 일이었다. 너, 죽어! 너, 죽을래? 너, 죽을 줄 알어! 어린 시절부터 죽음과 주검에 대한 공포에는 면역이 돼 있다. 주먹질과 발길질에 의해 가슴의 뼈가 굳었다. 두려운 것은 오히려 침묵이었다. 침묵 이상의 폭력과 공포는 없다고 생각했다.

레미콘 한 대가 골목길로 비집고 들어섰다. 대문간 계단 위로 올라선 나는 무심히 편지함을 열었다. 노란 서류 봉투 하나가 반으로 접힌 상태로 놓여 있었다. 나는 테이프로 봉해져 있는 봉투를 뜯어내다 말고 발송인을 확인했다. 그러나 발송자 주소와 이름은 적혀 있지 않았다. 먼저 겉봉투를 뜯어냈다. 검정 비닐봉지가 나왔다.

수많은 검은 그림자들이 눈가를 스쳤다.

비닐봉지 속으로 손을 집어넣었던 나는 흠칫 몸을 도사렸다. 침묵보다 무서운 전율이 명치끝을 때렸다.

나는 한참 뒤에야 타이어 자국 위에 나가떨어져 있는 회색 물체를 향해 침을 뱉고 골목을 나왔다. 거듭 골목길 주위로 눈길을 주면서…….

쥐를 잡읍시다! 오늘은 쥐약을 놓는 날입니다. 머리 속은 온통 쥐약 먹고 죽은 사람들과, 쥐약 먹고 죽은 개에 대한 소문으로 채워져 갔다.

'일단 정지'란 흰 페인트 글자가 횡단보도 표지 옆에 바리케이드를 치듯 길바닥에 누워 있었다. 빨간 신호등을 마주하고 섰다. 잿빛 물체의 잔영은 좀처럼 지워지지 않았다. 전선줄에 걸터앉아 있던 제비 한 마리가 건물 벼랑 너머로 낙하했다. 나는 쥐의 시체에 대한 잔영을 걷어내며 횡단보도를 건넜다.

버스는 경사가 급한 고빗길을 휘돌아 나갔다. 소변 금지. 벽보 금지. 주차 금지. 잔디를 밟지 맙시다……. 울긋불긋한 휘장이 드리워진 백화점 간판과 종합시장 건물이 스치고 지나갔다. 내릴 준비를 하기 위해 뒤쪽 승강구께로 몸을 뽑아 냈다. 손 대지 마시오. 출입구 벽면에 부착돼 있는 스티커가 끈끈이주걱처럼 눈가에 달라붙었다. 5일장터는 언제 봐도 생명력이 넘친단 말씀야. 박 사장의 목소리가 해조음처럼 밀려 왔다.

한라산 등반 계획은 중간에서 포기하고 말았다. 점심만 먹고 하산길에 올랐다. 그런데 시내에 도착하자 날씨는 활짝 갰다. 다른 직원들은 먼저 들여보냈다. 나와 박 사장만 5일장터 초입에서 내렸다.

5일장터의 풍물도 한 번쯤 특집으로 다룰 만하겠다고 생각했다.

"양 국장, 우리 모험 좀 해볼까."

"세계 무전여행이라도 하잔 겁니까?"

"4·3에 대해 본격적으로 파헤쳐 볼까 하는데, 양 국장 생각은 어때?"

나는 대답 대신 방금 들어와 앉은 사람들 쪽으로 시선을 돌렸다. 무방비 상태에서 면상을 얻어맞은 기분이었다.

"또 콩밥을 먹게 될 게 겁나는 모양이지."

빈대떡과 막걸리 주전자가 놓여졌다. 이 양반이 무슨 백을 믿고 이렇게 도도하게 나올까 하는 의구심이 지워지지 않았다. 그것도 사람들이 북적대는 5일 장터 한복판에서 4·3의 진상이니, 4·3의 조명이니 하는 말을 노상방뇨하듯 스스럼없이 까발리는 박 사장의 심중을 읽을 수가 없었다.

"처자식이 걱정돼서죠."

총성과 불기둥이 솟구치던 유년의 밤 하늘이 시야를 가렸다.

"이건 뜻밖인데……"

박 사장이 들어올렸던 막걸리 잔을 내려놨다.

"형님 입에서 4·3에 대한 모험을 제의하는 것도 뜻밖이군요. 설마

4·3을 구구법으로 착각하고 있는 건 아니시겠죠."

"솔직히 말하면, 잡지 판매량을 늘릴 궁리를 하던 끝에 생각해 낸 걸세. 요즘 들어서 좌경 쪽의 목청이 너무 드세어 가는 것도 그렇고……. 그러나 이건 어디까지나 내 의견일 뿐이고, 최종 결정은 편집국장인 자네가 알아서 하게."

구멍 뚫린 장막 틈으로 새어 든 햇살이 시선을 간질였다. 탐조등 같았다. 호미와 낫, 도마칼이며 연탄 집게, 꽃삽 등이 진열돼 있는 좌판대가 보였다. 너 하나쯤은 쥐도 새도 모르게 치워 버려도 뭐랄 사람 없어. 누구의 사주를 받고서 이 '4·3 진상규명동지회'란 걸 만들었지? 정말입니다. 저희들이 자발적으로 만든 모임입니다. 오직 억울하게 죽은……. 다시 군화의 주인공이 정강마루를 걷어찼다. 나는 나머지 언어들을 어금니 사이에 끼워 지그시 깨물었다. 진공이 돼 버린 머릿 속에는 오직 백열등 하나가 매달려 있을 뿐이었다. 이제, 대학 이학년밖에 안 된 자식들이 뭘 안다고 까불어, 임마! 삼십대밖에 안 된 당신네들은 뭘 안다고 쿠데탈 일으켰죠? 나는 하마터면 이렇게 고함을 지를 뻔했었다.

"양국장, 지금 쌍잔 받고 앉아서 위령제 지내고 있나."

"그러고 보니, 하다 못해 위령탑 하나라도 세울 수 있는 분위길 조성하긴 해야겠군요."

나는 유리잔 속에 가라앉아 있는 하얀 분말의 앙금을 젓가락으로 휘휘 저어댔다.

"어떡 할까?"

"생각해 보죠, 뭐. 사십 년 동안 방치돼 있던 고분 발굴 작업인데, 적어도 사십 일 동안의 준비 기간은 있어얄 게 아닙니까."

제 목구멍에 낀 땟국 씻어내기도 바쁜 세상에, 금지 구역에 있는 공동묘지를 파헤쳐 봐야 뼈다귀밖에 더 나오겠느냐는 말은 일단 보류하기로 했다.

"어쩜 자네 한풀이도 되지 않을까 해서 꺼냈던 말이니깐 부담스러워할 필욘 없네."

모험이 함정이 될 수 있다는 말로 받아들였다.

"그러나 만약 본격적으로 착수한다면, 내가 바람막이 구실은 하겠네. 대공 담당 책임자들에게도 이미 귀띔을 해뒀으니깐."

자기로서는 잡지사 판권은 물론이고 인쇄소까지라도 물 말아 먹을 마음의 준비가 돼 있다고 했다. 세상을 살아오면서 뼈저리게 체득한 것은, 자기를 가장 잘 아는 사람을 경계해야겠다는 생각이었다. 박 사장과는 이십 년 가까이 지내왔다. 신문 기자 시절만 해도 너나들이를 할 정도였다. 적어도 그의 인쇄사 잉크 묻은 월급 봉투 속에 갇히기 전까지는 그랬다.

"진짜 의도가 뭡니까? 지자제 시대를 위한 포석은 아닐 테고……."
"자네 전기 고문 물 고문 좀 당하게 해볼까 해서."

박 사장은 이내 웃음소리를 거두고 정색을 했다.

"작년에, 부친이 운명하기 며칠 전, 나에게 이런 얘길 하더군. 이 담에 인쇄업을 때려치우고 딴 사업을 해도 좋다마는, 4·3 사건에 대한 자료집이나 네 손으로 한 권 만들어 줬으면 여한이 없겠다구 말야. 처음엔 바짝 긴장을 했었지. 혹시 내가 모르는 집안의 비밀이 있는가 해서 말야. 그러나 나중에 알고 보니 그저 그렇고 그런 이야기였어. 그래놓고선 마을 사람들까지 동원해서 토벌작전과 선무공작을 벌일 때의 목격담을 들려주더군……. 하루는 지금의 백마목장 안에 들어 있는 '높은오름'까지 토벌을 나갔었다는 거야. 생포된 폭도에게서 얻은 정보를 갖고서 그들의 아지트를 표적지로 삼아 포위망을 좁혀 들어갔는데, 관목 숲에 있는 조그만 동굴에는 피 묻은 죽창 하나와 밑창이 떨어져 나간 농구화 한 켤레밖에 없었더라는 거야. 허탕을 치고 돌아오는 길인데 어디선가 어린애 우는 소리가 들리더래. 토벌대들은 또 한 시간여에 걸쳐 냇가 주변을 뒤졌다는 거야. 그런데 폭도라고 해서 붙잡은 건 젖먹이를 안고 있는 여자뿐이었어. 그 여자 머리챌 거머쥐고 닦달했지만, 산으로 끌려간 남편을 찾으러 나왔다는 말만 되풀이하더라는 거야. 헌데 폭도로 위장한 토벌대 한 명이 어린애를 나꿔채더니, 다른 동료를 향하여 휙 던지더래. 뭐라고들 하면서 웃어댔지만, 이북 사투리여서 무슨 말을 하는진 알아들을 수 없었다는군. 마치 배구를 하듯이 서너 명이 번갈아 가며 어린애를 던지고 받고 하더라는 거야."

나는 길게 담배 연기를 내뿜었다.

"그만 일어서시죠."

"막걸리 한 되만 더 하지."

"전 피곤해서 일찍 들어가 쉬어야겠습니다."

어린애를 업은 여인이 밥 공기만한 분재 하나를 사 들고 인파 속으로 사라졌다.

"금지 구역 팻말을 빼 던질 용기가 없다는 건가?"

"남을 위해 거짓 증언하는 것은 살인 행위나 마찬가집니다. 서로 좀 더 생각해 보기로 하고…… 차나 한 잔하고 헤어집시다."

잡지사 편집국장 감투를 쓰고 첫 출근을 하던 날, 아내는 나에게 침묵으로 살아가길 강요했다. 여보, 이제랑 제발 좀 조용히 살려고 하세요. 혼자 사는 세상 아니니깐……. 내가 언젠 웅변으로 살아왔느냐고 면박을 주려다 말았다.

신문사에서 쫓겨난 지 꼬박 일년 십 개월 동안 집지기 노릇을 했다. 1980년 여름은 나에게는 유난히 무더위와 권태를 느끼게 했던 계절이었다. 언론통폐합령에 의해 일간지 항도신문은 폐간됐고, 나는 일하는 즐거움을 박탈당했다. 아내가 출근하면서 건네주는 담배 한 갑과 천원권 지폐 한 장으로 하루하루를 죽여 갔다. 분필 냄새에 찌든 아내의 체취를 맡는 것이 유일한 낙이었다. 언제까지나 그렇게 아내 등에 업혀 살 참인가. 요즘에 태어나는 애들은 돌 전에 돌아다닌다네. 자존심이 허락한다면, 교정 일이나 좀 봐 주게. 나는 주저없이 박 사장의 요구에 응했다. 찬밥 더운 밥 가릴 처지가 아니었다. 놀고 먹는 남편, 아버지라는 자책감에서 벗어나야겠다는 생각뿐이었다. 내가 박 사장에게 존대어를 쓰기 시작한 것도 그 무렵이었다. 그리고 박 사장은 내가 입사한 지 일년여만에 빚더미에 쓰러진, 지금의 잡지사를 인수했다. 잡지는 전적으로 자네에게 위임할 테니, 밥을 하든 떡을 치든 맘대로 하라구. 박 사장은 잡지사 직원들과 더불어 취재도 다니고, 사진기자가 바쁠 때는 사진도 찍고, 일손이 달릴 적에는 교열도 거들어 줬다.

공장에는 벌써 인쇄 작업이 시작되어 있었다. 옥외 이층 계단을 따라 편집실로 걸음을 옮기던 나는 현관 앞에서 멈췄다.

"그렇게 생각할 수도 있겠죠. 그러나 회색분자니, 패배주의적 기회주의자로서의 역사관이니, 민중의 이름으로 투쟁 운운하는 건 너무 지나친데……. 보아 하니 젊은 양반 같은데, 그런 극단적이고 편협된 틀 속에 사로잡힌다면 사삼 세대를 두 번 죽이는 처사 아닐까요."

나는 전화를 받고 있는 김 기자 주위에 서 있는 동료들과 눈 인사를 나누고 자리에 앉았다.

"아까도 말씀 드렸듯이, 저희들도 무슨 이야기를 어디서부터 어떻게 풀어 갈까 고심한 끝에 그런 방향으로 시작한 거예요. 그래서 기존 자료들에 대한 현장 확인과 함께 자연부락별로 양쪽 피해자들의 목소릴 채집하려 하고 있는 겁니다. 지난번 세미나에도 참석해 봤다고 하니 잘 아시겠지만, 이번 호에는 그 날 참석했던 사람들의 육성을 전달하는 형식으로 편집을 했던 것도 그런 맥락에서……."

나는 팔꿈치를 책상에 받친 채 지그시 눈을 감았다. 자칫하다간 안팎곱사등이가 되기 십상이란 생각이 들었다.

"이거, 경호원이라도 채용해야 할 것 같은데요."

통화를 끝낸 김 기자가 서류 봉투를 들고 다가왔다.

"누군데?"

"이름은 안 밝히는데, 대학생이랍니다."

"뭐가 불만이래?"

"운동권 학생 같애요."

"그럴 수 있겠지. 허지만, 젊은 기분에 당초의 시점에서 벗어나면 안 된다구."

문득 국민학교 교과서에 실렸던 '팔려가는 당나귀'란 우화가 생각났다.

"관심이 많은 것 같긴 한데, 취재 작업이 제대로 진행될지 모르겠군요."

"왜, 또 무슨 일 있었어?"

"국장님 가신 뒤에 사장님과 사장님 장인이 한바탕 설전을 벌였다구요. 술은 어지간히들 취했었지만 딸을 데려가라, 말란 이야기까지 나올 정도였어요."

주먹질이 오가지 않았을 뿐이라고 했다.

"서청西靑이 도마 위에 올려졌었겠군."

나는 서류 봉투 속으로 손을 집어넣으며 중얼거렸다. 왕조 시대의 마지막 제주도 유배인의 딸인데 처갓집 고향이 어디 있겠나. 언젠가 박사장이 술자리에서 떠벌리던 말이 생각났다.

1·4 후퇴 때 제주도까지 표류해 와서 그냥 정착해 버렸다고 했다.
"이거 우리 잡지사에 아예 기증하라면 안 될까?"
나는 앨범을 김 기자에게 들어보였다.
"말도 마십쇼. 가보 일호라면서 밖으로 유출시킬 수 없다는 걸 겨우 사정해서 빌려온 겁니다."
늦어도 내일 저녁까지는 전해 줘야 한다는 것이다. 친구 할아버지의 유품이라고 했다.
나는 대충 훑어봤던 사진첩을, 골동품을 감정하듯 다시 겉표지부터 찬찬히 뜯어보기 시작했다.
4·3 사건 당시 제주도에 토벌군으로 왔었던 제2연대 제주도 주둔기였다. 단면으로 인쇄된 사십여 쪽 분량이었다. 검정 겉표지 중앙에 그려져 있는 제주도의 등고선에는 금박이 입혀져 있었다. 첫장을 넘겼다. 곰팡내와 함께 다섯 사람의 초상화가 십자형으로 자리잡고 있었다. 대통력 각하, 국방장관 각하, 국무총리 각하, 육군참모총장 각하, 수경사령관 각하, 그리고 철모를 쓴 연대장에 이어 미고문관, 부연대장······. 모두 제복 차림이었다.
"가만 있자. 이건 옛날 농업학교 자리잖아."
나는 그제서야 주위를 둘러봤다. 어느새 여섯 명의 기자들이 나를 에워싸고 서 있었다.
정문과 현관 정면에는 보병 2연대 본부라는 간판이 걸려 있었다. 다음 장으로 넘겼다. 내 심장은 시동이 걸린 엔진이 됐다. 피가 정수리로 몰려들었다. 사진첩에서 시선을 꺼냈다. 담뱃불을 댕기고 나서 길게 연기를 내뿜었다. 쇠사슬처럼 드리워져 있는 '山에 있는 同胞들에게 告함'이란 글자들이 담배 연기 속으로 흩어졌다.

尙今歸順하지 못하고 있는 武裝 非武裝同胞들이여, 그대들이 近一年 동안이나 사랑하는 家族과 정든 部落을 떠나서 눈비 오는 山中에서 苦生하고 있는 것은 다만 그대들이 知識이 不足한 緣故로 殘惡無道한 一, 二名의 共産主義者에 속았든 까달기다. 生覺해 보라, 그대들과 우리는 다같은 壇君始祖의……

"내일 취재에 필요한 자료들은 다 챙겼는지 모르겠네."
기자들을 따돌리고 나서 다시 사진첩으로 시선을 떨구었다.

……그러나 仁慈하신 大統領께서는 그대들의 어리석은 것을 불상이 역이시고 親히 婦人同伴來島하사 國防部長官을 불러 至今이라도 同胞에게 對해서는 그 生命을 保障하라고 命令을 내리셨다…….

檀紀四二八二年 四月九日
國防部長官 申性模

그 밑에는 석 장의 사진이 가지런히 배열돼 있었다. 흰 완장을 찬 남자가 허리 굽은 노파를 향하여 삿대질을 하고 있었고, 그 옆에 서 있는 젊은 여인은 손등으로 눈두덩을 가리고 있었다. 남자들은 모두 삭발 상태였다. 코흘리개에서부터 어른 할 것 없이……. 학교 운동장인 듯했다.

산사람들이 마을을 습격하고 난 다음날에는 어김없이 공회당으로 집합을 강요하곤 했었다.

나는 손놀림을 빨리 했다. 사진 설명 같은 건 읽어 보지 않았다. 세월의 뒤켠에 묻혔던 악몽의 나날들이 영화 필름처럼 뇌리를 스쳤다. 다음 사진은 확성기를 매단 지프 한 대가 들판을 질주하고 있는 모습이었다. 뽀족탑을 등지고 앉아 관을 짜고 있는 노인들도 보였다.

잠자지 맙서, 딱딱! 잠자지 맙서, 딱딱!……

통금이 시작되는 저녁 여덟시부터 야경꾼들은 각목을 두들겨대며 마을을 순회했다. 마을에서 자체적으로 조직한 야경꾼들은, 밤새껏 복음을 전하듯 잠자지 맙서, 딱딱! 하는 소리를 마당 안으로 내던지며 지나가곤 했다. 유난히 밤이 길었던 시절이었다.

처음 얼마 동안은, 이불 속에 몸을 숨긴 채 야경꾼의 소리를 흉내내는 재미로 어둠을 맞아들였다. 그것도 얼마 안 가서 시들해졌다. 동생들은 나에게 옛날 얘기를 해 달라고 졸라대기 일쑤였다. 나는 선생에게 얻어 들었던 이야기들을 그럴 듯하게 꾸며대며 들려주곤 했다. 그나마도 네댓 가지 이야기를 되풀이하는 게 고작이었다. 그러나 동생들과 나는 옛날 이야기보다는 차츰, 잠자지 맙서, 딱딱! 하는 소리가 더 그리워졌다. 씨이, 우리가 하느님인가, 잠을 자지 말게……. 야경꾼에 대한 불평은 차츰 침묵으로 바뀌어 갔다. 산사람들이 마을을 왈칵 뒤집어놓고 가는 날 밤에는, 잠자지 맙서라는 말을 들을 수가 없었다.

달이 차고 계절이 바뀔수록 잠자지 맙서라는 말은 차츰 졸면 죽는단 소리로 들렸다. 밤이 지나고 나면, 마을 길에 접한 처마에는, 괴상한 글귀가 씌여진 가마니터기가 깃발처럼 내걸리곤 했다. 투표하면 인민의 반역자이다! 단선單選 분쇄하고 단정單政을 절대 부인하라! 어른들은 날이 새자마자 가마니의 깃발부터 철거했다. 그게 무슨 뜻인지는 알 수 없었다. 아버지에게 물어 봐도 갑갑하기는 마찬가지였.

기껏 한다는 소리는, 아이들은 어른들 하는 일에 끼어드는 게 아니라는 말뿐이었다. 눈을 흡뜨거나 머리를 쥐어박으면서, 혹시 순경이 뭐라 물어도 입을 꼭 다물라고 했다.

어른들이 무서웠다. 무슨 괴물처럼 보였다. 밤마다 마을에 인접한 '오름岳'에서는 봉화가 올랐다. 시내 중심가에서 서너 참 떨어져 있는 마을에는 낮에만 순경들이 왔다가곤 했다. 밤은 산사람들의 세상이었다. 선거 이틀을 앞두고서 마을 사람들이 마을에서 쫓겨난 것도 산사람들에 의해서였다.

"이거 완전히 홈런인데……."

편집실에 나타난 박 사장이 나에게 봉투 하나를 내밀었다.

조의금 봉투였다.

"이걸 왜 저에게…?"

나는 의아해하며 박 사장을 쳐다봤다.

"꺼내 보라구."

박 사장의 얼굴은 굳어 있었다.

나는 봉투 안으로 손가락을 디밀었다. 겉봉에는 '근조謹弔'라는 글자만 쓰여 있었다. 손끝에 가벼운 전율이 일었다. 검은 비닐봉지가 생각났다. 접어져 있는 종이를 펼치자 만원권 지폐 두 장이 나왔다.

박지용 사장, 4·3 폭동은 어디까지나 불행한 역사의 뒷이야기에 지나지 않습니다. 폭도들의 손에 희생된 영혼들과 그 유족들의 입장을 무시한 채, 군경과 서북청년단을 싸잡아 매도하는 듯한 인상을 받았기에 드리는 말씀입니다. 영민한 박 사장이기에 더 이상 신상에 해로운 일은 하지 않으리라 믿습니다. 좋은 게 좋은 거 아니겠습니까.

나는 조의금 봉투 속에 들어 있는 쪽지 내용을 되풀이해서 읽었다. 어제 박 사장 부친 소기에 왔었던 문상객들 중 한 사람이라고 생각했다. 나중에는 한자로 쓰여진 글자들만 걸러 냈다. 매우 유려한 필치였다.

"전혀 감잡히는 사람 없습니까?"

"이 사람아, 우리 집에도 우편물 투시기가 설치돼 있는 줄 아나. 이건 우리 집 가보 제일호로 보관해 둬야겠어."

자손 대대로 물려주겠다고 했다.

"아무래도 4·3 사건 관계는 취재 방향을 수정해얄 것 같은데요."

"어이, 미스 문! 커피 두 잔……."

나는 박 사장을 따라 휴게실로 들어갔다. 휴게실이라곤 하지만, 암실을 꾸미다 남은 ㄱ자형의 공간에다 칸막이를 세워 놓은 곳이었다. 조그마한 탁자 하나와 안락의자 두 개가 있을 뿐이었다. 주로 나와 박 사장이 마주 앉아 차를 마시거나 편집 계획에 대한 의견을 교환할 때 이용됐다. 다른 직원들 사이에서는 밀실이라는 말로 통용되었다.

"양 국장, 아까 그 말 정말야?"

"예상했던 것보다 역풍이 너무 거세서 한 말입니다."

"시쳇말로 세월이 약이라더니……. 사줏셈이 든 건지 나약해진 건지 모르겠군."

나는 손에 들었던 찻잔을 내려놓았다.

"비겁해진 거겠죠."

"그럼, 아예 손을 대지 말아얄 것 아닌가."

"실은 저도 아침에 언짢은 전활 받고 나왔습니다……."

나는 잠시 말을 중단하고 찻잔을 마저 비웠다. 실은, 발송인의 신분이 밝혀져 있지 않은 우편물 이야기는 당분간 검정 비닐봉지 상태로 접어두려 했었다.

"내 예측이 들어맞았군. 내가 잠자리에서 일어나기 전에 우리 집사람이 전활 받았다는 거야. 나를 바꿔 달라고 실랑이를 벌이다가, 잡지를 만드는 실무 책임자의 집 전화번홀 말해 달라고 해서 말해 줬다더군."

잠시 침묵이 흘렀다.

"양 국장, 심각하게 생각할 거 없어. 사람이 지구를 지배하고 있는 한 폭력은 언제 어디서나 존재하는 것이니깐."

그냥 밀고 나가라고 했다. 나는 멍하니 이층 계단을 내려서는 박 사장의 뒷모습을 바라봤다.

"강 기자, 6월호 하고, 지난번 녹음 따놓은 테이프 좀 갖다 줘."

"어떤 테이프 말입니까?"

강 기자가 열쇠 꾸러미를 들고 들어섰다. 4·3사건에 대해 모두 녹음을 해두고 있는 것이다.

"달걀 사건."

"달걀 사건요?…… 아, 예."

나는 녹음기를 틀어놓고 앉아 잡지를 펼쳤다. 테이프를 가지고 초안한 원고만 훑어보고 만 것이 맘에 걸렸다. 잡지가 나온 뒤에도 여태 읽어 보질 못했던 것이다.

소란스러운 목소리가 걷히면서 사회를 맡은 내 육성이 흘러 나왔다.

—저희 영주瀛州지사가 ㅈ대학부설 백록사회문제연구소와 공동 주최한, 4·3사건 진상 규명을 위한 이 세미나는, 사십 년 만에 처음으로 거론되는 행사입니다. 사일구 직후 몇몇 대학생들이 주축이 되어 4·3 사건 진상 규명 동지회라는 것을 조직하고 4·3 사건에 대한 자료 조사에 착수했던 적이 있었습니다. 그 뒤에도 개인적으로 4·3 사건을 조명해 보려 했던 사람들이 있었지만, 번번이 당국에 의해 침묵을 강요당해 왔으며, 그 중에는 육체적 고통까지 받은 사람도 더러 있습니다…….

잠시 작동을 멈춘 나는 테이프를 앞으로 전진시켰다.

—그래서 이 자리에는 각각 입장을 달리하는 분들을 연사로 모셨습니다. 그럼 제가 한 분씩 연사를 소개하겠습니다. 맨 오른쪽에 앉아 계신 유관종 박사님을 소개합니다. 현재 극동문제연구소 소장이신 유 박

사님은 그 당시 9연대와 교체되어 토벌작전을 수행했던 2연대 소속으로 직접 진압 작전에 가담했었습니다. 다음은 전직 경찰관이었던 최두만 선생님을 소개하겠습니다. 최 선생님은 함경도가 고향이시고, 4·3사건이 나던 해부터 줄곧 이 곳에서 봉직하다가 정년 퇴임을 하셨습니다. 그 옆엣 분은 ㅈ대학교 사회학과 교수이며 백록사회문제연구소장이신 김옹찬 선생님이십니다. 이 밖에도 당시의 체험담을 들려주실 세 분 할아버지를 모셨습니다만, 본인들의 요청에 따라 개별적인 소개는 생략하겠습니다……

토요일 오후여서 그런지 삼백 석 규모의 공간은 발 디딜 틈 없이 꽉 들어찼다. 발표장 건물 마당과 골목길에 운집해 있는 사람들을 위해 옥외에는 확성기를 설치했다.

처음, 4·3 사건에 대한 세미나 개최 문제가 나왔을 때만 해도 나는 주저했다. 아무리 체육관 선거에서 컴퓨터 선거 시대로 바뀌었다곤 하지만 금단의 성역을 헤갈아대도록 방치해 두지 않을 것 같았다. 좌경 쪽의 극단적인 목청을 가라앉힐 겸, 산사람들에 의해 피해를 입은 사람들로부터 취재를 했으면 싶었다. 나를 아는 사람들에게서, 자신의 신상 발언을 위한 수작이라는 비아냥거림을 받고 싶지 않았다.

— 4·3 사건은 우선 호칭에서부터 좌익과 우익 쪽 입장의 견해가 다릅니다. 우익 입장에서는 4·3 폭동, 무장반란, 4·3 사건 등으로 명명 함에 반하여, 그 반대의 입장에서는 민중항쟁, 인민항쟁, 무장투쟁, 인민전쟁 등으로 호칭되고 있습니다. 희생자 숫자만 해도 그렇습니다. 정부측 자료는 축소되고, 이른바 민중항쟁측 자료는 확대된 감이 있습니다. 사천이백여 명에서부터 십만 명까지 거론되는 희생자 수에 비례하여 그 당시 제주도 인구도 이십칠만 육천 단위에서 삼십삼만까지 들쭉날쭉입니다. 그 다음 문제는 4·3 사건은 누구에 의해서, 무엇 때문

에, 그리고 어떻게 진행되었느냐는 점입니다. 한쪽에서는 제주도민 팔십 퍼센트 내지 팔십오 퍼센트가 빨갱이었다고 주장하고, 또 한쪽에서는 도민의 필십오 퍼센트가 궐기했던 민중항쟁이라 하고 있습니다. 양쪽 입장의 차이는 빨갱이들에 의한 폭동이었느냐, 외세에 항거한 민중항쟁이냐 하는 것뿐입니다. 참고로 말씀 드리면 당시 도민들 중 열 명에 여섯 명 이상이 문맹자였습니다. 그리고 지금까지의 기록을 종합해 보면, 해방 이후 제주도가 전국에서 제일 먼저 면과 리 단위까지 인민위원회 조직을 완료한 것으로 되어 있습니다. 이 곳에는 일천구백이십년대부터 이미 사회주의 운동의 온상이 돼 왔다는 이야깁니다. 도민들이 해방 후 일본에서 귀국한 노동자 계층과 학병 출신들에 의해 공산주의 환상에 젖게 했다는 것입니다. 그래서 당시 경무부장이었던 조병옥은, 대한민국을 위해서는 제주도 전역에 휘발유를 뿌리고 불을 질러 삼십만 도민을 한꺼번에 없애야 한다고 했는지 모릅니다. 그리고 처음 주둔했었던 십일연대장인 박진경 중령은, 구 제주농고 운동장에 수많은 시민을 집합시켜 놓은 자리에서, 머리털 끝만한 이적 행위라도 발각되면 즉석에서 총살시키겠다면서, 한라산 일대에 휘발유를 뿌리고 섬 전체에 불을 지르면 제주도의 빨갱이를 몰살할 수 있다고 하기도 했는데, 그는 해방 전에는 일군 학도병으로도 근무한 바 있어서 제주도 구석구석을 잘 알고 있던 사람입니다. 끝으로 에피소드 하나를 소개하고 제 이야길 마치겠습니다. 일천구백사십구년 여름에 신성모 국방장관이 내도를 했습니다. 그는 관덕정 광장에 모인 시민들 앞에서, 서북 청년회 등 육지 사람들이 관리로, 경찰관으로 들어와 도민들을 괴롭혔기 때문에 4·3 폭동이 일어난 줄 안다고 했다가 서북청년단의 거센 반발 때문에 해군 함정으로 대피하는 소동을 벌이기도 했습니다. 제주도에 사설 단체인 서청이 처음 들어온 것은 일구사칠년 봄인데,

인민위원회를 축출하는 데 충추 역할을 담당하기도 했습니다. 그리고, 이백여 명의 서청 단원이 4·3 사건 진압 과정에서 목숨을 잃었습니다. 그러나, 당시 좌경 단체에서는 서청을 백색 테러단의 시각으로 봤습니다만, 그들의 전투적 저돌성으로 말미암아 도민들이 감정을 악화시킨 점 또한 부인할 수 없을 것입니다. 일제 시대에는 서른 다섯 명의 일본인 관리와 칠십여 명의 순사만으로 다스려졌던 제주도였습니다. 그런데 4·3 사건 진압 과정에는 연인원 5개 연대 병력 외에도 백골대니, 아리랑부대니, 독수리부대니 하는 많은 독립 중대와 대동청년단, 민보단 등의 보조 군대를 조직했었는데도 일구오사년이 돼서야 한라산 금족령이 해제되었다는 것은 시사하는 바가 많습니다……

나는 녹음기 작동이 멈추는 소리가 나서야 창밖으로 던졌던 시선을 거뒀다. 잡지 내용은 이미 훑어본 뒤였다. 그러나 자꾸만 4·3에 대한 기호 풀이에 회의가 일었다. 퍼즐놀이를 하는 기분이었다. 도대체 이런 작업이 무슨 소용이 있다는 것인가. 한 개인의 삶에 있어서 역사는 무슨 도움을 줄 것인가. 부서진 오지 조각 같은 역사의 복원은 가능한가.

자꾸만 춘곤증이 온몸을 엄습해 왔다.

그 무렵 나는 점점 사람의 새끼로 태어난 것을 저주하고 있었다. 밤은 완전히 산사람들의 천국이 되었다. 유령의 세상이었다. 어둠을 몰고 나타났다가 첫닭이 울면 마을을 뜨는 유령들이었다. 검은 그림자들이 마을의 정적을 헤갈아 놓고 떠날 때마다 행방불명된 남자들이 늘어갔다. 산사람들은 젊은 남자들만 잡아가는 염라대왕이었다. 먹고, 입고, 덮을 수 있는 것이면 뭐든지 앗아갔다. 수많은 개, 돼지와 닭, 소와 말들까지도 산으로 끌려가 빨갱이가 되었다. 먹어라, 더 먹어라, 실컷 먹어둬라. 언제 어떻게 될지 모르는 세상, 배나 불려 둬라. 달걀 하나도 손대지 못하게 하던 아버지는 날사흘로 집에 기르는 닭의 모가지를 비틀어댔다. 세곗놈들에게 먹을 것 다 뺏기고서 빨갱이 누명을 쓰느니, 차라리 내 새끼들이나 실컷 먹여 두겠다고 했다. 돼지 추렴이 빈번했던 것도 이 무렵이었다.

선거 이틀 전 산사람들에 의해 '거문오름〔琴岳〕' 근처로 끌려갔던 마을 사람들은, 선거 다음날에야 귀가했다. 나흘 만에 마을로 돌아온 뒤에는 밤에도 옷을 입은 채 잠을 잤다. 꿈 속에서도 도망치고 숨는 연습을 하곤 했었다.

날이 밝아도 무섭고 두려운 것은 마찬가지였다. 토벌대나 순경들도 산사람들에게는 겁이 나서 그런지 낮에만 마을에 나타났다. 그러고선, 마을을 잘못 지켰다고 해서, 산사람들의 양식이 될 소금과 된장을 줬다고 해서, 식량과 가축을 뺏겼다고 해서 시달림을 받았다. 유격부대에 협력했다고 하여 토벌대에 끌려갔다가 송장이 되어 돌아온 사람들도 있었다. 마을길이 곧 저승길이었다.

마을에서는, 밤에는 폭도의 습격에 대비하여 보초를 섰고, 낮에는 군인이나 경찰이 나타나는 것을 마을 사람들에게 알리기 위해 망을 보게 했다.

낮에 토벌군이 들어오는 것을 망보는 일은 열 두서너 살 또래의 사내 아이들이 맡았다. 제일 큰 나무 곡대기에 대나무를 깃대처럼 꽂아 놓고 놀았다.

이 나무에서 저 나무로 옮겨다니며 원숭이 흉내를 내며 시간을 보냈고, 어른들은 일을 했다. 그러다가, 검은개 왐져! 누렁개 왐져! 하는 소리와 함께 나무에 꽂혔던 대나무를 눕히면 어른들은 일손을 멈췄다. 장정들은 아예 마을에서 멀리 떠났다가 토벌대가 돌아간 뒤에야 귀가하곤 했다. 폭도 왐져(온다), 뚝! 뚝 그치라, 순경 왕(와서) 심어간다(잡아

간다>! 막내동생의 울음을 그치게 하는 어머니의 에비 소리도 밤과 낮에 따라 바뀌었다.

그러나 그 해 겨울이 지난 뒤부터 어머니는 간장에 밥! 하는 에비로 막내 동생의 울음을 달래곤 했다. 소금에 조밥도 제대로 찾아먹지 못하던 때라서, 나에게는 고기에 밥! 하는 소리로 들렸다.

나는 결국 마지막 녹음 테이프까지 작동을 시켰다. 만약을 위해서, 그 날의 목소리 내용은 모두 확인해 두기로 했다.

오후 2시에 시작된 세미나는 세 시간이 지나도 끝나지 않았다. 우리가 예상했던 시간이 훨씬 지나 있었다.

마지막으로 극동문제연구소 소장이 등단했다. 막대한 경비를 들여가며 초청해 온 연사였다.

"……앞서 말한 분들의 주장에 대해 왈가왈부하진 않겠습니다. 그러나 현재 일본에 거주하고 있는, 당시 반란에 가담했던 사람의 기록을 맹신하는 듯하여 매우 염려가 됩니다. 해방되던 해 사월 하순이 되자 일본은 제주도민 중 부녀자와 노약자 등 오만 명을 본토로 대피시켜 놓을 계획을 세웠습니다. 미군이 한반도에 상륙할 것에 대비하여 미리 제주도를 전초기지화하여 일전을 벌이려 했던 겁니다. 그러나 일차로 목포 방면으로 이송하던 황화환晃和丸이 미 공군의 폭격을 받고 침몰해서 이백팔십 명이 희생당하는 등 본토로의 소개疏開 계획은 수포로 돌아갔습니다. 해방 당시의 전후 사정으로 봤을 때, 만약 미군이 제주도에 상륙하여 접전이 벌어졌었다면, 제주도는 아마 제2의 오키나와가 됐었을 게 뻔합니다. 결과론적인 이야기이긴 하지만, 미군들은 풍전등화의 처지에 있는 제주도민들의 생명을 구제해 준 해방군이었습니다……. 제가 알기로는, 제주도 4·3폭동에 대해 공개적, 공식적으로 거론되기 시작한 것은 작년 십일월 삼십일, 대통령 선거 유세차 이 곳에 내려왔던 평화당 대통령 후보자인 것으로 알고 있습니다. 그는, 내가 집권하면 인혁당 사건과 거창사건, 제주도 4·3 사건 등을 광주사태와 같은 차원에서 진상을 밝혀 억울한 사람들의 명예를 회복시켜 주겠다고 공언했었습니다. 그런데 그가 대권을 잡는 데 실패했으니, 폭동 희생자들에게는 여간 안타까운 일이 아닐 수 없습니다."

강당 바깥에서 날아들던 고함소리는 차츰 육두문자로 변해 갔다. 그러나 그의 자세는 흐트러짐이 없었다. 나는 다시 손수건을 꺼내 이마에서 흐르는 땀을 훔쳐 냈다. 아무래도 바깥 공기가 심상치 않았다.

"…… 아까 어떤 분은, 4·3 민중항쟁의 진상이 민족사적 차원에서 해결을 보지 못했을 땐, 국제사법재판소에 제소해서라도 진상을 밝혀야 한다면서, 당시 삼십삼만의 도민 중에서 십만이 죽었다고 말했는데, 환상과 착각도 이만저만이 아닙니다. 민주화가 됐다고 해서, 남로당에 의한 반란을 의거인 것처럼 도색시키려 할 때, 세계적인 관광지로 각광을 받기 시작한 제주도는 제2의 사삼폭동과 같은 비극을……."

유리창 깨지는 소리에 이어 누런 물체들이 날아왔다.

두런거리던 장내는 삽시에 수랑장이 됐다.

"여러분, 이러시면 안 됩니다. 제발…… 제발……."

그러나 달걀 세례는 계속됐다. 유리 조각 같은 고함이 노른자위와 함께 낭자했다.

마이크 줄은 이미 절단돼 있었다. 경찰관 두 명이 마지막 연사로 등단했던 극동문제연구소장을 강당 후문으로 호위하고 나갔다. 강당 주위는 서서히 평온을 되찾아 갔다. 제발 제발……. 나는 쓸쓸한 미소를 지었다. 제발 불은 지르지 말아줍서. 제발 어린것덜 목숨일랑 살려 줍서……. 내 머릿 속은 온통 불타는 고향 마을로 가득 찼다.

타앙탕! 탕!

"폭도들이 습격한 모양여!"

부엌 문짝을 고치던 아버지가 망치를 든 채 사방을 두리번거렸다.

"냐 둡서. 그 사람들도 조상이 있는 몸이니 제사 지낼 묵가루 가는 거야 흉봅네까."

어머니는 여전히 맷돌을 돌려댔다.

"한구야, 넌 얼른 숨어 있어라."

아버지가 집채만한 꼴단더미 쪽으로 시선을 줬다. 산사람의 습격이 있을 때마다 아버지는 나를 꼴단더미 속으로 숨게 했다. 다른 가족은 다 죽더라도 나만큼은 살아 남아야 한다는 것이었다. 우리 집안의 대들보라고 했다.

마을 곳곳에서 불길이 솟구쳤다. 비명과 통곡이 마을을 덮기 시작했다.

"아니, 이거 무슨 짓들이오."

"중산간 마을을 소개시키란 작전 명령이 내려졌으니 빨리 해변가 마을로 이주하시오."

햇불을 든 군인들이 처마끝에 불을 댕겼다.

"사전 연락도 없이 이래도 되는 겁니까?"

"마구간만이라도 제발…… 내일 저녁 집에 제사우다. 제발……."

맨발로 달려나온 어머니가 마구간 건물로 다가서는 군인의 다리를 껴안았다. 발길에 채여 넘어졌던 어머니가 몸을 한 바퀴 굴렸다.

"차라리 날 죽입서!"

어머니가 햇불을 든 군인의 상체에 매달렸다. 두 사람이 마당으로 나뒹굴었다. 어머니의 겨드랑이 사이로 총구가 삐쳐 나왔다고 생각되는 순간 한 방의 총성이 울렸다. 나는 비명을 내지르며 어머니에게로 달려갔다.

"아빠야! 아빠야!"

동생들의 울음 소리가 폭죽처럼 뿜어 올랐다. 나는 그제서야 마구간 앞에 곤두박질쳐져 있는 아버지를 발견했다. 고삐에서 풀려난 소들이 아버지를 밟고 마구간을 빠져 나왔다.
　"한구 아방아!"
　머리채를 풀어 헤친 어머니가 아버지를 부둥켜 안았다. 마당에는 먹물 같은 피가 흥건히 번져갔다.
　"내 서방 살려내라, 이 빨갱이 같은 놈덜아!"
　"당신이 방아쇠를 건드려 놓고선 누구한테 개소리 얏!"
　"이 여편네, 이거 적색분자 아냐, 이거."
　앞엣총 자세를 하고 있던 군인이 총부리를 돌렸다.
　"아이고, 제발 이 어린것덜 목숨만일랑 건드리지 말아 줍서!"
　어머니는 이내 통곡을 멈추고 양손을 삭삭 비벼댔다.
　아수라장이됐던 마을은 차츰 불꽃과 함께 사그라들기 시작했다. 간헐적으로 들리던 어린애 울음소리와 통곡도 멎었다. 불타는 마을은 대낮처럼 밝았다.
　어디선가 닭 우는 소리가 희미하게 들려 왔다. 바닷가 마을 쪽에서였다.
　동자석처럼 앉아 있던 어머니가 무릎 위에 얹어 놓았던 아버지의 머리를 내려놨다. 나는 비로소, 아버지는 함께 떠날 수 없음을 알았다.
　어쩜 지옥이라는 곳도 불타는 수련동 마을과 같을지 모른단 생각이 들었다.
　어머니는 땅 속에 저장되어 있던 고구마들을 구덩이 밖으로 내던졌다. 어머니와 나, 두 동생이 비집고 들어앉을 만한 공간이 동그라니 드러났다.
　"한구야, 느네 아방 저리로 모시라 보게."

어머니의 목소리는 여전히 차가웠다. 갑자기 어머니가 더 무서운 생각이 들었다.

어머니와 나는 아버지를 동여맨 멜빵 끝을 한 가닥씩 나눠 갖고 울타리 안으로 끌어다가 고구마를 저장했던 구덩이 안으로 떼밀었다. 몸을 뒤채듯, 아버지의 시신이 새우처럼 휘어졌다.

"이 어른아, 하다하다 저승길 떠나는디 맹물 한 대접 노잣돈 한 푼 없다고 구승허지 말아 줍서. 어찌하여 나의 저승 올래는 감저 구뎅이냐고 숭보지 말아 줍서. 이 수련동 마을이, 내 처자식덜과 정 섞으곡 시름 섞으멍 살던 땅인가 해서 돌아볼 생각 말앙 밤 하늘에 벨이 되곡 비구름 다스리는 해가 되곡 달이 되엉 이 어린 것들이나 보살펴 줍서……".

어머니는 상체를 잔뜩 움츠린 채 모래밭이나 다름없는 땅을 양팔로 구덩이 안으로 쓸어담기 시작했다.

다음 달에 실린, ㅈ면 ㅈ리에서의 4·3 사건 관계 취재를 끝낸 일행들은 저녁 늦게서야 시내에 도착했다. 김 기자 친구의 부친을 만난 나와 박 사장은 자정이 넘어서야 헤어졌다. 그러나 김 기자가 빌려 왔던 사진첩을 기증받으려 했던 기대감은 수포로 돌아갔다.

"양한구 씨!"

"누구시죠?"

아무도 보이지 않았다. 재차 등을 돌리는 순간, 어른 키가 넘는 바람벽과 쇠창살로 울타리를 두른 골목길 양쪽 입구에서 자동차 불빛이 내 몸을 덮쳤다. 나는 반사적으로 몸을 담벼락에 기댄 채 양 팔로 머리를 감쌌다. 검정 비닐 포장 같은 어둠이 내 의식을 덮쳤다. 탐조등 같은 불빛과 함께 밀려오는 구두징 소리가 서서히 내 심장의 박동을 조여오기 시작했다.

오성찬

버려지는 사람들

필자 소개
제주도 서귀포 출생. 1969년 〈신아일보〉 신춘문예 소설 당선.
신문기자와 박물관 큐레이터 역임. 도서출판 반석 대표(현)
소설집 『한라산』 『어두운 시대의 초상화』 『나볃로의 환생』 등.
요산문학상, 한국소설문학상, 한국문학상 등 수상.

버려지는 사람들

오성찬

시청 부녀복지계의 차석 이성숙李成淑 여사는 정각 아홉 시 오분 전에 근무처에 도착했다. 남편과 아이들의 뒷바라지를 해주고 자신도 준비를 해서 출근하다 보면 그녀는 이미 시작 전에 일의 한 파트를 끝내 놓은 듯한 기분이 들곤 했다.

간부회의에 들어갔는지 과장의 자리는 비어 있고, 여당의 선거운동을 해주고 두어 달 전에 부임해온 낙하산식 계장의 콤팩트를 보며 얼굴을 매만지다 곁눈질 인사로 그녀를 맞았다.

"이 여사, 강담동 파출소엘 가보세요. 난 바빠서 그러니까…."

그녀는 쿡 솟구치는 게 있었으나 눌러 참았다. 그녀에게 이제 참는 일은 다반사가 되어 있었다. 코트의 단추께로 가져갔던 손을 그냥 멈춘 채 걸레질 된 책상 위를 내려다보았다. 거기 어릉거리며 낯선 얼굴들이 들어와 박혔다가는 사라졌다. 한결같이 찌들고 지친 표정들—. 기아와 미아, 부랑인들을 관리하고 처리하는 일이 주업무인 이 과에서는 새벽 참에 이런 일이 드물지만은 않았다. 그러나 십오 년 가까이 이

분야의 일을 해오면서 요즘처럼 이런 일이 빈번한 적은 없었다. 이번에는 또 어떤 사람이 어떤 모양으로 버려진 것일까.

그녀는 다시 책상 위에 놨던 핸드백을 집어들었다. 그녀가 나오면서 뒤돌아보았을 때 계장은 비로소 안도의 표정을 짓고 있었다. 눈이 마주친 아동계의 강 계장이 삐죽 입술을 내밀며 눈을 흘겼다. 바쁘긴 뭘 바빠. 맨날 난 바빠서 바빠서…. 그녀의 험구를 이 여사는 환청으로 듣고 있었다.

이 여사가 강담동 파출소에 도착했을 때 벽가의 긴 의자에는 하얗게 머리가 센 할머니 한 분이 잠든 채 구겨 박혀 있었다. 그녀는 대번에 이 할머니가 자기를 불러내린 상대라는 걸 직감했다.

"뭐냔 말이야! 내가 내 돈 가지고 술 좀 마셨기로니 무슨 잘못이냔 말이야!"

한쪽 자리에서 심문을 받던 사내가 버럭 고함을 지르며 앞에 앉은 순경에서 삿대질을 해댔다. 사내는 옆에서 보기에도 위태롭게 보이만큼 몸이 흔들리고 있었다. 순경이 달래며 묻고 있었으나 그 말은 너무 작아서 들리지 않았다.

"아, 안 그래? 내가 뭘 잘못했어? 왜 내가 지서엘 끌려와야 돼?"

반문이 또렷한 걸로 보아 그의 과장된 흔들림은 일부러인 듯했다.

"허어, 이 양반. 아직도 잘못하면서 그러네!"

순경의 언성이 꽤 높아져 있었다. 이번엔 사내는 고개를 쳐뜨리고 아무 대꾸도 하지 않았다.

그때 얼굴이 익은 경장이 옆문으로 들어왔다. 그는 야근을 하고 막 세수를 한 참인 듯했다.

"아, 오셨군요…."

엉거주춤 서 있는 이 여사에게 그가 말했다.

"용두암에서 혼자 우는 걸 택시 기사가 실어왔어요."

경장은 턱짓으로 긴 의자에 구겨져 자는 할머니를 가리켰다.

할머니는 긴 여행이라도 나선 듯 입성이 깨끗했다. 그런데 자세히 보니까 머리가 센 것에 비해서는 나이가 덜 들어 보였다.

"기사가 무슨 얘기 않던가요?"

연고를 찾아주기 위해서는 아무 증거라도 잡아두지 않으면 안 되었다. 귀찮아서 내버리려는 사람과 가능한껏 되돌려서 떠맡기려는 정책, 그 팽팽한 줄다리기를 그녀는 늘 보아왔다.

"날이 저물어서 마지막 코스로 신혼부부를 안내하고 갔는데, 바다를 보며 혼자 울고 있더래요. 좀 이건가 봐요…."

경장은 검지를 곧게 펴서 귓등 위로 가져가 동그라미를 그려보였다. 그녀는 가볍게 고개를 끄덕이며 측은한 시선으로 구겨져 자는 할머니를 또 바라보았다.

"배 타고, 신랑이랑 왔는데 거기서 바다 구경하고 있으면 막걸리 한 잔하고 온다더니 종일을 기다려도 안 온다는 거였어요. 이 나이에 신랑도 그렇고…. 뭔 사연이 있나 봐요. 하도 배가 고픈 것 같아서 라면 하날 끓여드렸더니 이렇게 잠만 자네요…."

누가 버렸구나…. 그녀는 이내 기아성棄兒性 미아迷兒들을 떠올렸다.

―여기서 놀고 있거라. 맛있는 것 사갖고 올 꺼구마.

그리고 가서는 돌아오지 않는 아버지, 어머니. 그런 숱한 경우를 그녀는 접했고, 내력도 자세히 알고 있었다. 옛날 귀양지였던 이 섬은 이제 이상한 양상으로 바뀌어가고 있었다.

"그냥 데려가면 되지요?"

"그럼요. 우리도 고생하지만 수고가 많으시네요…."

"다 월급 받고 하는 일인데요 뭐…"

소설 • 오성찬_357

그녀는 이날 따라 자꾸만 자조적이 되어가고 있었다. 콤팩트를 보며 화장을 고치던 계장의 얼굴이 떠올랐다. 그녀는 떠오르는 영상을 밀어내며 잠든 할머니에게로 다가갔다. 너무 그 잠이 평온해서 깨우기 미안했으나 무작정 기다릴 수도 없었다.

"할머니…"

어깨를 흔드는데 얇은 스웨터 안으로 느껴지는 어깨 부위가 너무 야위어 있었다. 그리고 그만한 흔들림에도 할머니는 화들짝 깨었다.

깨어서 그녀를 쳐다보는 시선에 핏발이 서 있었다. 적의에 차 있는 시선이었다.

"할머니, 일어나셔요…. 가셔야지요."

그녀가 단호하게 말했다. 그녀는 경험으로 대개의 부랑인들에게 다소의 엄포와 냉정은 필요하다는 걸 체득하고 있었다. 그리고 이런 자세가 상대로 하여 수굴수굴 순복케 하는 요소라는 것도 잘 알고 있었다. 그녀의 냉엄한 표정에 질렸는지 할머니는 이내 기가 죽었다. 주섬주섬 일어나 의자에 바로 앉았다.

"할머니, 뭐 가진 거 없으세요?"

대개의 부랑인들의 팔에는 무엇인가 안겨 있게 마련이었다. 그런데 이 여자는 가진 게 없었다. 그녀는 대답 대신 자기 주변을 한 번 휘이 둘러보더니 홰홰 고개를 가로 저었다.

"아니…"

"아무 것도 안 가졌던가요?"

이번에는 경장에게 물어봤다.

"처음에 어쨌는지는 모르지만 기사가 데려왔을 때 가진 것은 아무 것도 없었어요. 모르지요. 그 신랑이라는 작자가 갖고 가 버렸는지도…"

"수고하셨어요. 고맙습니다."

"헤헤, 고마울 수야 없지요."

"그럼 뭐라고 할까요?"

"글쎄요. 헤헤…"

할머니의 옆구리를 끼고 파출소를 나설 때 이 여사는 다른 자리에 앉아 고함지르며 몸을 흔들어대던 젊은이가 신경 쓰였다.

"또로군, 또야…."

택시로 할머니를 태우고 사무실로 돌아왔을 때 의자를 돌려놓고 손톱을 다듬던 대머리 과장은 노골적으로 싫은 표정을 지었다.

이번에는 과장 자리 대신 계장의 자리가 비어 있었다. 이 여사는 아무 대꾸도 않고 책상 위에 핸드백을 놓고 코트를 벗어 옷걸이에 걸었다.

"할머니, 이쪽으로 와서 앉으세요."

말없이 들어선 그녀의 긴장한 표정이 부담이 되는지 주양이 일어나 미적미적 서 있는 할머니를 창가 자리로 데리고 갔다.

"어떻게 된 게야? 소지품 뒤져 봤어?"

나이 차이가 한참이긴 해도 과장의 이런 어투가 이 여사는 늘 속상했다.

"아무 것도 가진 게 없어요…."

"증명서도 전혀란 말야?"

"예…. 좀 어떻게 됐나 봐요…."

어쩔까 망설이다가 그녀는 토를 달았다. 코트를 벗어 놓고 자리로 돌아오면서 벽에 걸린 거울을 보니까 눈가의 달무리가 뿌옇게 되살아나 있었다. 그녀는 속을 끓였다 싶으면 되살아나는 이 달무리의 사연을 스스로도 모르겠는 것이다.

"거기 모셔두면 어쩔 거야? 이리 좀 보내 봐…."
 이 양반이 또 심심했나 보구나. 늘 자기가 사회로부터 부당한 대우를 받고 있다고 생각하는 일급 상이용사인 과장은 지난 연초 복지과장 발령을 받아 가지고 부임해 와서도 늘 불만이었다. 이런 불만이 어떤 때는 직원들에게나 업무 상대로도 터졌다. 주양이 겁먹은 시선으로 할머니를 과장 곁으로 데리고 갔다. 손님 접대용 안락의자가 놓여 있었으나 할머니는 쳐다보았을 뿐 거기 앉으려 하지 않았다.
 "할망, 어디서 옵디가?"
 과장이 서 있는 할머니를 위아래로 훑어보며 물었다. 그러나 그녀는 무슨 말인지 못 알아듣는 듯 적의에 찬 시선만 디룩거리고 있었다.
 "할머니, 어디서 왔느냐니깐?"
 이번에 그의 목청은 높았다. 그러나 할머니는 아무 대답도 하지 않았다. 대신 말뜻을 알아듣기는 한 듯 고개를 살래살래 가로저었다.
 "그렇지. 그러고 보면 육짓 할망은 맞군. 어떤 놈이 배를 태워 가지고 왔나? 부두 검문소에서는 뭣들 하는지 원…"
 "혼자 오진 않은 모양이에요. 신랑이 데리고 왔다니까…."
 이 여사가 대답하자 방 안의 어린 직원들이 쿡쿡거리며 웃었다.
 "유기된 장소가 어디야?"
 아예 과장은 그녀를 유기된 것으로 취급하려나 보았다.
 "유기됐는지 어쨌는지 어젯밤 늦게 용두암에서 울고 있는 걸 발견해서 파출소에 신골 했대요…."
 "유령 같았겠군…."
 과장이 이번엔 혼잣소리처럼 뇌며 할머니의 표정을 면구스러울 정도로 뜯어보았다.
 "그 한적한 곳에 저녁 늦게 혼자 앉아서 우는 여자가 심상치는 않았겠죠….”

"글쎄 말이야. 이런 할머니가 금년 들어서 몇 건이야?"

"노인들이 벌써… 대여섯 건 되지요, 아마…"

"따루 통계를 뽑아놔야겠어. 이건 절대루 보통 일이 아니라구. 지에미 애비를 쓰레기 버리듯 버리는 세상이니 원…"

"말세 아닙니까 말세…"

기사 최 씨가 앞질러서 과장의 지론을 내놔버렸다.

"누가 아니랬어? 정말 말세야 말세…"

그는 맞장구를 쳐놓고 확인을 하려는 듯이 방안을 휘이 둘러보았다. 그러나 쿡쿡거리던 말단직원들은 꺼병이 대가리 처박듯 서류뭉치 위에 엎드려 있었다.

"주양, 몸을 한번 뒤져 봐!"

벽가에 엉거주춤 서있는 그녀에게 과장이 빽 고함을 질렀다.

그녀가 다가가 상대가 와락 덤벼들기라도 할 것 같은 표정으로 할머니의 옆구리와 가슴께를 만져봤다.

"없는데요….”

"에이, 그래서 숨긴 물건 찾아내겠다. 쯧쯧…"

과장은 직원들 행동에도 불만이었다. 그가 벌떡 일어나 할머니의 가슴께를 툭툭 쳐봤다. 그 거친 행동에 그녀는 움찔움찔 했으나 그런 행동에도 길들여져 있음이 분명했다. 과장을 바라보는 시선이 잔뜩 어두워져 있는 걸 이 여사는 느꼈다.

"어떻게 하지?"

그제야 과장이 그녀를 돌아보며 처리 문제를 의논했다.

"글쎄요…. 우선 소망원에 보내 놓고 연고자를 찾아보는 수 밖에요….”

소망원은 이 시의 부랑인 일시보호소였다. 각지에서 떠들어온 부랑인들이 남녀노소 함께 '보호'되고 있었다. 그러나 거기는 '거지 집합소'라는 별명답게 시설도 형편없고 지저분했다.

사람들은 왜 일체의 소망이 없는 곳에다 〈소망원〉이란 이름을 붙였을까.

그것이 지독한 패러독스라는 걸 그녀는 갈 적마다 느꼈다.

"지금 거기 수용 인원이 몇 명이지요?"

"어제 현재 인원이 103명입니다."

소망원 담당 직원이 얼른 대답했다.

"꽉 찼네."

"예, 좀 불편할 지경이지요. 그러나 아직은 괜찮습니다…."

직원의 말투에는 그 사람들이야 그만 것쯤 견디는 게 당연하지 않느냐는 투가 배어 있었다.

"일단 소망원에 인계를 하세요. 그리고 연고자를 꼭 찾아내야 합니다. 용서할 수 없어요, 나쁜 놈들…"

과장은 용사답게 손가락 두 개가 날아가 버려서 붕대로 감은 오른손을 쳐들어 보이며 부르짖었다.

"그렇긴 해도 찾아내려면 증거나 꼬투리라도 있어얄 거 아니야…. 예? 할머니 고향이 어디세요, 고향?…"

그래도 할머니는 멀뚱멀뚱 그를 쳐다볼 뿐이었다.

"온 데, 살던 마을 모르겠어요? 저어기 말예요…"

과장은 창 너머로 멀리 바다 건너를 가리켰다. 그래도 그녀는 고개를 가로저을 뿐이었다. 이번엔 그녀는 몸까지도 함께 흔들렸다.

"이런 판이 있나. 증명도 일체 없어, 살던 데, 낳은 데도 모른다…. 참 한심스럽네…"

한심스럽다는 시선으로 과장은 한참이나 무표정한 할머니를 올려다보고 있었다. 그러더니 포기한 사람처럼 내뱉았다.

"최 기사가 주양과 함께 소망원엘 다녀오지. 이 할머니를 태우구 말이야…"

"예. 다른 공문서 보낼 것들 없으세요?"

"소장더러 이르세요. 어떻게라도 연고자를 찾아서 귀향시킬 생각들을 하라고…"

"예."

그들이 양쪽에서 할머니를 부축하듯 하고 나가자 이 여사의 입에서는 훅 하고 짧은 한숨이 나왔다. 이제 비로소 두 번째 몰려온 일의 파도를 넘어선 셈이었다.

계장이라는 작자는 바쁘다는 핑계로 어느 과를 싸돌아다니며 잔사설을 까고 있을까. 돌아와서는 멋대로 했다고 걸고 넘어지지나 않을까. 허긴 과장이 결정한 문제니까 그쪽으로 밀어버리면 그만이지만 일의 처리가 영 마음에 걸렸다.

그러나 점심 후에야 들어온 계장은 그런 일에는 아무 관심도 없었다.

"별 수 없잖아요. 우선 소망원에 놔두고 연고를 찾아볼 수밖에요. 수고하셨어요."

그녀는 의외로 선선했다. 아, 이런 데가 그녀의 정치적인 점이로구나. 그녀는 시인했다. 자기편을 가르고, 상대를 밀어내고, 또 필요한 사람을 자기편으로 끌어들이고…. 이런 산술적 작업이 어떤 때 그녀의 눈에 뚜렷하게 보였다.

"대신 연고를 찾는 작업을 서둘러야 할 겁니다…. 머잖아 연말도 다 가오잖아요. 가능한껏 연말에 시설들을 비울 수 있었으면 좋겠어요…."

그건 그녀도 동감이었다. 가능한껏 연말 전에 가족들을 찾아갈 수 있으면 얼마나 좋을까. 저들 중에는 애타게 가족들이 찾는 상대도 있을 것이다. 현상 심인… 사람 찾음. 여보 돌아와 주오, 현복이가 울고 있오. 신문지의 하단마다 얼룩진 심인尋人 광고들이 떠올랐다가 사라졌다. 담뱃갑에 박힌 천연색 사진의 또릿또릿한 아이들 표정도 떠올랐다가 사라졌다.

그런가 하면 기를 쓰고 떼어버리려는 악연惡緣들도 있었다. 그녀는 언젠가 공무원 교육을 받으러 갔다가 같은 업무를 하는 딴 도의 부녀복지계 직원을 만난 적이 있었다. 며칠 같이 잠을 자고 식사를 하는 동안에 가까워지자 못하는 소리가 없었다.

"우리는 어떻게 하는지 아세요?"

시선을 반짝이며 은밀하게 그녀가 다가왔다.

"……"

그녀는 대답은 안 했지만 과연 그들이 부랑인을 어떻게 처리하는지 관심거리였다.

"밤중에 차를 타고 타도의 경계까지 가는 겁니다. 다리 하나만 건너가면 우리 구역이 아니니까요…."

"그래서요?"

그녀는 다급해져서 물었다.

"귀향 여비만 손에 쥐어주고 거기 부려놓는 거지요."

"저런…"

그녀의 입에서 이 한마디가 터져 나왔다.

"귀향 여비가 몇 푼 되나요?"

이번에는 이 여사가 물었다.

"사실 윗분들이야 그런 사업에 돈을 쓰려 하나요. 다리 하날 놓던가 건물을 세우면 눈에 띄니까요…."

"실제로 집에까지 돌아가고, 일단 안정되게 살림을 시작할 수 있게 보조가 되는 게 옳아요."

"사회복지, 사회복지 말만 했지…."

"행정기관이나 종교단체나 말만 번지르르 했지…. 모두들 같이 살겠다는 생각이면 문제가 없을 거에요."

"그런데 그렇게 쫓아버린 사람들이 도로 돌아오는 경우는 없나요?"

"왜 없겠어요. 돌고 도는 거지요. 우리만 그러겠어요? 우리 구역에도 새벽이면 어디서 떨어졌는 지도 모르게 부랑인들이 득시글거리는데…."

"서로 응급조치로 내다버리기 작전을 벌이는 거군요…."

"그런 셈이지요."

그들은 더 아무 말도 하지 못했다. 그저 쓰겁게 서로의 표정을 쳐다보았다.

그녀는 항만상담소에 전화를 걸어보았다. 할머니의 인상착의를 이야기하고 언제 들어왔는지 기억이 나느냐고 물었다.

"그런 할머니 여기로 들어온 적 없어요. 아시다시피 우리는 부랑인들은 철저히 도로 배를 태워 보내고 있지 않습니까?"

껄껄한 사내의 목소리는 변명에 급급했다.

"아니, 우리는 지금 책임을 묻는 게 아니에요. 이 할머니를 연고를 찾아줘야 하니까 혹시 인적사항을 알 수 있지 않을까 해서 그런 겁니다. 배를 탔다면 그때까지는 증명서가 있었을 테니까…."

그녀는 자연히 설득조가 된 자신을 깨닫고 있었다.

"글쎄 모른다니까요. 정말이에요. 그런 할머니가 항만을 거쳐간 적은 없으니까요…."

휑, 수화기 저쪽의 공간이 느껴졌다.

"알겠어요…."

이렇게 되면 별 도리가 없었다. 전화를 끊고 한참을 앉아 있다가 하릴없이 공항 쪽에다 전화를 걸었다. 이번에는 공항상담소의 전양이 전화를 받았다.

"예, 공항상담소입니다.…"

그녀의 가성이 귀청을 간지렀다.

"여기 시청 복지관데요. 사실은… 연고 없는 할머니 한 분이 들어왔거든요…."

그녀는 할머니의 인상착의와 그간의 경위를 쭈욱 이야기했다.

그러나 가만히 듣고 있던 저쪽도 빠질 구멍에는 민첩했다.

"증명 없이 비행기 탈 수 없다는 거야 이 여사님이 더 잘 아시잖아요? 철통같으니까요…."

딴은 그랬다. 그 할머니 주제로 봐서 비행기 타고 왔을 것 같지는 않았다. 그러면 어디서 떨어졌다는 말인가.

"알았어요… 혹 증거 될만한 건이 있으면 전화 주세요…."

그녀는 그만 수화기를 놓았다.

"혹 떼려다가 혹 하나 더 붙이겠수…."

어디들을 갔는지 방 안은 텅 비어 있었고 마주앉아 서류 정리를 하던 아동계의 강 계장이 참견을 하였다. 그녀는 험구였지만 오래 같이 근무한 만큼 속을 잘 알았고, 서로 통했다.

"너무 속끓이지 마우. 이 여사 눈가에 또 달무리가 둘렸어…."

"오래 일을 해서 면역이 될 만도 한데 일이 터지면 남의 일 같지가 않다니까요…."
 "글쎄 이놈의 세상이 어떻게 된 셈인지…."
 강 계장이 펜을 던지듯 상 위에 놓더니 지익직 슬리퍼를 끌며 밖으로 나갔다. 그 사이 그녀는 소망원으로 전화를 걸었다.
 "예."
 성격이 본래 퉁명스러워서 선물을 가지고 갔던 사람들로부터 민원까지 사는 소망원장이 전화를 받았다. 그러나 그녀는 오래 사귀어 봐서 퉁명스런 이 사내의 속에 깊은 정이 있는 걸 잘 알고 있었다. 할머니의 상황을 묻자 그가 갑자기 목소리의 톤을 높여 대답했다.
 "말도 맙서. 그 할머니 육자배기 목청이 기가 막힙디다."
 "노래를 그렇게 잘 불러요?"
 "들어선 모르니까 이 여사도 한 번 와서 들어봅서…."
 어쨌든 안정을 되찾은 건 다행한 일이었다. 수화기를 놓는데 밖으로 나갔던 강 계장이 자판기에서 뽑은 커피 두 잔을 들고 들어서고 있었다.

 퇴근시간에 맞추어 이 여사는 용두암으로 갔다. 거길 가봤자라는 걸 뻔히 알면서도 용머리는 이상한 인력으로 그녀를 끌었다.
 횡포한 관원들에 의해 장수가 죽임을 당한 후 그 주인을 따라 바위로 굳어졌다는 용마龍馬의 전설이 깃든 바위는 이 날도 파도와 바람에 의연히 버티고 서 있었다. 비수기였으나 철 늦은 관광객들이 드문드문 해변가의 계단을 내려가서 사진을 찍는 모습들이 보였다. 계단으로 내려가는 바위벽 여기저기에는 다녀간 사람들이 자기 이름을 새겨놓은 것들이 조잡하게 널려 있었다. 사람들은 얼마나 짧은 세월 세상에 왔다간 흔적들을 남기고 싶어하는가.

마치 그것들은 자기가 세상에 머무는 순간이 촉박하다는 것을 스스로 자인하는 것만 같았다.
　그런데 그 번데기 같은 인상의 할머니가 앉아서 울던 자리는 어디쯤일까. 그 신랑이라는 사내는 어디쯤에서 바다를 보며 기다리라고 했을까. 그녀는 하릴없이 빈 인조석 의자들 주변을 두릿거렸다. 그러나 아무 데도 그럴싸한 흔적들은 떨어져 있지 않았다. 그런 기대조차가 전혀 허망한 것이라는 걸 그녀 자신이 더 잘 알고 있었다.
　멀리 수평선을 향하여 망원경이 하나 설치되어 있었다. 신혼부부 몇 쌍이 그 주변을 거쳐갔지만 아무도 그것을 들여다보려 하지 않았다. 멀리를 내다볼 만큼 그들은 한가하지가 않은 것이리라. 그녀는 계단을 내려가 망원경 앞에 섰다. 백원 짜리 동전을 넣으면 시계視界가 트이게 된 장치였다. 그녀는 주머니를 뒤져 구멍 속에 동전을 집어넣었다. 눈을 갖다 대니까 시야에는 요동하는 물굽이가 확대되어서 다가들었다. 그런 파도 위를 갈매기 한 마리가 외롭게 날아가는 게 스쳤다. 저 갈매기의 외로운 비상은 무슨 의미가 있는가. 동체를 트니까 우뚝한 섬이 시야에 잡혔다. 아, 저 섬이 귀양오던 옛 선비들이 관을 벗었다던 관탈冠脫이지. 그렇긴 하지만 어찌 귀양객들 관이 저기까지 남았을까. 어쩌면 그 시대에 망명을 오던 사람들이 저기까지 와서는 의연히 버티고 섰는 한라산에 압도되어 그때까지 쓰고 있던 관을 벗었을 수도 있지 않을까. 그나저나 조선시대 이 섬까지 귀양왔던 사람의 수가 몇 백명이나 된다지 않은가. 섬은 그 시대에도 바른 소리나 하고 귀찮은 백성들을 쫓아내는 땅이더니 이제 또 한차례 사람들의 악연을 떼어버리는 장소가 된 느낌이었다.
　섬은 1960년대 말께부터 갑자기 개방되었다.
　신제주엘 가면 주로 일본의 관광객들을 상대로 웃음도 몸도 파는 가

런한 여자들 숫자가 천 명이 넘는다는 걸 그녀는 잘 알고 있었다. 구제주의 동·서 부둣가에도 쫓아도 쫓아도 몰려드는 철새들의 숫자가 꽤 된다는 걸 파악하고 있었다. 그녀들뿐만 아니라 소매를 잡아끌기만 하면 어디서나 따라나서는 여자들이 사방 널려 있다는 걸 그녀는 느끼고 있었다. 숫자뿐만 아니라 그들의 생활상, 그들의 의식까지도 어느 정도는 파악하고 있었다.

이렇듯 섬은 개방되면서 성도덕 면에서도 무방비의 천지가 되어 있었다. 새벽 참에 출근해 보면 어느 공중변소 옆, 어느 놀이터의 빈 의자 위에 라면박스에 담긴 아기가 내버려졌다는 신고가 들어와 있는 날이 적지 않았다. 여관의 타월 같은 것에 싸여서 울다가 지쳐서 버르적거리던 새빨간 핏덩이들. 아직 탯줄이 달린채 눈을 지리 감은 그것들은 태어난 세상에 감정이라도 있는 듯이 조그만 주먹을 부르쥐고 발악을 하고 있곤 했다.

더 심한 경우도 있었다. 어느 날 새벽에는 시내의 한 여인숙에서 신고가 들어왔다.

—아이고게. 어멍은 달아나 버리고 아기는 다 죽어가난 빨리 옵서게.

수화기에서 여인숙 주인여자의 목소리는 잦아져 가고 있었다.

그리 먼 거리가 아니었으므로 그녀는 달려가 보았다.

그런데 인가 끄트머리의 외진 여인숙은 마당에서부터 골마루와 문지방까지 온통 피투성이였다. 여인숙 요 위에 아기는 피투성이 인 채 버려져 있고 태반은 바로 문지방 가에 떨어져 있었다. 그때까지 아기와 탯줄은 연결된 상태였다. 아기를 낳아놓고 겁결에 도망가는 순간 문지방 가에서 태반이 떨어졌다는 상황이 판단되었다.

—밤중에 여자 손님 혼자가 들어왔수게. 이상하다고는 생각했지만

이런 변이 나리라고야 생각했수과? 새벽에 일어나 보니까 피가 널려 있어 우린 사름 죽은 줄 알았수게.

수다스런 여주인은 떠벌렸다. 그녀는 가위와 실을 가져오게 해서 이미 말라버린 탯줄을 잘랐다. 탯줄을 자를 때 아이는 몇 차례 발길질을 했는데 고추가 달린 놈은 체중도 튼실하고 이목구비가 번듯했다.

—아이고, 이렇게 잘 생긴 아이를!

여인숙 타월을 빌어 아이를 싸안고 나올 때 주인은 한편 아쉬운 듯 소리 질렀다. 만명에 한 명 꼴로나 튼실하게 생겼다고 진단을 받은 이 아이는 그러나 제때에 탯줄을 안 잘라준 때문에 시각·청각의 장애자로 일생을 살 수 밖에 없게 되었다. 영아 일시 보호소인 영익보육원에 맡겨졌던 그 아이가 최근 미국으로 입양된 사실을 그녀는 알고 있었다.

그녀가 허탕을 치고 구름다리께를 돌아서 용담로터리 부근까지 왔을 때 그녀는 문득 자기 앞서 걷는 한 거지를 만났다. 얼른 봐서는 남자인지 여자인지 잘 분간이 안 되는 그 거지는 옷 위에 옷을 껴입고 머리에도 얹을 수 있는껏 모자를 얹어놔서 마치 털북숭이 외국종 개를 연상시켰다. 그를 처음 봤을 때부터 그녀의 가슴은 쿵 내려 앉아서 마구 방망이질을 치기 시작했다. 시내의 부랑인들은 대개 한번씩 소망원에 붙들려갔다 나온 경우들이어서 눈에 익었지만 이 거지는 생판 처음이었다. 저 거지는 어디서 왔지. 저를 어째야 되는 거지? 그녀는 속에서 안달이었지만 좀체 결정을 내릴 수가 없었다. 그런 상태로 그녀는 인력에 끌린 듯 거지의 뒤를 쫓아가고 있었다. 거지는 갈지자之로 휘청거리며 걷다가 쓰레기 더미가 보이면 주룩 그쪽으로 달려가서 뒤졌다. 두 번째 쓰레기 더미에는 팔 한 짝이 뜯겨나간 오버가 내버려져 있었는데 그걸 쳐들고 살펴보더니 대뜸 한쪽 팔을 꿰어 입어버렸다. 등대기에 소금기가 내비친 오버가 그녀의 시야 앞을 우줄우줄 걸어가고 있었다. 아, 그런데 로터리 막 못 미쳐 쓰레기통 있는 데에 닿았을 때였다. 뒤따라오던 그녀는 우욱 치밀어 오르는 토기를 억제하며 골목으로 내빼기 시작했다. 그는 마침 비닐봉지에 넣어서 내버려져 있던 자장면 부스러기들을 손으로 움켜서는 입으로 가져가고 있었던 것이다.

아아, 그녀는 한참을 내빼와서야 자신의 눈에 담뿍 눈물이 고여 있는 걸 깨달았다. 아아, 저 사람을 어찌할 것인가. 가슴까지 치밀어 오른 토기는 그대로 멍이 되어서 묵중하게 명치끝을 누르고 있었다. 바람은 거슬러 불어오고 있었다. 그녀는 그 바람을 맞으며 천방지축 걸었다. 그녀는 그녀 자신이 모래먼지에 함께 휩쓸려 가는 느낌이었다. 아무 데나 구원을 청하지 않으면 안 되었다. 그녀는 문득 청송원의 진 원장을 떠올렸다. 그는 그 스스로가 고아이면서 이제는 고아원의 젊은 원장이 되어 있었다. 한때 고등학교 교사로 지낼 때 그녀도 가르침을 받은 스승이었는데 여러 인연으로 그녀의 인생 지표가 되어 있었다. 거리의 전화박스에서 수화기를 들고 다이얼을 돌렸을 때 그는 마침 자리에 있었다.

"내 곧 나가지. 거기가 어디야?"

목소리가 다급하게 들렸던지 원장은 선선히 응했다. 그녀는 기억 되는대로 다방 이름 하나를 대고 수화기를 고리에 걸었다.

지하다방으로 내려가서 원장을 기다리는 동안에도 그녀에겐 비참한 영상만 떠올랐다. 밀감나무 과수원에 영아가 유기 되었다는 신고를 받고 달려간 것은 지난 해 팔월의 일이었다. 차에서 내려서 두 밭 거리를 걸어가는 데도 몇 번이나 땀을 훔쳐야 되는 무더운 날씨였다.

―그저께부터 고양이 소리 같은 게 들리긴 해도 누게가 그런 줄이나 알아서….

그녀들을 안내하고 가는 과수원 주인은 어이가 없는 모양이었다. 주인의 뒤를 따라 샆짝 안으로 들어서니까 더운 김이 확 몸에 끼얹혀 왔다. 나무들 몇 줄 사이를 헤쳐 들어가니까 정말 어디서 고양이 울음소리 같은 게 들려왔다. 아아, 이럴 수가, 아기는 여학생의 블라우스 위에서 버르적거리고 있었다. 말라붙은 아이의 몸뚱어리 위에 귤나무 이파리의 그림자가 어룽거리고 있었다. 엎드려 들여다보던 그녀는 아기의 발꿈치가 헤져 피멍이 들어 있는 것을 보았다.

―시상에, 시상에 목숨도 모질지…

주인 여자가 또 넋두리를 하였다.

―악!

그런데 그녀는 더 아기를 관찰하다가 고함을 지르며 뒤로 물러 앉고 말았다. 이럴 수가, 이럴 수가, 세상에 이럴 수가. 그녀는 세차게 고개를 내저었다. 그녀가 본 것은 아기의 그 작은 조개에서 꼼실꼼실 기어 나오던 구더기들이었다.

―에미가 어떤 년인지!

주인 여자도 알아채고 욕지거리를 했다. 그녀는 스물스물 그 구더기들이 자기 뇌 속으로 파고드는 듯한 착각을 떨쳐버릴 수가 없었다. 주인 여자는 나이를 먹은 만큼 당찬 데가 있었다. 머리에 쓰고 있던 수건을 벗어 몰려드는 쇠파리를 쫓는 한편 기어 나오는 구더기를 제거한 다음 블라우스와 수건으로 아기의 몸을 쌌다.

사흘을 땡볕 아래서 견딘 그 아기도 어느새 보호소에서 돌을 지내놓고 있었다. 아아, 생명이란 얼마나 모진 것인가.

"웬 일이야, 이 여사가 나를 다 찾구?"

앞에 와 앉은 진 원장이 그녀의 얼굴을 찬찬히 뜯어보고 있었다. 그녀는 웃으려 하는데 표정이 잘 풀리지 않았다.

"어째 이 여사 자신이 미아가 된 것 같네…."

예, 그래요. 제 자신이 미아가 되었어요. 그러나 이 말은 밖으로 새어나오지는 않았다. 차가 날라져 왔을 때 그녀는 오늘 아침부터 있었던 이야기를 죽 했다.

"작은 일은 아니야. 80년 팔천 오백이던 기아가 83년에는 일만 이천 백, 87년에는 일만 삼천 삼백으로 계속 증가추세라니까…."

진 원장도 침울하게 말을 받았다.

"아이들뿐만 아니라 어른들까지 내다버리게 되었으니 이 일은 어째야 좋죠?"

"빈민계층에 대한 보다 적극적 경제 지원과 가족의식의 변화가 시급히 바라지는 시점이지. 상호간에 연대의식이 절실한 때라고 봐…."

"그런 의식의 변화들을 어떻게 일으키죠?"

"그래도 포기할 수야 없지. 종교와 교육과… 모든 분야에서 최선을 기울이는 수밖에…. 그런데 시설을 운영하다 보면 아직도 도처에 살아있는 샘들이 보이거든. 숨어서 좋은 일 하는 사람들이 드물지 않게 있어."

"……"

그녀는 의지에 찬 원장의 표정을 보며 연신 고개를 끄덕이고 있었다. 그제서야 그녀는 남편에게가 아니라 그에게로 다이얼을 돌렸던 이유를 깨달아가고 있었다.

"자, 우리 나가지. 나가서 찬바람이라도 쐬구 저녁이라도 먹자구. 세상이 어두운 구석들로 차있기 때문에 우리가 힘을 비축해둬야 하는 거야."

그가 앞장서 일어나서 카운터로 가 찻값을 치렀다. 그리고 활발하게 계단을 오르는 그의 인력에 끌리듯 그녀는 따라가고 있었다.

육자배기 할머니의 연고자를 찾는 마지막 방법으로 시청 부녀복지과에서 보낸 지문조회는 일주일만에 회보가 왔다. 주소가 확인되자 그녀는 장거리 전화로 그쪽 면사무소 총무계에 전화를 걸었다. 두 번, 세 번 전화를 걸어서야 겨우 그녀의 가정사정을 파악할 수 있었다.
"아아, 그 할머니요. 딱하게 되었는데요…."
저쪽은 우선 기피하는 소리부터 했다.
"왜 그러세요, 왜 딱합니까?"
"그 할머니는 남편도 자식도 없고 거택구호 대상자입니다."
거택구호 대상자…. 그들의 처지가 어떻다는 건 어느 지방이나 피차 일반일 것이었다. 그녀는 이런 절대빈곤층이 이 사회의 저변에 가을날 낙엽처럼 깔려 있는 걸 잘 알고 있었다. 선거철이 되면 쌀 한 가마니씩의 선심을 감지덕지 받아들이는 이들. 이들을 상대로 선물 나누는 일을 그녀 자신도 한 경험이 있었다.
"할머니의 말로는 신랑이 자기를 이곳까지 데려왔다는데요?"
그녀는 따졌다.
"그 할머니 정신 나간 소리를 어찌 믿으세요? 그 할머니는 어릴 때부터 정박精薄으로 결혼은 했으나 이내 돌아왔었어요. 신상명세서를 우리가 잘 파악을 해 놓고 있습니다…"
"그런데 어떻게 그런 할머니가 이 먼 섬에까지 왔을까요?"
"말하기 거북합니다만 그 할머니에게 또 여든 넘은 노모가 있습니다. 요즘 들어서 발작만 일으키면 신랑을 내놓으라고 머리끄덩이를 잡고 행패를 부렸답니다. …그래 일가에서 한푼 두 푼씩 돈을 모았던 모양이에요. 육십만 원을 모아 기도원엘 데려간다고 갔는데 데리고 간 사람이 이모 아들이었던 모양이에요…."

거기까지 듣자 모든 상황이 확 알아졌다. 그녀의 귓청에 쨍, 이명耳鳴이 왔다. 그녀의 어깨를 세찬 것이 내려쳤다. 탈진해서 앉았던 그녀는 전화 내용을 사실대로 써서 보고하는 수밖에 없었다.

"하는 수 없어요. 우리로서도 연말까지는 한 사람이라도 시설인원을 줄여야 하니까…. 이것도 인연이니 이 여사가 그 지방엘 다녀옵시다…."

보고서를 들고 부시장실엘 다녀온 과장이 그녀에게 윽박지르듯 말했다. 책상을 지키고 앉은 계장의 표정도 그녀에게 강요하고 있었다. 주양 쪽을 돌아다봤으나 그녀는 아직 거친 업무를 떠맡길 만큼 미덥지 못했다.

남편과 아이들에게 번번이 미안했으나 없을 동안 친정어머니께 와서 돌보아달라고 부탁하고 그녀는 할머니의 귀향여비를 끊었다. 생각해 준다고 며칠 분 급식비까지 얹어 끊어줬으나 자기 여비를 보태도 실비가 될까 말까한 액수였고, 게다가 그 길은 미친 할머니와 동행해야 하는 위태로운 여정이었다.

그녀들이 배를 타던 날도 바람은 거세게 거슬러 불었다. 옛날 귀양오던 사람들의 심정이 이랬을까. 옷을 입을 만큼 껴입었는데도 몸이 부룩부룩 떨려왔다.

배가 부두를 떠나 한참 바다로 나갔을 때 뱃전에 기대서서 바다를 바라보던 할머니의 입에서 흥얼흥얼 육자배기 가락이 들려오기 시작했다. 그 소리를 듣자 그녀는 퍼뜩 귀가 트였다.

간다아, 가기는 간다마는
내 돌아갈 곳이 어디드냐

그것은 전혀 미친 여자 같지 않은 또렷한 음성이었다. 그 홍얼거리는 소리를 듣자 그녀는 왈칵 가슴으로 치받쳐 오르는 게 있었다. 아아, 이 일을 어찌해야 할 것이냐. 그녀는 파도를 붙잡고 기도하는 심정이 되었다.

 갈매기 한 쌍이 파도를 거슬러 날으며 외로운 싸움을 싸우고 있었다.

아동문학

등대 · 한라산 2
마라도 · 한라산
종이피아노
해맞이
설문대할망

김영기

등대
한라산 2

필자 소개
1984년 아동문예 신인문학상 당선.
동시집 『날개의 꿈』 『작은 섬 하나』 『새들이 주고받는 말』 등.

등대 외 1편

김영기

갈매기가
바다 위를
자맥질 할 때면

등대도
파도를 일으켜
하늘을 나는
하이얀 새가 된다.

아버지가
밤바다에
그물을 던질 때면

등대도
그물을 던져
바다에 뜬 별을
건져 올린다.

한라산 2

비 맞고 속 잎 자라듯
몰래몰래 꾸는 꿈
날개를 갖고 싶대요
안개에 젖어 고사리 움트듯
쏘옥쏘옥 크는 꿈
하늘을 날고 싶대요.
탐라의 아기 장수
겨드랑이에 감춰둔
날개의 꿈
빗줄기 뒤에 숨어 키운대요.
안개 속에 숨어 날아본대요

마라도
한라산

필자 소개

1976년 《소년》지에 동시 추천. 전남아동문학가협회, 제주아동문학가협회 회장 역임. 한국문협 제주도지회장(현)
한국아동문학상, 소청문학상, 전남아동문학가상 수상.
시집 『사는 게 뭣산디』 『햇님이 사는 꽃밭』(동시집) 외.

마라도 외 1편

김종두

오늘같이 좋은날
마라도는 출항하지 않는다.
해종일 빛화장으로 단장한
한라산을 바라보기 위하여
마라도는 무적을 울리고 해무를 걷어낸다.

시시각각 변하는 빛의 얼굴 한라산
오늘같은 날
한라산은 마라도를 유혹한다.
잔잔한 파도의 자맥질과
파아란 하늘의 눈웃음
그리고 눈부신 태양의 빛으로
마라도 순진한 섬처녀를 유혹한다.

오늘같은 날
마라도는 닻을 내리고
마라관산馬羅觀山 영주비경瀛州秘境 바라보며
사랑노래 부른다.
산자락 그늘이 섬에 닿을 때까지

마라도는 태역밭에서
숙객들과 어울려 쐬주잔을 비운다.

오늘같이 좋은날
마라도는 등대불마저 꺼놓고서
영원한 고향 한라산 품에서 단잠에 빠진다.

한라산

제주 섬아이들은 한라산 품에서 큰다.
바닷가 아이들이나
중산간 아이들이나
제주 아이들이라면 그 어디서나
한라산을 바라보며 커간다.

날마다 산을 오르며
날마다 한라산을 맴돌며
날마다 한라산이 흘려 내보내는 샘물을 마시며
한라산이 들려주는 이야기를 들으며 자라는
제주의 아이들.

한라산은
섬 제주에서 태어난 아이들을
섬 제주에서 자라는 아이들을
섬 제주에 터잡고 살아갈
제주 사람으로 키운다.

강순복

종이피아노

필자 소개
한국문인협회, 국제펜클럽, 한국아동문학회 회원(현)
한국피부관리사협회 제주지회장(현)
동화집 『종이피아노』 『키 크는 요술안경』 『네 발로 걷는 아이』 등
E-mail : ksb1234@hanmail.net

종이피아노

강순복

　아름다운 음악이 흐르던 문예회관 대극장 안은 난리가 났습니다. 눈 깜짝할 사이에 일어난 신기한 일 때문입니다. 도저히 있을 수 없는 일이 일어난 것은 피아노 연주를 하던 반지라는 소녀 때문이었습니다.
　청각장애아인 반지는 오늘 연주회를 위해 손이 저릴 만큼 연습을 했습니다. 쇼팽의 연습곡을 눈을 감고서도 쳐낼 정도로 열심히 연습한 것입니다.
　연주 순서를 기다리는 동안 반지는 마음 속에서 몇 번이고 같은 기도를 드렸습니다.
　'하나님! 잘할 수 있도록 도와주세요. 제 손가락 마디에 지혜를 주셔서 실수하지 않도록 도와주세요.'
　반지는 후! 하고 심호흡을 해가며 차례가 될 때까지 기도를 했습니다.
　드디어 반지 차례가 되었습니다.
　"다음은 하효초등학교 오학년 이반지 어린이 순서입니다. 연주할 곡목은 쇼팽의 연습곡입니다."

사회자의 말이 끝나자 반지는 무대 위에 있는 피아노를 향해 걸어갔습니다. 반지가 피아노를 향해 걸어갈 때 약간씩 뒤뚱거리는 걸음을 앞쪽 관객들은 보았습니다.

반지는 관객들의 눈이 커지는 것을 알았지만 다소곳이 인사를 한 후 피아노의 건반에 손을 올려놓았습니다.

"야아! 나를 도와 줘. 음표야, 쉼표야, 나를 도와줘!"

반지는 건반을 향해 아주 작게 중얼거렸습니다. 반지는 피아노 건반과 악보를 친구처럼 생각해 왔습니다.

딩동댕, 딩동댕, 딩동 딩동댕.

강단 안에는 반지가 치는 피아노 소리가 퍼지기 시작했습니다.

관객들은 이제 겨우 열두 살짜리가 어려운 곡을 참 잘 친다고 생각하며 음악 감상을 했습니다. 그런데 어느 순간 반지가 천천히 일어섰습니다. 반지의 손은 이제 피아노의 희고 검은 건반이 아니라 허공에 떠 있었습니다. 손가락만 부지런히 움직이는 것, 그런데 이상한 것은 여전히 음악이 흐른다는 사실이었습니다.

"아니? 저… 저 애가…?"

"저건 쇼야. 녹음기를 틀어 놨나 봐."

여기저기서 소란이 일어났습니다.

반지를 지켜보던 선생님도 부모님도 식은땀이 났습니다.

"아니야. 녹음기를 틀어 놓은 건 아닌 거 같아."

눈을 감고 감상하던 관객들도 세상에 이럴 수가, 놀라서 일어섰습니다.

반지는 차츰 허공을 건반 삼아 계속 손가락을 움직이며 무대 중앙으로 걸어 나갔습니다.

도저히 있을 수 없는 일이 벌어지고 있는 것입니다. 도대체 치지도 않는 피아노가 소리를 낸다면 믿을 수가 있을까요?
 관객들이 입을 벌린 채 멍하니 서있는 데도 반지는 계속 허공에서 피아노를 치는 중입니다.
 반지는 일학년 때까지만 해도 정상적인 아이였습니다. 유난히 피아노를 좋아했지만 반지네 집안 형편이 피아노를 사 줄 수는 없었습니다.
 "피아노가 얼만 줄이나 아니? 네가 갖고 있는 돈 백 개씩 백배는 내야 돼."
 천 원짜리 용돈이 생기자 그 걸로 피아노를 산다는 반지의 말에 엄마가 웃으며 말씀하셨습니다.
 반지는 그 날부터 군것질을 전혀 하지 않고 돈이 생기는 대로 꼬박꼬박 저금을 했습니다.
 반지가 피아노 치는 꿈을 거의 밤마다 꾸기 시작한 것도 그 무렵부터입니다. 심지어 날개 달린 피아노를 타고 날아다니는 꿈도 꾸었습니다.
 반지가 초등학교에 입학하고 보니 많은 친구들이 피아노학원을 다니고 있었고, 그 친구들이 바이엘이니 체르니니 할 때면 주눅이 들었습니다.
 "엄마! 피아노학원 보내 주세요."
 반지가 떼를 썼지만 엄마는 선뜻 대답을 못 했습니다. 그러던 하루, 엄마가 하얀 표지에 피아노 건반을 그려 책상 위에 올려놓더니 투명 스카치테이프로 붙여 주었습니다. 도 레 미 파 솔 라 시에다 빨 주 노 초 파 남 보 무지개 색깔로 표시도 해 주었습니다.
 반지는 도미솔도 대신에 빨노파빨하고 색깔 이름으로 부르기도 했습니다.

"엄마! 종이피아노라 소리가 안 나."

"종이라고 생각 말고 진짜라고 생각하렴. 그러다 보면 정말로 소리가 날 수도 있는 거야."

반지는 아침에 일어나면 제일 먼저 피아노를 쳤습니다. 아는 것이라고는 도레미파솔라시 뿐이었습니다. 그래도 아주 열심히 하니까 차츰 동요도 칠 수 있게 되었습니다.

엄마는 종이피아노가 다 닳아지면 다시 새것을 그려 붙여 주었습니다.

"엄마! 윤근이네 옆집에 피아노 학원이 생겼어요. 시내도 거기 다닌대요."

반지가 이학년이 되었을 때 동네에 피아노교습소가 생겼습니다. 그렇지만 엄마는 반지를 학원에 보낼 엄두도 못 냅니다.

아이엠에프 때문에 살림이 더 어려워진 탓도 있습니다. 그래서 엄마는 반지보다 더 마음이 상했지만 형편이 조금만 나아지면 보내준다고 했습니다.

딩동댕 딩동댕

교습소에서 울리는 피아노 소리는 날씨가 맑은 날은 반지네 집까지 들립니다. 그런 날이면 엄마는 짜증이 났지만 반지는 신이 납니다.

"엄마! 피아노 소리 곱지?"

반지는 일요일에 교회 가는 일이 참 즐겁습니다. 일찍 가면 더러 피아노를 만져 볼 수도 있었기 때문입니다. 피아노 치는 선생님 곁에 서 있다가 슬며시 만져보는 것입니다.

"치고 싶은 모양이구나. 한번 쳐볼래? 괜찮아. 눌러 봐."

선생님은 반지의 작은 손을 건반 위에 올려놓아 주기도 했습니다.

하지만 반지의 손은 갑자기 뻣뻣해져서 제대로 건반을 누르지 못하곤 했습니다.

봄이 되자, 반지네 마을에는 밀감꽃이 무더기로 피어 향기를 날렸습니다. 부모님은 과수원 일을 하느라 저녁 늦게 돌아 오셨고, 반지는 숙제도 못한 채 피아노교습소 주위를 뱅뱅 돌았습니다.

안개가 자욱한 어느 날 저녁, 반지는 어디선가 들려오는 고운 소리를 듣게 되었습니다. 그 소리는 아직까지 한번도 들어보지 못한 음색이 아주 맑은 소리였습니다. 반지는 자신도 모르게 소리나는 곳을 향해 천천히 걷기 시작했습니다. 얼마쯤 걸었는지, 어디쯤 왔는지 알 수가 없었습니다. 그런데 천천히 움직이던 반지가 악, 하는 외마디 비명과 함께 철컥하는 쇠 부딪치는 소리가 났습니다.

"아악, 엄마야! 엄마야! 아야…"

반지는 쥐를 잡으려고 놓아 둔 덫에 발목이 치인 것입니다.

반지가 어른들에게 발견되었을 때는 이미 반지의 왼쪽 발목은 거의 잘려나간 상태였고, 울다 지쳐 의식을 잃은 후였습니다.

이 사고로 반지는 다리를 절뚝이게 되었고, 소리가 잘 들리지 않더니 청각장애자가 되어버린 것입니다.

엄마는 더 이상 반지에서 종이피아노를 그려 주지도 않았고 책상 위에 붙인 종이 피아노마저 찢어 버렸습니다.

텔레비전에서 피아노 치는 장면이 나오면 채널을 다른 곳으로 돌렸습니다. 그러나 반지는 여전히 피아노교습소 담벼락에 매달려 소리 듣기를 좋아했습니다. 소리가 잘 들리지 않을수록 더 가까이 귀를 갖다 대었습니다. 그런 반지를 지켜본 교습소 선생님은 가끔씩 반지를 불러서 피아노를 만져 보게 했는데 한번은 반지 엄마가 화를 벌컥 내는 바람에 다시는 반지를 못 본체 했습니다.

"반지야! 기도하렴. 예수님은 반지가 원하는 일이라면 무엇이든 들어주시는 분이시니까 옳은 일이면 무엇이든 기도하면 들어주실 거야."
 교회 학교 선생님은 언제나 부드러운 음성으로 감싸주셨습니다.
 반지는 새들의 우는 소리도 더 이상 들을 수 없었으며 시냇물이 졸졸졸 흐르는 소리도 듣지 못했습니다.
 "소리를 듣지 못하니까 정말 갑갑해. 보지 못하는 애들은 얼마나 갑갑할까…"
 반지는 자기보다 더 힘들고 어려운 친구들의 마음을 이해하게 되었습니다.
 어느 날 교회학교 선생님이 반지네 집엘 찾아 왔습니다.
 "반지 엄마! 반지는 영혼이 너무 곱고 착한 아이에요. 피아노를 치도록 해 주세요. 제가 가르칠게요. 틀림없이 할 수 있을 거예요. 반지는… 피아노를 치게 해야 돼요. 물론… 속이 상하시겠지만… 반지가 할 수 있는 일을 하게 해야해요."
 반지는 교회 선생님 덕분에 피아노를 배우게 되었습니다.
 반지가 오학년이 되었을 때는 반지의 피아노 연주 솜씨가 놀랄 정도로 나아져 있었습니다.
 말소리는 들리지 않는데 피아노 소리는 들린다는 반지를 데리고 이비인후과를 찾은 엄마는 또 한번 낙심했습니다.
 "청각장애입니다. 이 어린이의 경우는 일종의 착각 현상인데요. 가끔씩 이런 경우가 있지요. 어떤 일에 깊이 몰두하다 보면 꼭 들리는 것 같은, 일종의 이명현상이죠."
 병원을 나서며 엄마는 이제 반지가 피아노를 치려고 별 거짓말을 다 하는구나 싶어서 속이 상했습니다.

전도 초등학교 피아노 콩쿠르대회
주최: 삼다일보사
장소: 문예회관 대극장
일시: 1999년 9월 9일

반지에게 찢겨진 신문광고를 보여준 교회학교 선생님은 매우 흥분해 있었습니다.
"반지야! 너 할 수 있지? 그치?"
멀뚱히 쳐다보는 반지에게 시간이 없다며 선생님은 피아노연습을 시키기 시작했습니다. 발표회 날은 그 날로부터 두 달 후였습니다.
선생님은 전부터 연습했던 쇼팽의 연습곡을 치게 했습니다.
"선생님! 오선지가 필요 없는 악보가 있었으면 좋겠어요. 까만 음표 대신에 무지개색 옷을 입은 음표를 마구 섞어 놓아도 색깔만 보면 음 이름을 알 수 있거든요. 우리 엄마가 가르쳐주신 것처럼…"
반지는 연습 도중 잠시 쉬면서 말을 했습니다.
"어떻게?"
"도는 빨강, 레는 주황, 미는 노랑…, 높은 도는 진빨강, 낮은 도는 연빨강…, 그러면 악보가 없어도 꼬리만 달아주면 악보가 되잖아요."
"그거 좋겠다. 그러면 어린 아이들이나 지능이 조금 낮은 애들도 쉽게 익힐 수 있겠구나."
선생님은 반지 생각에 맞장구를 쳤습니다. 엉뚱한 것 같지만 그런 생각을 하는 것만으로도 반지는 틀림없이 무언가 해낼 것 같았습니다.
잘 알아듣지 못해서 말하는 것조차 잊어 가는 반지가 과연 많은 사람들 앞에서 피아노를 칠 수 있을지 엄마는 불안했지만 밥 먹는 것도 잊을 만큼 피아노 치기에 열중인 반지는 어서 빨리 연주회 날이 오기만 기다렸습니다.

드디어 대회 날이 돌아왔습니다.

문예회관 대극장에는 많은 사람들이 모였습니다. 반지는 순서를 기다리는 동안 쉬지 않고 기도를 드렸습니다.

'제발 저를 도와주세요. 잘 들리지 않아도 피아노 치는데 큰 어려움이 없도록 그래서 부모님과 선생님을 기쁘게 할 수 있도록, 제발 도와주세요.'

마음속에서 몇 번이고 기도를 드린 후 무대에 오른 반지는 처음에는 아무탈 없이 쇼팽의 연습곡을 잘 쳐나갔습니다. 그런데 한참을 열심히 건반을 두드리던 반지의 손이 무엇에 이끌린 듯 자연스럽게 피아노에서 떨어진 것입니다.

그런데 자세히 보니 반지의 작은 몸을 무지개 빛 동그라미들, 언뜻 보면 비누방울 같기도 한 꼬리 달린 음표들이 둥그렇게 감싸고 있는 것이 아닙니까. 비누방울 같이 동그란 꼬리 달린 음표들은 관객들의 머리 위까지 날아왔다가 사라지기도 했습니다.

"어? 어? 저… 저런 일이…"

도저히 믿을 수 없는 일이 일어난 강당 안은 이제 술렁거리기 시작했습니다. 그렇지만 음표들은 아무 일도 아니라는 듯이 너울너울 춤을 추었고, 반지는 어느새 피아노 연주를 끝내고 다소곳이 고개 숙여 인사를 하고 있었습니다. 누군가 먼저 짝 짝 짝 하고 박수를 치니까 이윽고 관객들이 하나 둘 일어서면서 박수를 치기 시작했습니다.

반지의 가슴은 불타는 듯 뜨거웠지만, 아직도 음표들은 음악이 다 끝나지 않은 듯 너울대며 춤추고 있었습니다.

박재형

해맞이

필자 소개
제주아동문학회 회장, 제주문인협회 부지회장 역임.
계몽아동문학상 수상.
동화집 『검둥이를 찾아서』 『내 친구 삼례』 『다랑쉬오름의 슬픈 노래』 등.

해맞이

박재형

바람이 불어 왔다. 쪽빛 바다를 건너온 바람이 불어 와 뺨을 어루만지고 자꾸만 머리를 쓸어넘겼다. 파도가 이는 바다 멀리 수평선에 관탈섬이 걸려 있었다. 나는 외로이 서 있는 관탈섬을 한참 동안 바라보았다. 축 늘어진 내 어깨를 바람이 불어 와 어루만져 주었지만, 나는 슬픔을 털어 버리지 못했다.

아버지께서 돌아오지 않으셨다. 그제 저녁, 바다로 나간 아버지께서는 돌아오실 줄을 몰랐다. 생선 비린내와 바다 냄새를 안고 대문을 들어서시던 아버지께서, 장화를 신은 발로 성큼성큼 들어와 반찬거리로 남겨 온 고기를 내밀던 아버지께서 거짓말처럼 모습을 보이지 않으셨다.

어머니는 아버지께서 마치 돌아가시기라도 한 듯이 눈물을 흘리셨다. "뱃사람은 언제 죽을지 모른다."라는 말씀을 가끔 하셨는데, 그 말이 씨가 되었나 보다고 하시며 굵은 눈물을 죽죽 흘리시며 부둣가로, 해양경찰서로 종종걸음을 치고 다니셨다.

나도 가슴이 아팠다. 내가 아버지를 차가운 겨울 바다로 밀어 낸 것 같아 정말 가슴이 아팠다. 아버지께서 돌아오시지 않는다면 그건 모두 내 탓이다.

그 날, 청소 시간에 선생님이 몇 번이나 조용히 하라고 야단을 치셨다. 그런데도 우린 선생님의 눈치를 보며 틈만 나면 이야기보따리를 풀어 놓았다.
은정이가 탑동으로 놀러 가자고 하였다.
"얘들아, 자전거 타러 가자. 바다도 구경하고."
은정이의 말에 우린 모두 찬성을 했다. 탑동 넓은 광장에서 자전거를 타거나 롤러 스케이트를 타면 즐거울 것 같아 나도 찬성을 했다.
교실 청소가 끝나자마자 탑동으로 향했다.
우리는 동문 시장 과일 가게와 옷 가게를 지나 동문 로터리를 거쳐 산지로를 따라 걸어갔다 대밭 속의 참새들처럼 웃으며 떠들며 갔다.
바다를 건너온 싸늘한 바람이 옷깃을 스쳤지만, 추위를 느낄 만한 날씨는 아니어서 발걸음이 가벼웠다.
"우리, 고깃배 구경하면서 가자."
수협 공판장 옆을 지날 때쯤 유진이가 말했다.
"그렇게 하자."
은정이가 좋다고 하자, 아이들은 별말 없이 어선 부두로 발길을 돌렸다. 나는 작은 동력선들이 빼곡히 들어선 어선 부두로 가기가 싫었지만, 하는 수 없이 친구들을 따라갔다. 그리고 그 곳에서 아버지를 만나고 말았다.
"샘이야, 어디 가니? 친구들과 같이 왔구나."
아버지께서는 고기가 담긴 상자를 들고 배에서 내리다가 우리를 발견하고는 반가운 듯이 말씀하셨다.
"네, 저, 저, 놀러……."
나는 친구들 앞에서 아버지를 만난 게 부끄러워 말을 잇지 못했다.
"너희들, 우리 샘이하고 사이좋게 지내야 한다."
아버지께서는 활짝 웃는 낯으로 말씀하셨다. 그리고 호주머니에서 돈을 꺼내어 나에게 내미셨다.
"샘이야, 이 돈으로 친구들과 빵이라도 사 먹어라."
나는 얼른 자리를 피하고 싶었다. 아버지 몸에서 나는 비릿한 생선 냄새를 아이들이 싫어할 거라는 생각에 얼른 아버지 곁을 떠나고 싶었다. 아버지나 어머니께서는 늘 생선 냄새를 달고 사셨다. 어머니께서는 그게 바다 냄새라고 하며 아무렇지도 않다는 듯이 말씀하셨지만, 나는 그 냄새가 화장실 냄새보다도 더 싫었다. 그래서 얼른 돈을 받지 못하고 머뭇거렸다.
그러자 빛나가 손을 내밀었다.
"감사합니다. 잘 먹을게요."
빛나는 횡재나 했다는 듯이 돈을 넙죽 받았다.
"고맙습니다."
아이들도 덩달아 인사를 하였다.
"재미있게 놀다 가거라."
아버지께서는 행복한 웃음을 지으며 고기 상자를 어깨에 메고 공판장으로 걸어가셨다.
아버지와 헤어진 우리들은 골목길을 빠져 나와 서부두 쪽으로 나섰다. 그런데 빛나가 엄지손가락과 집게손가락으로 돈을 집고 높이 들더니 얼굴을 찡그리며 말하였다.
"어이구, 이 비린내! 돈에서 냄새가 나. 샘이 아버지 몸에서 나던 냄새야. 이래서 우리 어머니께서 돈이 제일 더러운 거라고 하셨구나."
빛나는 아버지께서 주신 돈이 더러운 물건이라도 되는 듯이 얼굴을 찌푸리며 코 앞에다 대고 손부채질을 하였다.
"너, 정말 이럴래?"
나는 와락 화가 치밀어 빛나를 쏘아보았다.
"왜? 내가 어쨌는데? 돈에서 냄새가 난다고 해서 화났니? 그럼 내가 거짓말한다는 거니? 내가 거짓말했니? 한번 맡아 봐. 얼마나 지독한 냄새가 나는지."
빛나는 돈을 거칠게 내 코 앞에 내밀었다.
"왜들 이러니? 그까짓 걸 가지고."
지연이가 말렸지만, 나는 분을 참지 못했다.
"우리 아버지께서 주신 돈이 더러운 돈이란 말이지? 그렇게 더러운 돈을 왜 받았니? 왜 받았어?"
"뭐라고? 주시니까 받았지. 내가 달라고 했니? 네가 안 받으니까 내가 대신 받은 거 아냐? 자, 가져. 더러운 돈."
빛나는 마치 쓰레기라도 버리는 것처럼 돈을 내던졌다. 돈은 떨어져 내리다 바람에 실려 날아갔다.
나는 돈을 주울 생각도 못 하고 울면서 집으로 돌아와 버렸다. 친구들의 목소리가 따라왔지만, 나는 뒤도 안 돌아보았다.
"재미있게 놀았니?"
저녁에 돌아오신 아버지께서는 호두과자를 내밀며 다정하게 말씀하셨다. 나를 위해 아버지께서는 시장 옆 구멍가게에서 호주머니를 뒤져 생선 냄새가 나는 돈을 꺼내 호두과자를 사셨을 것이다.
"샘이 아버지는 정말 좋은 분 같아요. 샘이는 좋겠다."
가게 아주머니는 아버지를 추겨 세우면서 호두과자를 봉지에 담아

주셨을 테고, 아버지께서는 호두과자를 받고 기뻐할 나를 생각하면서 기분 좋게 시장길을 따라 오셨을 것이다.
 구수한 호두과자 냄새가 풍겨 왔지만 나는 얼굴을 펴지 않았다.
 "친구들 앞에 그런 모습으로 나타나면 어떻게 해요? 창피하게."
 내 입에서는 엉뚱한 말이 튀어나왔다. 아버지 몸에서 나는 비릿한 냄새가 싫었고, 친구들이 작업복 차림의 아버지를 보는 게 싫기는 했지만 아버지를 창피하다고 생각해 본 적은 없는데, 내 입에서는 마치 대사 연습이라도 한 배우처럼 자연스럽게 창피하다는 말이 튀어나온 것이다.
 "창피했니? 난 그런 줄 몰랐다."
 아버지께서는 갑자기 당한 일이라 그런지 머쓱한 표정을 짓더니 얼굴을 붉히셨다. 그리고 밖으로 나가셨다. 아버지께서 돌아오신 건 밤이 이슥해서였다 아버지께서는 술에 취하셨다.
 "난 창피한 놈이야. 난 창피한 놈이야."
 아버지께서는 주정을 하듯이 혼잣말로 말씀하셨지만, 나는 그게 나 때문에 하시는 말이라는 걸 단번에 알아챘다.
 "당신이 왜 창피한 사람이에요? 우리 집 기둥인데. 아이들 앞에서 이게 뭐예요?"
 어머니께서는 술주정이라고 생각했는지 타박을 하셨다. 아버지께서는 술주정을 하시는 게 아니고, 내가 들으라고 하시는 말씀일 것이다.
 나는 아버지께 큰 잘못을 저질렀다는 걸 알면서도 이불 속에서 나갈 수 없었다.
 아버지께서는 이틀이나 더 술을 드셨다. 바다에도 나가지 않고 술을 마시고 돌아와 말없이 슬픈 표정으로 앉아 계시곤 했다.
 어머니께서는 자꾸 술을 마시는 아버지에게 짜증을 내셨다.

"당신 왜 그래요? 설날이 돌아오는데, 차례 준비도 해야 하고, 애들 양말이라도 사 줘야 할 거 아니에요?"

"알았어. 내가 돈을 벌어 와야지. 나는 돈만 벌어다 주는 돈벌레니까"

장사를 하고 늦게 돌아오신 어머니 말씀에 아버지께서는 나 들으라는 듯이 말씀을 하시고 바다에 나갈 채비를 하셨다. 바다로 가시는 아버지의 어깨가 무거워 보였지만, 나는 죄송하다는 말 한 마디 하지 못하고 아버지의 무거운 발걸음 소리만 들어야 했다

그런데 아버지께서는 돌아오지 않으셨다. 밤배를 탔으니 아침에는 돌아오셔야 하는데, 아버지께서 탄 금성호는 모습을 드러내지 않았다.

먼바다에 돌풍이 불었다고는 하지만 다른 배들은 아무 일 없었다는 듯이 씩씩하게 물살을 헤치며 돌아왔는데, 아버지께서 탄 배는 돌아오는 걸 잊기라도 한 것처럼 나타나지 않았다. 아버지께서 탄 배가 실종되었다는 소식이 뉴스 시간마다 흘러나오고, 어머니께서는 장사도 못하고 부두와 해양경찰서를 오락가락하셨다.

나는 정말 가슴이 아팠다. 아버지께 죄송하다는 말씀도 못 드렸는데, 돌아오시지 않으니 눈앞이 캄캄하였다. 만일, 아버지께 무슨 일이라도 생기면 어떻게 하나 하는 걱정으로 입이 바작바작 말랐다. 그래서 어젯밤은 한잠도 이루지 못하였다. 눈만 감으면 슬픈 빛을 띤 아버지의 얼굴이 떠올라 잠이 오지 않았다.

해님이 바닷속으로 들어가려는지 구름 낀 서쪽 하늘이 붉은 빛을 띠었다.

'지금 아버지께서는 어디에 계실까? 기관이 고장나 바람과 파도에 밀려다니고 계실까? 아니면, 판자에 의지해서 물 위를 떠다니고 계실

까?'

　나는 저녁 바다를 바라보며 아버지께서 무사하시기를 빌었다. 나는 아버지를 위해 무언가를 하고 싶었다. 아버지께서 돌아오실 때까지 기다리고만 있을 수는 없었다.
　'어떻게 하지? 어떻게 하면 아버지를 돌아오시게 할 수 있을까?'
　나는 관탈섬을 멍하니 바라보며 아버지의 얼굴을 그려 보았다. 바닷바람에 그을어 검붉은 얼굴과 하얗게 바래어 가는 아버지의 머리털을 그리다가 나도 모르게 눈물을 주르륵 쏟았다.
　나는 한참 동안 관탈섬을 바라보다가 동화책에서 읽었던 이야기를 떠올렸다. 떠오르는 해님에게 소원을 빌면 그 소원이 이루어진다는 내용의 이야기였다.
　'해맞이를 하며 해님에게 빌면 아버지께서 돌아오실까? 정말 아버지께서 돌아오실까? 그래, 돌아오실 거야. 아버지께서는 꼭 돌아오실 거야.'
　해님에게 빌면 소원이 이루어진다는 말을 믿고 싶었다.
　어둠이 밀려와 나는 힘없는 발걸음으로 집으로 향하였다. 시장에는 불빛이 환하고 슬픔을 모르는 사람들이 물건을 사고 팔고, 어딘가로 바삐 걸어가고 있었다. 아버지께서 잡아 온 고기를 파시던 어머니의 자리는 비어 있었다. 어머니께서는 집에도 안 계셨다.
　"누나, 아버지 꼭 돌아오시는 거지?"
　동생 승빈이도 걱정이 되는지 근심스러운 표정으로 물었다.
　"그럼, 아버지께서는 꼭 돌아오실 거야. 걱정 말고 저녁이나 먹자."
　나는 승빈이와 저녁을 먹고 설거지를 하고 나서 책을 읽었다. 글자는 눈에 들어오지 않고, 귀는 밖으로만 열렸다. 그러나 아버지의 장화 소리는 들리지 않았다.

어머니께서는 한밤중에 돌아와 저녁도 들지 않고 잠자리에 드셨다.

나는 밤새 뒤척이다 일찍 일어났다. 어머니께서는 피곤하신지 베개도 안 베고 정신 없이 주무시고 계셨다.

문을 열고 밖으로 나가자, 찬 기운이 몸 안으로 확 파고들었다. 나는 가로등이 불을 밝히고 있는 골목길을 나와 큰길로 나섰다. 사람들이 지나다니지 않는 새벽길을 걷는다는 생각에 두려움이 밀려왔다.

그러나 나는 아버지 얼굴을 떠올렸다.

'아버지께서 돌아오시길 빌어야 해.'

나는 하늘에 뜬 별을 보며 사라봉을 향하여 잰걸음을 내디뎠다. 기도하는 마음으로 계단을 올라갔다. 그리고 정자에 올라가 동쪽 하늘을 바라보았다. 원당봉 위로 샛별이 밝게 빛나고 있었다. 머지 않아 둥근 해님이 수평선 위로 고개를 내밀 것이다. 바다는 어둠 속에서도 흰 이를 드러내며 파도를 만들어 해안가로 밀어 내고 있었다.

나는 동쪽 하늘을 바라보며 손을 모았다.

'샘이야, 걱정 마. 꼭 돌아갈게. 큰 고기 떼를 만나 못 돌아간 거야.'

바람결에 아버지께서 웃으며 하시는 말씀이 들려오는 것 같았다.

정말이다. 아버지께서는 꼭 돌아오실 것이다. 나는 해님이 솟아오를 동쪽 하늘을 보며 자꾸 빌었다. 동쪽 하늘이 어슴푸레 밝아 오고 있었다.

장영주

설문대할망

필자 소개
저서 『구연방법론』, 동화집 등 다수.
한국아동문학상, 한국아동문학작가상, 녹색문학상 등 수상.

설문대할망

장영주

머어언 옛날 호랑이가 담배 피우던 시절보다 더 머어언 옛날, 제주에는 설문대할망(설문대 할머니)이라는 사람이 살았었지요.

설문대할망의 몸집이 얼마나 컸는지 아세요?

한라산을 베개 삼아 누우면 다리 하나는 제주모관 앞바다에 있는 관탈섬에 걸쳐야 편히 잘 수 있었지요. 빨래를 하려면 한라산을 깔고 앉아야 할 수 있었다니 그 몸집이 얼마인지 상상이나 되겠어요?

설문대할망이 심심해서 한라산 꼭대기에서 바윗돌을 하나씩 집어서 획획 던지면 섬이 되었다니 그 힘 또한 어마어마했던 모양이에요.

이처럼 거대한 몸에 무지무지한 힘을 가진 설문대할망은 여자이지요. 그래서 치마를 입고다녔는데 글쎄요? 그 치마를 무엇으로 만들었으며 누가 만들었는지, 크기는 얼마인지 아는 사람은 없답니다.

설문대할망이 한라산을 만들려고 치마에 흙을 담아 나르는데 구멍이 뚫린 치마여서 흙이 떨어졌지요. 흙이 떨어진 곳은 360여 개의 오름(산)이 되었지요. 마지막 한 곳에 부은 흙은 한라산이 되었답니다.

한라산을 다 만들고 좀 쉬려고 앉았는데 뾰족한 돌멩이가 엉덩이를 찌르는 것이었지요. 화가 난 설문대할망은 꼭대기를 쑥 홈파내어 휙 던져 버렸답니다.

참, 한줌 잡아 팬 곳은 어찌 되었냐구요? 그건 백록담이 되었지요. 돌멩이는 떨어져서 산방산이 되었고요. 그래서 백록담의 둘레와 깊이하고 산방산의 둘레와 높이가 같은 것이랍니다.

어느날이었지요. 설문대할망이 한라산에 앉아 바다를 바라보다 오줌이 마려워 그냥 그 자리에서 오줌을 눕고 말았지요. 그 오줌이 얼마나 많고 힘이 셌는지 홍수가 되어 물난리를 겪었고 땅 한 쪽이 끊겨 나갔지 뭐예요. 그게 우도랍니다.

성산읍 일충봉에 우뚝 솟아 있는 기암이 있는데 이 바위는 설문대할망이 접싯불을 켰던 등잔이지요. 처음엔 밑에 있는 바위 위에 불을 켰는데 얕아서 바위를 하나 더 올려 놓은 것이라는데, 설문대할망이 등잔으로 썼다 하여 지금도 등경돌이라 부르지요.

이처럼 몸집이 크지, 힘도 당할 자가 없이 세었지만 그래도 여자였지요. 설문대할망은 늘 속옷을 입고 싶어 했지요. 설문대할망은 사람들을 모아 놓고 내기를 하였지요.

"여러분, 나하고 내기 하나 합시다. 내가 입을 속옷을 하나 만들어 주면 그 대가로 육지까지 걸어 다닐 수 있게 다리를 놓아주겠소."

설문대할망이 내기를 걸어오자 사람들은 서로 얼굴만 쳐다보며 아무 말도 못했지요. 글쎄 속옷을 만들려면 명주가 몇 동이 있어야 할 지 도저히 분간이 안 될 뿐 아니라 어느 정도 크기로 만들어야 할지 짐작도 못할 일이 아니겠어요?

"어떻든 수가 생길 거요. 우선 내기부터 합시다."

사람들은 육지에 편히 오고가기를 원했지요. 그 당시는 교통이 불편

해서 조그만 배로 육지를 드나들려면 여간 불편하지 않았고 사고도 많이 생겼거든요.

사람들은 설문대할망에게 속옷을 만들어 주기로 하고 명주를 모으는데 아무리 모아도 어림없었지요. 속옷을 만들려면 명주 백 동은 있어야 하는데 그게 그리 쉽지 않았거든요. 여기서 한 동은 오십 필이라고 합니다. 그 어마어마한 명주를 짜서 속옷을 만드는데 그만 한 동이 부족했지요. 사람들은 난처했어요.

"어떻게 사정 얘기를 해 봅시다."

사람들은 설문대할망을 찾아가서 그간의 사정을 얘기했지만 대답은 아주 냉정했어요.

"이 사람들아, 어찌 구멍 뚫린 속옷을 창피하게 입고 다닌단 말인가?"

예나 지금이나 창피한 건 매한가지이지요.

사람들이 아무리 사정해도 듣는 둥 마는 둥 흙장난을 하다 내버린 곳이 있어요. 조천읍 조천리 바닷가에 있는데 육지까지 다리를 놓으려다 만 흔적이라고 해요.

그 때 사람들이 조금만 더 열심히 명주 백 동을 마련하고 설문대할망의 속옷을 만들었다면 부산인지 목포인지는 몰라도 육지까지 고속도로가 생겨 씽씽 자동차가 달리고 있을지 모르는 일이지요.

그런 설문대할망이 어느날 흔적도 없이 모습을 감추었지요. 어디갔냐구요?

한 여름이었어요. 불볕더위가 기승을 부려 큰 몸집을 움직이려니 땀이 많이 나고 마땅히 쉴 만한 그늘도 없었지요. 그래서 더위를 피할 겸 피서도 할 겸 물을 찾아 길을 나섰지요.

"참 시원하겠군."

설문대할망은 두리번거리다가 물을 발견했지요.
"여기서 목욕이나 할까?"
설문대할망은 아무 생각 없이 '풍덩' 물 속에 뛰어 들었는데 그 후 영영 물 밖으로 나오지 못했답니다. 그 만큼 물이 깊었나봐요. 지금도 그곳을 물장오리라 부릅니다.

희곡

강신무 降神舞

장일홍

강신무降神舞

필자 소개

1950년 제주시 출생. 1985년 《현대문학》 추천으로 데뷔.
〈한국일보〉 신춘문예 당선. 문화관광부 창작희곡 공모 최우수상 수상.
대한민국문학상. 한국희곡문학상, 《월간문학》 동리상 수상.

강신무降神舞

장일홍

〈나오는 사람〉
  탄실
  에미
  금례
  준오
  고수

〈무대〉
무대 오른 편에 이엉으로 엮은 초가집 한 채. 객석에서 잘 보이는 것은 마루와 툇마루인데 마루 양쪽이 방이고 부엌은 마루 끝에 딸렸다.
무대 왼 편에 정낭(대문). 정낭에서 초가집 뒤꼍까지 돌담이 뺑 둘러쳐졌고 마당에는 멀구슬나무 한 그루가 덩그라니 서 있다.
막이 오르면 어느 여름날의 새벽. 에미와 탄실이 마루에서 곤히 자는 중이다. 마루벽의 쇠못에 걸린 북·장고·신칼·요령이며 울긋불긋한 쾌자 등은 이 집이 심방(무당)의 거처임을 은연 중에 알려준다.

에미 : (잠꼬대로) 폭도야! 폭도야! 아이고오, 살려줍서. 우리 아방은 죄가 없수다. 우린 산사람들 편이우다게.(사이) 병정들이 온다! 토벌대가 온다! 아이고오, 살려줍서. 우리 애기 아방은 폭도가 아니우다. 제발 목숨만 살려줍서. 으흐흐흑….

탄실 : (일어나 에미를 흔든다) 엄마, 엄마!

에미 : (눈을 뜨고) 으응? 왜 그래?

탄실 : 꿈 꿨어요?

에미 : (일어나며) 꿈? 아니 … (하다가) 맞아, 꿈을 꿨지.

탄실 : 울고 불고 생야단이 났어요.

에미 : (픽 웃고는) 내가 울어? 굿이 시작되는 날은 늘 똑같은 꿈을 꿔.

탄실 : (질린 표정으로) 오늘도…굿이 있나요?

에미 : 이런 등신, 영등굿도 몰라? (주먹으로 어깨 탕탕 치며) 흐유, 온 삭신이 그냥 녹작지근하네. 얘, 내 등 좀 자근자근 밟아다오. (엎드린다)

탄실 : (등허릴 욱신욱신 밟는다)

에미 : 에구구, 시원하다. 어, 조오타. 그만 하거라. (앉아서 어깨 주무르며) 밟을 때 우드득 우드득 뼈 갈라지는 소리 나지 않던?

탄실 : 아뇨.

에미 : 내 뼉다귄 갈라졌다 붙었다 지 맘대로여, 제에길…. (별안간 정색을 하고) 오늘은 하늘이 두 쪽 나도 나랑 같이 굿판에 가야 한다.

탄실 : 난 안 가요. (툇마루로 나온다)

에미 : (따라 나오며) 에미 말을 거역했다간 마른 날에 벼락 맞고 뒈질 줄 알어!

탄실 : (맥없이) 그래도 할 수 없죠, 뭐.

에미 : 이 년이 정말 잡귀에 씌워도 오지게 씌웠군.

탄실 : (심드렁하게) 딴 소리 말고 꿈 얘기나 해줘요.

에미 : 꿈?… (생각에 잠긴다) 참 희한한 일도 다 있지. 고깔 모자를 눌러쓴 심방이 어디선가 불쑥 나타나서 신칼과 요령을 나한테 맡

기고는 홀연히 사라져 버리는 거여. 한참 후에 보면 높은 동산에 올라가 날 오라고 불러. 애타는 손짓에 이끌려 밤새도록 지치게 언덕을 오르다 꿈에서 깨곤 한단다.… 헌데 묘하게도 그 꿈을 꾸고나면 꼭 굿할 일이 생기거든.

탄실 : 에이, 그따위 맹랑한 게 아녜요. 폭도가 나오는 무시무시한 꿈이라구요.

에미 : 폭도? … (끄덕끄덕) 그럴 테지. 4·3 사태 때 우리 아버진 폭도들의 죽창에 찔려 창자가 튀어나와서 죽었고 첫 남편은 토벌군에게 총살을 당했는데 이틀만에 시체를 찾고 보니 까마귀떼가 두 눈과 코를 파먹은 뒤였어. 그건 다행이었는지 몰라. 두개골이 허옇게 드러난 시신들이 골짜구니를 메웠으니까….
(절래절래) 끔찍한 광경이었지. 생각만 해도 치가 떨려.

탄실 : 첫 남편이라면…?

에미 : 니 애비가 아녀. 그 화상은… (입을 다물어 버린다)

탄실 : 아버지 얘기라면 기를 쓰고 꽁무닐 빼는 이유가 뭐예요?

에미 : 까발겨선 뭘해, 다 지나간 일인데.

탄실 : 아, 기억나요! 난 성을 세 개씩이나 가지고 있었죠. 국민학교에 입학할 당시는 김씨였고 삼 학년 땐 강씨였다가 육 학년 이후로는 엄마의 성을 따라 박씨가 됐어요. 호호호…난 복도 되게 많은 년이지 뭐유. (갑자기 싸늘해지며) 대관절 난 누구의 씬가요?

에미 : …….

탄실 : (다그치듯) 누구에요?

에미 : 죽었어.

탄실 : (발딱 일어서며) 거짓말! 새빨간 거짓말쟁이!

에미 : (노해서) 망할 년! 버르장머리 없이 어따 대고 함부로 주둥아릴

놀려!

탄실 : 더 이상 날 어린애 취급하지 마세요. 숨기려 하지 말고 사실대로 얘기해 달란 말예요!

에미 : (노려보다가) 오냐, 말 하마. 똑똑히 들어둬라. …그해 겨울은 유난히도 추웠다. 동짓달 열 아흐레, 널 낳고 몸도 채 풀기 전인데 술에 취한 니 애비가 와락 방문을 열어제끼며 어떤 잡놈이 싸지른 구정물로 생긴 애새끼냐고 고래고래 악을 쓰더라.
(울음이 북받쳐서)… 눈보라 치던 그날 밤 핏덩일 안고 울면서 친정으로 돌아왔다. 이래도, 이래도 니 애비가 누구냐고 묻겠냐?

탄실 : (냉소적으로) 흥, 그랬군요. 난 잡놈이 싸지른 구정물로 태어났군요.

에미 : 그 화상은 하루에도 스무 번씩이나 손을 씻었다. 마누라가 똥 누는 데까지 따라가서 무얼 하는지 살펴봐야 마음이 놓이는 그런 위인이었어. 한시도 놔주지 않고 숨통을 죄는데… 어휴, 콧구멍이 두 개니까 숨을 쉬었지.

탄실 : 다신 아버지 얘기 꺼내지 말아요.

에미 : 그 화상 생각을 하면 지금도 오금이 저리고 등골이 오싹해지는구나.

탄실 : (말머릴 돌리려고) 실은 나도 싱숭생숭한 꿈을 꿨어요.

에미 : 무슨 꿈?

탄실 : 귀양풀이 하는 꿈.

에미 : 귀양풀이? 니가?

탄실 : 응.

에미 : 누가 죽었는데?

탄실 : 남자.

에미 : 어떤 남자?

탄실 : ……

에미 : 감질나게 할 거야?

탄실 : (헛소리처럼) 해바라기・맨드라미・다알리아・백일홍・나팔꽃・분꽃 …… 아, 행복하다, 행복해….

에미 : (눈이 번쩍) 어라? 그게 뭔 소리여? 아무래도 애가 성한 정신이 아녀. 두린굿을 한판 걸쩍하게 벌여야 쓰겄어.

탄실 : (불쑥) 외할아버진 토벌군 편이었나요?

에미 : 니 편 내 편이 어딨냐? 우린 아무 편도 아니었다.

탄실 : 폭도들한테 죽임을 당했잖아요.

에미 : 폭도들이나 병정들이나 매한가지였어. 그 자들은 개구리나 메뚜기 잡듯이 양민들을 잡아 죽였단다. 그때 이웃 마을에선 이런 일도 있었지. 병정들이 학교 운동장으로 사람들을 죄다 모이게 해놓고선 느닷없이 총을 마구 쏴 갈겼어. 병정들이 가버린 후, 모질게 명이 긴 남정네 하나가 우리 마을로 기어와 숨겨주기를 간청했는데… (망설이다가) 누군가가 밀고를 하는 바람에 그 남정넨 찌프차 꽁지에 매달린 채 살려달라고 울부짖으면서 끌려갔지. 차가 멎었을 땐 온몸이 걸레 조각처럼 갈가리 찢어져서 숨져 있었다더라.

탄실 : 세상에 어디 그럴 수가…!

에미 : (점점 가슴이 더워 온다) 병정들이 이웃 마을을 휩쓸고 지나간 뒤, 불알 달린 사람은 모두 다섯밖에 남지 않았어. 그때 죽은 사람들의 피는 시내를 넘치게 했고 살아남은 사람들의 눈물은 강을 이루었다. 개처럼 죽어간 망자들의 원혼은 구천을 헤매다 돌아와 아직도 이 땅의 어드메를 떠돌고 있겠지… 얘야, 원혼들의

피맺힌 한을 누가 풀어주겠냐? 오직 심방들만이 그 일을 해낼 수 있단다.

탄실 : (도리질하며) 난 절대로 심방은 되지 않을래요.

에미 : (어르고 달랜다) 이것아, 니 외할미도 심방이었어. 우리 집안은 오 대째 내려오는 세습무란 말여. 자손이 무업을 잇지 않으면 조상신이 노해서 재앙을 내린다구. 니가 서울서 공장살이 하다가 비루먹은 강아지 꼴이 되어 내려온 게 삼시왕의 노여움이란 걸 몰라?

탄실 : …….

에미 : 니가 요사이 걸핏하면 헛소릴 하는 게 영락없이 헛것에 홀린 모양인데 헛것은 다 도깨비여.

탄실 : (멍해서) 나도 도깨비야, 엄마…….

에미 : 미친 년! 니 몸엔 호색하는 도깨비신이 씌웠다니까. 두린굿을 해서 도깨빌 물리치지 않으면 제 명에 못 죽어, 이것아….

탄실 : 이렇게 사느니 차라리 죽는 게 나을 걸.

에미 : (애가 타서) 애야, 넌 내 뱃속에 열 달씩이나 들어앉아 있었으면서 에미 속을 어찌 그리 몰라주냐?

탄실 : 엄만 내 속을 알아?

에미 : …….

탄실 : 내 어렸을 적 꿈이 뭐였는지 알아요? 흰 모자를 쓴 간호원이 되는 거였죠. 난 그저 평범하게 살고파요.

에미 : 조상신이 그냥 놔둘 것 같으냐? 널 꼭 붙잡아 와서 수종들게 하고 말 거여. 넌 그로부터 한 뼘도 달아날 수 없단 말이다. 이것아, 넌 내 씹으로 난 년이 아녀. 삼신 할마님께서 신딸로 점지해주셨어. 그게 니 운명이여….

탄실 : (독백) 돌아오는 게 아닌데, 아닌데….
에미 : (확신에 찬 어조로) 넌 반드시 돌아오게 돼 있었어.
탄실 : 엄마! 부탁이에요. 제발 날 놔줘. 다시 육지로 나가서 가정부가 되든지 점원을 하든지 아무 일이라도 할래요.
에미 : 그건 안돼! 매운 공장밥 먹고 병들어서 겨우겨우 집구석에 기어 들어온 년이 또 어딜 나간다고? 죽대같이 말라비틀어진 그 몸으론 취직은 커녕 물 한 모금 빌어먹기도 힘들 거여.
탄실 : (두 손을 삭삭 비비며) 엄마, 이렇게 빌겠어요. 딸자식 하나 없는 셈치고 날 보내줘요.
에미 : (눈알을 부라려) 망할 년! 어디 도망쳐 보려무나. 땅끝까지라도 쫓아가서 뒷덜미 나꿔채 올 테니까. 저번엔 가야호 선상에서 머리 끄댕일 잡고 끌어내렸지만 이번에 잡히면 아주 인두로 가랭일 지져버릴 거여. 여편네 구실도 못 하게시리….
탄실 : (도리도리) 심방은 안돼. 저엉 끝끝내 강요하면 죽어버릴 테야!
에미 : (악에 받쳐서) 이 개좆을 핥을 년아, 그러찮아도 넌 뒈싸지고야 말어! (순간 핏발선 눈으로) 그래, 너 같은 애물, 차라리 죽어버려! 오냐, 죽는 게 소원이라면 내 손으로 없애주마.

　에미, 마루에서 나일론 줄을 갖고 나와 우악스럽게 딸의 두 손을 묶는다. 어리둥절한 탄실이 저항하려 했지만 이미 늦었다.
　에미, 이번에는 백지와 바가지를 들고 나와서 넋들임굿에서 하는 것처럼 딸의 얼굴에 물을 뿜고 백지 한 장을 바른다.

탄실 : (숨이 막혀) 음,음,음!
에미 : 어쩔 테야? 심방이 될 거여, 안 될 거여? 속 시원히 대답을 해,

대답을-!

　　탄실, 버둥거리다가 툇마루 아래로 굴러 떨어진다. 에미, 맨발로 마당에 뛰어내려 물을 뿜고 또 한 장의 백지를 겹쳐 바른다.

에미 : (표독스럽게) 이 년아, 이래도! 이래도 고집을 못 꺾어, 그 쇠고집을-!
탄실 : 음,음,음… (일어나려고 안간힘을 쓰다 혼절해 넘어진다)
에미 : (와락 달려들어 백지를 벗기며) 어이구우, 내 새끼 죽는다, 죽어! (머리를 받쳐들고) 아가, 정신 차려! 이 년아, 퍼뜩 정신 차려!

에미, 바가지 물을 한꺼번에 탄실의 얼굴에 쏟아붓는다.

에미 : (옴쭉달싹 하는 기색이 있자) 어이구우, 살았구나! 내 새끼 살았어! 다신 심방 되라고 안 할게 목숨만 부지해다오. (딸의 손을 풀고 툇마루에 눕힌 다음) 탄실아, 에미다. 눈 좀 떠다오, 이것아…. (체신머리없이 엉엉 운다)
탄실 : (숨을 크게 내쉬고 일어난다)
에미 : (어쩔 줄 몰라) 얘, 너, 너….
탄실 : 내가 여기서 잠들었었나요? (하품)
에미 : (훌쩍거리며) 에미가 잘못했다, 용서하거라, 이젠 안 그럴게.
탄실 : 네에?
에미 : 너, 괜히 사람 놀라게 해놓고선 시침 뚝 떼기냐?
탄실 : 시침떼다니, 뭘 말예요?
에미 : 아녀, 저어… 너, 참말로 에미 곁을 떠나서 멀리 가고 싶으냐?

탄실 : ……．

에미 : (목이 메어) 말해 봐, 이것아. 니 소원을 들어줄 테니까. 토란 잎에 구르는 이슬 같은 우리네 인생인데 아옹다옹 하면서 살면 몇백 년을 살겠어? 얼른 얘기해 봐.

탄실 : (기어드는 목소리로) 가고 싶어요, 엄마… 바닷가 언덕 위에 초가집을 짓고 내 동무 길녀처럼 물질을 하면서 호오이 호오이 숨비질 소리를 지르며 긴긴 하루 해를 보내고 싶어요 (꿈꾸듯) 아이들의 밥상엔 전복이며 소라, 물꾸럭, 해삼, 날미역… 싱싱한 해산물이 철따라 오르겠지요. 붉은 햇덩이가 물마루 너머로 떨어지고 나면 호롱불을 켜서 귀여운 꼬마들의 해진 양말을 깁구요. 그이가 만선을 하고 먼 뱃길에서 돌아오는 날, 포구까지 단숨에 달려나가 목이 터져라 아빠의 이름을 외칠 거예요. (사이) 하지만 내가 없으면 엄만 어떻게….

에미 : (덥석 딸의 손목을 잡고) 이것아, 내 걱정일랑 하지 마. 난 아직 젊단 말여.

탄실 : 쉰 둘의 나이가 젊어요?

에미 : 제 팔자 제 복인 걸. 아무렴 내 몸 하나 건사하지 못 하겠냐? 영등굿만 끝나면 여비를 마련해 줄 테니 멀리 떠나. 니가 가고 싶은 곳이 있으면 어디든지 가란 말여. (혼잣말로) 아암, 죽는 것 보다야 백 번 낫지. 아무데 가든지 그저 몸성히 잘 살아야 해…. 에미가 바라는 건 오로지 그것뿐…. (돌아서서 옷고름으로 눈물을 닦는다.)

탄실 : ….

에미 : (한숨) 내 나이 쉰 둘이면 서천 꽃밭 구경갈 날도 멀지 않았어. 무어 그리 칭원하고 원통할 게 있냐. 탯줄 사른 땅에 묻히면 그

만인 것을….

탄실 : 엄마, 그런 말씀 마시고 오래오래 사셔야 해요.

에미 : 일점 혈육 너 하나 믿고 의지하면서 반 평생을 살아온 거여. 온갖 멸시 천대 받으면서도 이를 악물었던 건 너 때문이었어.

탄실 : (가슴이 뭉클해서) 나도 알아요, 엄마. 새벽잠 설치며 공장에 나갈 때나 밤하늘의 별과 벗해서 자취방으로 돌아올 적마다 그리운 건 주름진 엄마 얼굴뿐이었어요.

에미 : 자식 새끼가 뭔지… 니가 없는 사이, 에미가 벤 베개는 밤마다 눈물로 홍수를 이루었단다. (타령조로) 석탄 백탄 타는 데는 연기도 김도 나지만 오장간장 타는 데는 연기도 김도 아니 난다. 저 산천으로 내리는 물을 나무등걸 다 썩은 물. 내 눈으로 내리는 물은 오장간장 다 썩은 물… (회한에 잠겨) 첫 서방은 난리통에 총 맞아 죽고, 둘째 서방은 의심 많아 갈렸고, 셋째 서방은 개차반이 망나니에다 술푸대라, 섣달 그믐 밤에 불타 죽고 말았어. 동네 사람들이 우 몰려가 불을 끄고 보니까 그 망나닌 숯이 되었더라. 그때 우리 어머니가 생전에 남긴 말이 확 떠오르더구나. 심방은 팔자를 그르쳐야 한다고 말여. 그 길로 난 이 서방, 저 서방 다 버리고 심방이 됐단다….

탄실 : (불현듯) 아! 생각나요, 엄마. 상만이네 처마 밑에서 추위에 발을 동동구르며 우리 집이 불타는 걸 봤어요. 무섭고 몸서리나는 밤이었죠. 날 구박하던 아버지의 시체며 타다 남은 필통, 엄마의 옥양목 치마, 내가 아꼈던 고동색 블라우스 … 아니, 제일 애석했던 건 꼬박꼬박 써 두었던 일기장이 불타버린 거였어요.

에미 : 그 망나닐 묻고 돌아오면서 다짐하고 또 다짐했지. 묻자, 지나간 모든 날들을 내 마음속 깊은 웅뎅이에 파묻어버리자. 잊자, 해묵

은 상처를 잊고 지내노라면 언젠가 새 살이 돋아나겠지….
탄실 : (문득) 엄마, 오늘 영등굿 한다면서 굿판에 안 나가세요?
에미 : (하늘을 올려다 보곤) 아유, 내 정신 좀 봐. 벌써 해가 중천에 떴네. 속히 가야겠다. 넌 들어가서 찬 밥이라도 찾아먹고 한숨 푹 자거라.
탄실 : 네, 알았어요.

  에미, 바삐 방안으로 들어가 무복과 무구가 든 보따리를 들고 나온다.

에미 : 다녀오마, 떡이랑 실과를 듬뿍 얻어올게.
탄실 : 다녀오세요.

  에미, 퇴장하고 탄실이 마루로 들어가 눕는다. 잠시 후 동네 처녀 금례가 주위를 살피며 살금살금 등장.

금례 : 언니, 언니! (대답이 없자) 아무도 안 계세요?
탄실 : (툇마루로 고갤 내밀고) 누구세요? 어머, 금례가 웬일이야?
금례 : 그냥 … 심심해서 놀러 왔어. 어머님은 어디 가셨나요?
탄실 : 해안가에 굿하러 가셨어.
금례 : 오오라, 영등굿이 시작된다더니…
탄실 : (툇마루에 나앉으며) 앉아. 농사일로 바쁠 텐데 용케 짬을 냈구나.
금례 : (앉는다) 부모님 몰래 살짝 빠져 나왔어. 언니에게 물어볼 것도 있고 해서 말야.
탄실 : 나한테 물어볼 게 있다구?

금례 : 응.
탄실 : 뭔데?
금례 : 저어…언닌 서울서 공장 다니다 내려왔잖아?
탄실 : 애두, 새삼스럽긴.
금례 : 공장이 어디 있지? 뭘 만들어?
탄실 : 그건 알아서 뭐 하게?
금례 : 그냥…
탄실 : 청계천에 있는데 피복공장이지. 가죽옷을 만드는 곳이야.
금례 : 월급은 얼마나 줘?
탄실 : 글쎄, 대중없지 뭐. 시다로 금방 들어가면 10만 원쯤 받다가 고참이 되면 20만 원이 넘기도 하구….
금례 : 나도 공장에 취직할까 하는데 언니 생각은 어떠우?
탄실 : (멍하니 보다가) 얘…너, 가지 마. 큰일 나.
금례 : 어머나, 왜 그래?
탄실 : (힘없이) 고향처럼 좋은 덴 없어.
금례 : (뾰루퉁해서) 치잇 누가 그걸 몰라서 묻나, 뭐… 난 농사일이 진절머리가 나. 농약, 비료값, 인부삯, 씨앗대금 제하고 나면 남는 게 하나도 없다니깐. 언니, 우리 남동생 머리 좋은 거 알지? 걔가 금년에 고등학생이 됐는데 수업료 낼 돈이 없어서 휴학해야 할 판이야. 부모님은 아들놈 하나 공부 시킬 능력이 없는 사람들이라구. (결연히) 공장 다니면서 동생 학비를 벌 테야. 내가 못 배운 한을 동생에게까지 물려주고 싶진 않단 말야.
탄실 : 넌 서울이 어떤 곳인지 알기나 해?
금례 : 사람 잡아먹는 호랑이굴 속은 아니잖아. 언니도 갔다 왔으면서 뭘….

탄실 : 몸 버리고 마음 상하기에 딱 알맞은 곳이 바로 그 동네야.

금례 : 아, 아닌 말로 나 하나 망쳐서 우리 동생 떳떳하게 자라준다면 난 그걸로 족해.

탄실 : (격앙하여) 이 멍텅구리야! 너만 손해지, 그런다고 누가 널 알아준다든?

금례 : 알아주지 않아도 상관없어.

탄실 : 기름밥은 아무나 먹는 게 아니야. 농사일처럼 생각했다간 큰 코 다친다구. 하루 14시간 손발이 퉁퉁 붓도록 3년 동안이나 일했는데 내게 남은 건 보증금 50만 원짜리 방 한 칸에다 헐어빠진 몸뚱아리 뿐이었어. 달동네 판자집에서 겨울을 세 번 넘겼는데 해마다 한 번씩은 연탄가스 중독으로 죽을 뻔 했지. 어디 그뿐이야? 작업장 기계소리 때문에 가는귀가 먹어버렸고 먼지를 너무 많이 마셔 폐가 망가져서 경증 폐결핵 진단을 받았어. (조소를 띠며) 그래도… 제발로 걸어서 그 지옥으로 갈 셈이야?

금례 : (기가 질려서) 하지만 언니도 지옥에 갔다 왔잖아?

탄실 : 내가 겪었으니까 말리는 거야.

금례 : 두고 봐, 난 기어코 하고야 말겠어. 월급 타면 몽땅 동생 학비로 보내줄 거야.

탄실 : (비꼬듯) 월급? 그래, 월급이란 걸 타긴 타지. 한데 가불한 거 빼고 매점 외상값, 방세, 일수돈 찍고나면 거덜이 난다구. 난 그 흔한 세일 치마 하나 못 사입고 외식 한 번 못 해봤어. 야간일 끝내고 허기지고 지친 몸으로 시장에 가서 500원어치 순대 한 접시 시키고나면 까닭없이 눈물이 왈칵 치밀곤 했지…. 너, 진짜로 갈 거야?

금례 : (무겁게 고개를 끄덕인다)

탄실 : 언제?

금례 : 내일이라도 당장.

탄실 : 가려거든 맘 단단히 먹고 가. 가서 누구한테 헤프게 정 주지 말고.

금례 : 정 주긴… 난 독한 맘 먹었어.

탄실 : 아무리 그래도 객지에 나가면 외롭고… 흔들릴 때가 많아.

금례 : 언닌 서울서 남자랑 사귄 적 있어?

탄실 : (얼굴이 화끈해서) 나? 아니…

금례 : 호호호… 우리 사이에 감출 게 뭐 있어? 나한테만 살짝 귀띔해 봐.

탄실 : …….

금례 : 어느 놈팽이에게 실연 당했지? 그래서 고향에 내려온 후론 문밖 출입도 삼간 채 틀어박혀 있는 거지?

탄실 : (머뭇거리다가) 사실은 그런 일이 있었어. 몸도 아프고….

금례 : 어떤 일? 구체적으로 알면 안돼?

탄실 : 그쯤이면 됐어. 더 이상 캐려고 하지 마. (풀죽은 소리로) 난 이제 사람 구실 제대로 못할 거야.

금례 : 동네 사람들이 서울 공장에서 일하다 폐인이 되어 돌아왔다고 입방아를 찧던데…그리고 보니 언니, 부쩍 야윈 것 같아. 얼굴이 많이 상했어.

탄실 : (충격을 받고) 폐, 폐인이라구…! 나, 머리가 어질어질 해서 좀 누워야겠어. (툇마루에 드러눕자 멀리서 굿소리 들려온다)

금례 : (일어서며) 언니, 그럼 다음에……

탄실 : (손을 허우적이며) 아 또 저 소리, 저 소리…!

금례 : 무슨 소리? 아무 소리도 들리지 않는데…. (굿거리 장단이 빠른

속도로 고조돼 간다)

탄실 : (귀를 틀어막으며) 아, 아, 악!

금례 : (질겁해서) 왜 그러는 거야!

탄실 : (입에 거품을 물고 온 몸을 비비꼬며) 아, 아악!

금례 : (안절부절 못하여) 에그머니, 이를 어쩌나?

    금례가 엉겁결에 탄실의 팔을 잡는 순간, 거센 힘에 떠밀려 마당으로 나동그라진다. 금례, 땅바닥에 퍼질러 앉아 멀뚱히 탄실의 발작을 지켜본다. 이윽고 장단이 잦아들면 탄실, 툇마루에 쭉 뻗은 채 가쁜 숨만 할딱인다.

금례 : (가까이 다가가서) 어, 언니…이젠 괜찮아? 어휴, 저 비오듯 쏟아지는 땀 좀 봐. 이러고 있을 때가 아냐. 어머님께 알려야지. 언니, 조금만 기다려, 후딱 가서 어머님을 모셔올게.

    금례, 서둘러 퇴장한다. 사이, 무대 차츰 어두워지고 전면 중앙에 두 개의 톱 라이트가 떨어지면 왼편에 준오가 들어선다.

준오 : 바쁠 텐데 나오라고 해서 미안해. 다른 게 아니라 손수건을 전해 주려고… 탄실의 손수건은 아무리 빨아도 핏물이 지워지지 않아서 새 걸로 하나 샀지. (사이) 어젠 정말 고마웠어. 내 평생에 그처럼 따스한 손길을 느껴보긴 처음이야. 어렸을 때 코피가 터지면 어머닌 꼭 솜으로 콧구멍을 틀어막고 뒷목을 가볍게 두드려 주시곤 했지. 탄실이가 바로 어머니처럼 날 치료해 줬거든. 솜대신 손수건이었지만…. (손수건을 꺼내) 이거 성의니까 받아줘.

탄실 : (오른편 조명 속으로 들어오며) 주시는 거니까 받지요. (받는다) 하지만 고마워 할 것까진 없어요. 준오씨도 내가 다쳤을 때 도와주셨잖아요?

준오 : 참, 그랬지. 미싱 바늘이 손등에 꽂혔었지? 그만 하기가 다행이야. 공단 전자회사에 다니는 어떤 애는 컨베이어 벨트에 팔이 감겨 어깻죽지까지 절단하는 대수술을 받았대. 프레스에 찍혀 손목이 뎅강 잘려나가는 건 다반사고… 어때, 손은?

탄실 : (재빨리 감추며) 나았어요, 다섯 바늘을 꿰매긴 했지만….

준오 : 미싱대에 앉아서 깜빡 졸았구먼.

탄실 : (무심결에) 네, 졸다가 굿소릴 들었어요.

준오 : 굿소리?

탄실 : (당황해서) 아, 아뇨…아무 것도 아녜요.

준오 : 졸음이 올 땐 노랠 부르면 되지. 탄실이가 잘 부르는 노래가 있다던데?

탄실 : 무슨 노래요?

준오 : 뭐, 이어도….

탄실 : (킥킥거리다가) 이어도사나.

준오 : 그래, 이어도사나. 재단반에 소문이 쫙 깔렸던데… 탄실이가 그 노랠 기똥차게 부른다고 말이야.

탄실 : 한많은 제주도 해녀들이 가슴을 쥐어짜며 부르는 노래에요. 그 노래만 들으면 왠지 난 눈물이 나요.

준오 : 어쭈, 나도 한 번 듣고 싶은데….

탄실 : 싫어요, 내가 뭐 가수가요. 아무 때나 노랠 하게.

준오 : 허허… 오랜만에 구성진 민요가락을 듣는가 했더니 틀렸군. (사이) 피곤해 뵈는데 일이 고되지?

탄실 : 선적 날짜가 다가오니깐 작업 독촉이 빗발치듯 하네요. 어차피 올라간 방세를 메꾸고 밀린 곗돈을 부으려면 밤일을 해야죠.
준오 : (자조적으로) 흐흐… 우린 따뜻한 피를 가진 인간이 아니야, 스위치만 넣으면 무한정 돌아가는 차디찬 기계지.
탄실 : 나랑 친하던 경희는 이렇게 비참하게 살아서 뭐 하냐며 엊그제 룸살롱으로 팔려 갔어요.
준오 : 그애는 늘씬한 몸매에다 곱상한 얼굴하며 팔 거라도 있으니… 에라, 쉽고 편하게 살려면 그럴 수도 있겠지.
탄실 : 선적이 끝나면 사장님께서 특별 보너스를 준댔어요.
준오 : 체… 그까짓 사탕발림에 감지덕지하지 마. 우리 사장은 명색이 교회 장로야. 한 달에 한 번씩 공장으로 목사를 초청해 합동예배가 뭔가를 드릴 때, 설교 제목은 언제나 「도둑질 하지 말라」, 「계명을 지켜라」 따위지. 그건 공원들이 회사 물건을 훔쳐내 밖으로 빼돌리는 걸 막기 위한 정신 교육에 다름 아니라구. (적개심이 활활 타올라) 개새끼들! 헐벗고 굶주린 노동자들에겐 비인간적인 몸수색에다 생계비에 훨씬 미달되는 저임금을 주면서, 교회당 신축헌금 5천만 원, 무슨 무슨 성금 1억 원 기탁… 흥, 하나님의 것은 하나님에게, 가이사의 것은 가이사에게로 바친다 이거야!
탄실 : 며칠 전에 야간 일 할 때 쪽지를 받았어요.
준오 : 쪽지?
탄실 : 파업에 찬성하면 이름을 써 넣으라는 설명이 있더군요.
준오 : 그래서?
탄실 : 이름을 쓰지 않았어요.
준오 : 어째서?
탄실 : 두렵고 떨렸기 때문이죠.

준오 : 용기를 내야 해. 우리 한 사람, 한 사람은 연약한 풀잎처럼 힘이 없지만 뭉치고 일어서면 쇠처럼 강해질 수 있다구. 질경이는 수레바퀴에 찍혀도 죽지 않고 민들레는 말발굽에 밟히면서 꽃을 피워낸단 말이야!

탄실 : (시무룩해서) 어려운 말은 잘 몰라요. 섬 무지렁이가 뭘 알겠어요. 난… 아무래도 파업에 동조할 수 없을 것 같네요.

준오 : (의외라는 듯) 으응? 그럼 소문이 사실인가….

탄실 : (날카롭게) 어떤 소문인데요?

준오 : 아, 아냐… 난 그저… 실은 말이야, 나 공장을 그만 두게 됐어.

탄실 : (어리벙벙하여) 그만 두다뇨…?

준오 : 오늘 회사로부터 해고 통지서를 받았지.

탄실 : …….

준오 : 이유는 묻지 마.

탄실 : 그 이유를 알아요.

준오 : 안다구?

탄실 : 며칠 전 동료들의 농성이 있었을 때 앞장선 사람이 한 방에 사는 숙자였어요. 숙자가 어디론가 사라져 버리고 난 뒤, 사무실에서 날 부른다기에 가보니 생산부장과 노무과장이 숙자의 행방을 대라는 거예요. 내가 모른다니까 준오씨 얘길 꺼내대요.

준오 : 내 얘길?

탄실 : 준오씨 하고 가까운 사이냐고 묻길래 동료일 뿐이라고 했더니 접촉하지 말라는 거예요. 준오씬 위험인물로서 노동자를 가장한 불순 학생이요, 위장 취업자라구요.

준오 : (분노해서) 미친 놈들! 난 회사를 위해서 누구보다도 열심히 일했어. 코피를 쏟으면서까지 내가 받은 더러운 돈보다 더 많은 노

동을 했다구!
탄실 : 파업에 끼지 않는 날 보고 동료들은 스파이, 동료를 팔아 먹은 년이라고 욕하고 있다는 걸 잘 알아요. 준오씨도 그렇게 생각하시겠죠?
준오 : 그만 둬. 난 이제 떠나야 할 사람이야.
탄실 : 처음부터 준오씨가 이런 데서 일할 사람이 아니란 걸 알아챘어요.
준오 : 알아채다니?
탄실 : (준오의 손을 보며) 그 손… 작고 하얀 손. 기집애 손보다 예뻐요.
준오 : (주저하다가) 후련히 다 털어놓고 가겠어. 난 이번 파업의 배후 조종자로 지목돼 해고된 거야. (타는 시선으로) 이 추악한 세상에서 때묻지 않은 한 떨기 들꽃 같은 탄실이를 오래도록 잊지 못할 거야. 잘 있어…. (퇴장)
탄실 : 주, 준오씨…!

안타까이 준오가 나간 쪽을 바라볼 때 톱 라이트 꺼지고 무대 밝아오면 에미와 금례, 헐레벌떡 마당으로 들어선다.

에미 : 아가! 도대체 어찌 된 영문이냐?
탄실 : (누운 채 기진해서) 괜찮아요.
금례 : 맙소사. 이게 무슨 조화야! 난 언니가 급살 맞은 줄 알았다니깐.
에미 : (딸의 이마를 짚어보고) 허이구, 이 열 좀 봐. 불덩이 같구먼. 이거 야단났네, 야단났어! 암만해도 의원을 불러와야 쓰겠어. 이것아, 꼼짝말고 누워 있어, 알았지?

탄실 : (겨우 몸을 일으키며) 가지 마, 엄마가 곁에 있으면 금세 나을 거예요.

에미 : 그래도 뭔 수를 내야지. 옳지, 냉수 찜질이라도 해야겠어. (부엌으로 들어간다)

금례 : 언니… 정말 괜찮은 거야?

탄실 : (억지로 웃어보이며) 응.

금례 : 갑자기 무서워졌어, 서울 가는 거… 언니, 어쩜 좋지? (에미, 수건과 대야를 들고 나온다) 나, 갈게, 몸조리 잘 해. (에미에게) 안녕히 계세요. (나간다)

에미 : 오냐, 니가 고생이 많았다.

탄실 : (에미 팔을 붙들고) 엄마, 아무 데도 가지 말고 내 곁에 있어줘요.

에미 : 알았어, 이것아. (마루에 있는 목침을 갖고 와서) 마음을 착 갈아앉히고 눈을 붙여봐. (탄실, 눕는다. 물수건을 딸의 이마에 얹으며) 초감제를 끝내고 요왕맞이 굿을 한참 하는 도중에 금례가 와서 숨넘어 갈듯이 니가 위급하다는 바람에 수심방에게 알리지도 않고 부랴부랴 달려왔지 뭐야. 헌데 너… 금례 얘기론 서울서 남자랑 불장난을 했다는데, 그게 사실이냐?

탄실 : ……

에미 : 엉? 단맛 다 빨아먹은 사내놈이 널 버렸다면서?

탄실 : 아녜요. 엄마.

에미 : 아니긴 뭐가 아녀? 그래서 내 새끼 여린 가슴에 한이 맺혔지. 육실헐 놈… 두고 봐라. 그 백정모 횡액을 만나고 말 거여. 난리 때 이야기 해줬지? 피투성이가 돼서 우리 마을로 기어들어와 살려달라고 애원하는 남정네를 몰래 고자질한 게 누군지 아냐?… 내

첫 남편이었어. 저혼자 살겠다고 악착같이 발버둥 치더니만…폭도와 내통했다고 어떤 놈이 모략질해서 끝내는 죽고 말더구나. 남의 눈에 눈물을 흘리게 하면 제 눈에 피를 흘릴 때가 오고, 남의 가슴에 못을 박으면 제 가슴에 창을 박을 날이 오는 법이여, 기필코 오고야 말어….

탄실: 난 버림받지 않았다니까요.

에미: 그럼…?

탄실: (천천히 상체를 일으키고) 남자의 시체를 봤어요.

에미: (눈이 휘둥그레져서) 뭐여!

탄실: 혀를 길게 빼물고 눈을 뜬 채 축 늘어져서… (몸서리친다)

에미: 목을 맸더란 말이냐?

탄실: 우리 공장에 다니다가 그만두고 떠난 남자에게서 편지가 왔어요. 내가 보고 싶다구요. 물어물어 산동네로 찾아갔는데…… 시신을 본 후론 머리가 멍해지고 뼈속까지 흐물흐물 해지데요. 미싱대에 앉으면 미싱틀이 그 남자 얼굴로 변하고, 미싱소리가 울음소리로 들리더군요. (진저리치며 웅크린다) 밤마다 시체가 꿈에 나타나고… 비명을 지르며 꿈에서 깨어나면 온몸에 식은 땀이 흥건했어요.

에미: 것 봐, 내가 뭐랬어? 도깨비신이 홀라당 니 몸에 씌운 거여.

탄실: 어젯밤 꿈에선 내가 죽은 남자의 귀양풀이를 해줬어요. 귀양풀이를 한 다음날은 왼종일 굿소리가 귀에 쟁쟁 울리죠. 굿소리가 나면 꿈에서처럼 나풀나풀 춤을 추어야 할 텐데 춤을 못추니 자꾸 사지가 뒤틀리고 숨이 컥컥 막히는 거예요.

에미: 암만해도 넌 일만 팔천 신을 청해 놓고 삼시왕 앞에 몸을 매어야 할 팔자여. 쯔쯔 … 운명을 비껴갈 사람이 따로 있지.

이때, 고수 등장. 우락부락하게 생긴 40대의 아낙이다.

고수 : (볼멘 소리로) 아니, 탄실 엄마. 뭘 하는 거유? 요왕맞이가 끝나서 영감놀이를 할 차례인데, 다 큰 처녀 끼고 앉아 한가히 노닥거리게 됐수?
에미 : 글쎄, 탄실이가 난데없이 몸이 아프다잖우. 그래서 조마조마 하면서도 자리를 뜨지 못하고 앉아있는 거라우.
고수 : (나무라듯) 어허, 말만한 비바릴 너무 그렇게 호호 해가며 키우는 게 아녜요. 아, 옛날 같으면야 벌써 애새낄 두엇씩이나 까고도 남을 나인데 굿하다 말고 젖 주려고 왔수?
에미 : (울화가 치밀지만 참는다) 그게 아니고…… 그럴 사정이 좀 있었다우.
고수 : 팔팔하던 성님도 이젠 늙어서 굿 한마당을 놀 기력이 없는 게로군. 아무튼 빨랑 가요. 수심방이 노발대발이라구요. 알잖우? 그 양반 성질나면 물도 씹어 먹는 거.
에미 : 이걸 어쩌나, 우리 애기가 이렇게 열이 화덕처럼 펄펄 끓는데…
탄실 : (보다 못해) 엄마, 내 걱정 말고 다녀오세요.
고수 : 거 봐요, 얼른 갑시다. (비아냥거린다) 아, 나같은 고수야 북장고나 두드리면 그만이지만, 성님은 영감놀이에서 없어선 안될 귀하신 몸인데 빠져서야 되겠수?
에미 : 애야, 내 가서 얼굴만 비치고 금방 돌아오마. 안으로 들어가 누워 있거라.
탄실 : 여기가 시원해서 좋아요.
에미 : 아파도 꾹 참아야 한다, 알았지?

탄실 : (가느다랗게) … 네.
고수 : (탄실에게) 어디가 아파서 그래? 나한테 통그만 있는데 몇알 줄까?
탄실 : 아뇨, 됐어요.
고수 : (알약을 꺼내) 먹어봐, 두통엔 백발백중이니깐.
에미 : (버럭) 불난 집에 부채질 하지 말고 냉큼 가!
고수 : (자존심이 팍 상해서) 이거 왜 이러슈? 내가 준 약을 먹으면 어디 동티라도 난답니까? 남은 기껏 생각해서 주는 건데 성의를 그렇게 무시해서야, 원….
에미 : 임자나 많이 잡수시구랴. (홱 돌아선다)
고수 : 헹, 싫음 관두슈. 고자는 평양감사도 사양한답니다. (약을 도루 집어넣으며) 쳇, 더럽고 아니꼽고 치사해서….
에미 : 아니꼬우면 이녁이 심방 노롯 하면 될 거 아녀!
고수 : (얼굴이 벌겋게 달아올라) 뭐요? 이거야 원, 밸이 꼴려서 어디… 성님, 너무 큰 냥 하지 마슈. 아니, 심방될 종내기가 따로 있답디까? 서당개 삼 년에 풍월 읊는다는 소리도 못 들어봤수? 나도 이 지랄같은 고수생활 삼 년에 굿패 따라 다니면서 어깨 너머로 배운게 많다우. 영감놀이에 나오는 영감역 쯤은 나도 할 수 있다구요. (입을 삐죽이며) 잘한다, 잘한다 해주니까 기고만장해 가지구선… 뭐 성님이 없으면 굿판이 거덜나고 고수들 죄 굶어 죽을 줄 아슈? (코를 휭 푼다) 천만에 말씀이우다.
에미 : 흥, 할 줄 안다니까 임자가 내 대신 하면 되겠구랴.
고수 : 암은요 한번 해볼까요?
에미 : (콧방귀만 퐁퐁 뀐다)
고수 : (점점 약이 올라서) 어렵쇼? 이거 보자 보자 하니까 사람 괄시해

도 유분수지. 그 단추 구멍 만한 눈깔이나 사타구니 벌리듯이 활짝 벌리고 자알 보슈.

에미 : 육갑 떨지말고 해보더라고.

고수 : (곰방대를 문 시늉으로 이리 비틀 저리 비틀 하며) 하하하…… 우리는 서울 남산 먹자골에 사는 허 정승의 아들인디 우리 마지막 일곱째 동생이 제주 한라산에 유람차 와 있다고 하길래, 그 동생을 찾아보려고 왔소. 한라산에 올라가서 살펴보니 오호라! 어디서 징소리가 나고 향내가 그윽한지라, 다가가서 보니 영감! 영감! 어서 이리로 드시지요, 하고 날 청하는 소리가 들리길래 이렇게 부리나케 왔소이다. 하하하… (한 손엔 곰방대를, 한 손은 뒷짐을 지고 뒤뚱뒤뚱 걷는다)

에미 : (차갑게 쏘아보며) 그게 영감놀이여, 병신춤이여?

고수 : (기가 차서 말문이 막힌다)

에미 : (스스로 근엄해져서) 나라의 임금과 고을의 심방은 하늘이 내리는 거여. 사람이 되려고 해서 되는 일과 안 되는 일이 있다는 걸 명심하오.

고수 : 얼씨구? 그야말로 점입가경이로군. 성님은 저 혼자 하늘이 내린 심방인 줄 착각하고 있네에.

에미 : (불끈해서) 닥쳐요!… 조천댁과 더 이상 다투고 싶지 않으니 속히 갑시다. (황망히 나간다)

고수 : 젠장, 꼴린대로 해 보슈. (약을 다시 꺼내) 탄실아, 이거 세알만 먹고 푹 자. 뭐니 뭐니 해도 대갈통, 이빨통, 월경통엔 통그만이 최고니께, 으헤헤헤….

탄실 : (받으며) 고마워요, 아줌마.

고수 : 에끼, 고맙긴… 니 에미 성질이 꼭 불여우 같아서 나랑 가끔씩

티격태격 하긴 한다만… 우린 입속에 들어간 사탕도 칵 뱉아서 쪼개가지고 나눠 먹는 사이여.
탄실 : 알아요, 엄만 괜스레….
고수 : 나도 알어. 니 에미 보통내기가 아니란 걸. 평소엔 빌빌거리다가도 신자리 위에 올라서서 요령과 신칼을 잡으면 눈빛부터 달라진다니까. 수덕 좋고 영험 있는 심방으로 이 근동에선 모르는 이가 없지. 니 할머닌 더 유명했다더라. 그 할망을 따를 심방이 여태 태어나지 않았다고 노친네들이 쑤근대는 걸 엿들은 적이 있어. 느이 집안은 차암 이상타. 신주를 잘 모셨나, 산터를 잘 썼나…? (고갤 외로 꼬다가 이마를 딱 치며) 아이고야, 내가 시방 오도방정을 떨고 있을 때가 아닌디… 나, 갈란다. (퇴장)

사이. 먼 함성처럼 굿소리가 들려오자 탄실, 귀를 틀어막지만 질탕한 굿소리는 더욱 커지고 그에 따라 온몸을 뒤틀며 뒹군다.
일순, 감전된 것처럼 사지가 뻣뻣해지더니 용트림하듯 서서히 몸을 일으켜 비상하려는 새처럼 하늘을 향해 두 팔을 뻗을 때 한 줄기 신비한 섬광이 그녀의 육신을 관통하면 그 얼굴에 희열과 패기가 용솟음친다.
돌연, 미친 듯이 마루로 내달아 송낙을 쓰고 쾌자를 걸치고 요령과 신칼을 들어 마당으로 뛰어내리면서 굿장단에 맞춰 너훌너훌 춤추기 시작한다.

탄실 : (신칼을 휘두르며)
　　　잡귀야, 잡신아,
　　　요건 보니 잡귀로다

요건 보니 잡신이로다
어떤 것이 잡귈런고
저승도 못 가고
이승도 못 오고
허공 중에 놀던 것이 잡귀로다
받아라, 천하명장 쓰던 이 칼을!
이 칼은 사람 잡는 칼 아니고
귀신 잡는 칼이로다
시왕대번지 둘러받아
너른 마당 번개치듯
좁은 마당 벼락치듯

나가면서 들어오면서 풀어내자
쑤어나라, 쑤어나라, 헛쉬!
쾌자 자락을 휘날리는 탄실의 춤사위가 신명을 더해 갈 때 보따리를 든 에미 등장.
에미, 어리둥절 소스라쳐 입을 딱 벌린 채 그 자리에 붙박혀 있다가 절규하듯 외친다.

에미 : 우와, 신 내렸다! 신 내렸어! 우리 애기한테 신 내렸어-!

징소리 바라소리 낭자하다. 에미, 두 손 비비며 사방 팔방에다 대고 절 하다가 탄실이와 한데 어우러져 춤춘다. 이윽고 해일 같은 장단이 잔잔해지면 모녀는 황홀경에서 깨어난다.

탄실 : (달려가 에미품에 안기며) 엄마아!

에미 : (딸의 등을 토닥이며) 참말, 용타. 신이 내렸으니 너도 이젠 어엿한 신딸이여, 하늘이 내린 심방이란 말여.

탄실 : 엄마, 그 사람, 귀양풀이…꼬옥 내 손으로 해주고 싶어요. 미치도록 좋아했는데… 말 한마디 못하고…헤어졌어요. 어, 엄마… (흐느낀다)

에미 : (눈물이 핑 돌면서) 불쌍한 것, 우리 설운 애기….

눈으로는 울고 입으로는 웃는 에미 얼굴에 스폿 라이트 점멸 하면서.
막.

수 필

파리채
별 쏟아지던 밤
난분 속의 작은 생명

강태국

파리채

필자 소개
국제펜클럽, 한국문인협회 회원. 현대수필 이사. 제주대 명예교수(현)
수필집 『낙서의 조각들』『추억의 조각들』『너 그래도 돼』
논문집 『수필인가 소설인가』

파리채

강태국

　대학시절부터 인연을 맺은 산사에서 참선을 하고 있다. 벽을 향해 눈을 45도로 내려깔고 무념무상의 심정으로 결과부좌했다.
　점심 후였고 게다가 눈이 그런 각도라 자연히 눈이 감겼다. 꾸벅꾸벅 단잠의 삼매경으로 몰입했다. 새소리와 꽃향기에 섞여 과거 잠시 거치고 간 여인들이 한 데 모여 원을 그리면서 내 주위를 맴돌며 덩실덩실 춤추고 있다. 빠져 나오려고 한 발 옮기는 찰나 누군가가 허리를 꾸욱 찔러왔다. 순간 잠이 깨었다.
　흐트러진 자세를 고치고 경책警策 한 대를 맞으라는 신호다. 발소리를 죽여 경행經行하면서 참선자들을 격려해 주는 당번 승려에게 들킨 것이다.
　합장을 하고 고개를 약간 눕혔다. 경책 맞을 때 귀가 다치지 않도록 함이다. 오른쪽 어깨로 날아왔다. '차악' 여운을 남기면서 고요함은 깨어지고 꿈도 깨어졌다. 꿈 속의 꿈이었다.
　아내가 파리채 들고 내 주위를 응시하고 있다. 파리를 쫓고 있는 눈치다. 설마 그럴 리는 없겠지만 한 방 얻어맞을세라 손을 저어 파리를 쫓아냈다.

어깨를 만져보니 달라붙는 게 있어 집어보니 납작해진 파리였다. 뒷벽을 확인해 보니 핏자국이 있었다. 꿈 속 경책 소리가 파리채 소리였나보다.

아내는 공중에서 맴도는 파리를 후려갈기는 운동을 내리 하고 있다. 투박하다고나 할까. 소박한 아내를 바라보면서 꿈의 여운을 정리 재구성해 보려는 의식이 꿈틀거리고 있었다.

나는 일본에서 태어났다. 태평양전쟁 말기 할아버지는 일본에 건너가 장손을 구출한답시고 어린 나를 품에 품고 B29 폭격기로 아수라장이 된 현해탄을 건너왔다.

고향에서 중학을 나와 부모님 곁에서 공부한답시고 또 다시 건너갔다. 부모님은 돌아가셨고 사업가로 출세한 숙부님 댁에서 대학까지 다닐 수 있었다.

선禪에 흥미를 느껴 길게는 1년 짧게는 한 달 휴학을 해가며 후꾸이 福井에 있는 영평사永平寺에서 참선을 하였다. 이 경험은 큰 힘이 되고 있다.

몇 년 새에 조부모님을 비롯하여 아껴주시던 숙부님, 막내 삼촌까지 돌아가시는 불행이 겹쳐 귀향을 생각했다.

산사에서 면벽하며 가느냐 마느냐 화두였다. 등뒤에서 새소리 개울소리 나뭇가지를 스쳐 지나가듯 바람소리가 정겹고 아름답게 들려왔다. 때때로 처량하고 마치 조상님들 속삭임과도 같았다.

60년대 말 제주 농촌은 전기, 수도, 가스도 없었다. 도쿄와 견주어 50년도 1백년도 뒤떨어진 문화수준이었다.

하나 어찌하리. 증손으로 제사 명절 때 여기저기 흩어져 있는 선묘

들을 돌아보고 내 손으로 벌초해 드리자고 마음먹고 귀향했다.

조상님들 담배연기에 그을린 벽 천장, 할머님께서 눈물 흘리면서 보리짚으로 밥 짓던 부엌, 초가 처마에 둥지 튼 참새들이 짹짹 환영해 주었다.

친족들은 종손 며느리 고른답시고 연일 모였다. 고을 일대 처녀를 대상으로 집안 특유의 선택법으로 골라갔다.

다산계냐 자녀가 많으냐, 김장과 된장, 간장 맛은, 밭일 물질은 잘하는지, 침쟁이와 점쟁이, 무당, 정신질환은 있었는지……

미모나 맵시, 학력, 우아함은 아예 따지지 않는다. 도회지에서 갈고 닦은 나의 여성관은 무시당했다.

신부가 간택되었으니 그리 알라고 일러왔다. 옛 궁중에서나 쓰던 '간택'이란 말도 우스웠지만 심정이 착잡했었다. 짐작한 대로 자연 그대로 오리지널 신토불이였다. 꼼짝없이 그 규수와 결혼했다. 2남 2녀를 낳았고 요리솜씨도 좋아 식솔 모두 건강하다.

다른 것들은 약간씩 까먹으나 생일 제삿날은 잘 기억해 둔다. 친화력도 있어 친족의 중심이 되고 있다. 그들의 절대적 지지에 힘입어 내 위에 군림하여 관리하는 느낌이 든다. 나는 늘 이방인이고 조금이라도 눈을 떼면 무슨 일을 저지를지 모르는 요주의 인물로 비쳐지고 있는 셈이다.

밭 잠수일도 야무지게 하여 어려운 고비 고비마다 잘 내조하여 조강지처로 자리를 굳히고 있다.

하나 남편 글이 수없이 활자화되어도 읽지를 않는다. 읽어보겠노라고 손에 쥐어보나 금방 단잠에 빠져버린다. 요즘은 원고 읽어주고 웃을 대목에서 웃는지, 슬픈 곳은 슬퍼하는 지로 원고 됨됨의 가늠자로 삼고 있다. 이 글도 읽어주면 어떤 얼굴을 할까. 즐거움이 하나 생겼다.

자극제가 되어 지금부터 열심히 찾아 읽을 것이리라.

고갱, 쇼팽, 멘델스존, 헨델, 나타리 우드, 클린트 이스트우드, 춘원 이광수, 마광수 교수, 버너드 쇼, 데칸쇼(데카르트, 칸트, 쇼펜하우어)니…… 는 떡이 되니 밥이 되니다. 아내에게는 다 부질없는 공염불 자장가에 불과하다. 아무런 지적 방해를 하나도 안 받는 강점強點이 파리채인 셈이다. 그에 비해 나는 나약하다. 철학, 문학, 음악 잡동사니 같은 지적 양심이 가득 차 있으니 허약하고 취약하다.

그러나 둘 사이 침묵은 깊다. 대화의 회로가 막힌 고독감 속에서 방황의 계절도 있었다.

영화 주인공이 섬에 표류되어 원주민 처녀에게 발목 잡혀 몸부림치며 탈출하다가 도로 잡히는 그림처럼 자기를 미화하면서 자기 자신과의 투쟁도 있었다.

그래서 요주의 남편으로 비쳤으리라. 소처럼 느릿느릿 곰처럼 묵묵히 정리하고 청소하며 끄떡없이 버티고 서 있다. 젊은 날 내 주위에 파리 떼와 같이 맴돌던 멋진 현대 여성들도 아내는 파리채 하나로 깨끗이 물리치고 있다.

방황의 계절, 그 풍경화 속에는 해인사, 범어사, 낙산사 등지로 찾아 헤매는 초췌하고 고달픈 젊은 나의 초상도 담겨져 있다. 어쩌면 체관諦觀이나 달관을 확인해 보려는 고행이었으리라.

이따금 '다방에라도…….' '식당에서 갈비는' 하면 그 돈으로 집에서 차라리 며칠 푸지게 먹을 수 있다며 마다한다. 분위기 깨고는 있으나 알뜰하고 착한 면모로 받아들인다. 흙과 바다 그리고 땀에 배인 제주 농촌의 원형적인 여성으로 새겨본다. 고아 아닌 고아로 자란 나에게는 안정감 같은 것으로 느껴진다.

춘몽에서 덜 깬 눈에 파리채 들고 마치 승무를 추듯 너울너울 아른

거리고 있다. 기분좋게 즐기는 춘몽을 깨게 하여 미안해하는 기색도 없이 그 무던한 동심의 얼굴은 주름져 있지만 티없이 해맑다.

　나 혼자 헤아려 주면 편안한 것, 새겨가며 썩은 지 어언 30년, 꿈인지 생시인지…

　지난 겨울 스물일곱 난 큰 딸을 시집보냈다.

김가영

별 쏟아지던 밤

필자 소개
제주수필문학회 회장(현). 한국문인상 대상 수상
수필집 『여자가 남자를 사랑할 때』 『남자 운이 좋은 여자』 등.

별 쏟아지던 밤

김가영

　사랑하는 사람의 변심으로 상처 입은 나는 함덕 바닷가로 갔다. 여름이 끝날 무렵이었다. 바다는 죽은 듯 잔잔했다. 여름의 끝을 알리는 신선한 바람이 바다 저편에서 불어왔다. 나는 끼고 있었던 반지를 빼서 힘껏 바다에 던졌다. 그리고는 조금 울었다. 고아가 된 기분이었다.
　그 날 이후 내게는 바닷물이 차갑게만 느껴졌다. 바닷가에서 태어나서 그 이후 한번도 바다를 가깝게 접하지 않았던 여름은 없었는데. 헤엄치는 일도 없어지고 말았다. 지글대는 태양이 견딜 수 없을 때면 석양이 질 무렵 바다에 손과 발을 가만히 담가 보는 정도로 지냈다. 그럴 때마다 아직도 남아 있는 물 속의 따뜻함이 발끝으로 느껴졌다. 그러면서 눈을 감고 있으면 용서하기 어려운 배신이랑 거짓이랑 슬픔이랑 불안이 이상하게도 없어지는 느낌이 들었다.
　답답하면 함덕 바닷가엘 간다. 간혹 배신감 때문에 반지와 던져 버린 추억을 되새겨 보기도 하면서.
　지난 여름, 함덕 바닷가에는 밤인데도 체온보다 뜨거운 바람이 불어

왔다. 더위가 극성을 부렸지만 피곤을 모르는 젊은 남녀들이 바닷가에서 기타를 치고 춤을 추며 놀고 있었다. 젊은 남녀들이 물고기들같이 바다에 뛰어 들어가 헤엄을 치고 나오고 다시 들어가고 하는 모습이 정말 아름다웠다. 나도 젊었다면 남자 친구들의 기타 소리를 들으면서 물 속에 들어가 멋있게 헤엄을 치고 나올 텐데, 그런 생각을 하면서 문득 하늘을 올려다보았다. 함덕 바닷가의 밤하늘을.

까만 비로드에 수많은 핀을 꽂아 놓은 것처럼 헤아릴 수 없을 만큼의 별들이 밤하늘에 강을 만들고 있었다. 그런 밤하늘을 보며 나는 빠져 들어가듯이 해변을 걸었다. 갑자기 그 밤의 바다에 몸을 적시고 싶어졌다. 그것은 정말 욕망이었다.

다행스럽게도 달도 없었다. 해변 끝에는 사람도 없었다. 나는 입고 있던 옷 그대로 샌들을 벗어 던지고 바다 속으로 들어갔다. 바다 속에 허리를 담그고 가만히 앉았다.

그때였다. 달이 구름 사이로 얼굴을 내밀었다. 그러고 보니 마치 반짝이는 야광충바다였다. 언젠가 보았던 야광충보다도 커다랗게 빛나는 야광충이었다. 순간 나는 바다에 안겨 있다는 실감에 기뻤다. 아니 행복하기도 하고 외롭기도 했다. 그 아름다움에 울고 싶어졌다. 문득 아름다운 광경을 함께 나눠 볼 사람이 없다는 것이 너무도 아쉬웠다.

그런데 난 혼자가 아니었다. 어느 사이엔가 한 남자가 다가와 있었다. 난 내 생각에만 정신이 팔려서 그 남자가 다가왔는지도 몰랐다.

그 남자도 옷을 입은 채였다. 나이도 용모도 달빛으로는 알 수가 없었다. 나는 은근히 겁이 났다. 느낌으로 제주 사람이 아닌 것만은 확실했다.

"이렇게 많은 아름다운 보석을 본 일이 없어요" 하고 나는 조심스럽게 중얼거리듯 말했다. 그러자 내가 겁을 먹은 것과는 달리 그 남자는 조금 생각한 뒤 부드럽게 대답했다.
"좋으시다면 당신에게 전부 드리지요. 저의 선물입니다. 하하하"
그리고는 그 남자는 저만큼 헤엄쳐 가 버렸다.
나는 여태껏 남자한테서 보석을 받아 본 적이 없다. 그런데 세계의 어떤 여자보다도 많은 보석을 그 밤 낯선 남자한테서 받았다.
나는 26년 전 연인의 변심으로 반지를 버렸던 상처를 비로소 아름다운 기억으로 간직할 수 있는 여유가 생겼다. 그 밤, 함덕 바닷가에서.

조명철

난분 속의 작은 생명

필자 소개
《문예사조》에 수필로 등단. 한국수필가협회, 한국문학회 이사(현)
수필집 『아내의 미소 웅녀의 미소』 『신호등과 돌하르방』 『가는 바람 오는 빛』 등.

난분 속의 작은 생명

조명철

나는 난을 좋아한다. 오랜 세월 난을 가까이에 두고 살아왔으니, 사랑한다고 말하고 싶지만, 차마 그럴 수가 없다. 지난 겨울 난들의 고통을 덜어주지 못했으니 어찌하랴. 초등학교 은사님으로부터 선물이라며 준 제주 한란, 이제도 가족히 두고 날마다 바라보고 있다. 어느새 30여 년의 긴 세월이 흘렀다.

봄이 오면 어김없이 싹을 틔우고, 낙엽이 질 무렵이면 꽃을 피웠다. 천 년 노송을 박차고 비상하는 학의 모습을 닮은 꽃도 그러려니와 때로 풍겨오는 향기는 생명의 환희를 느끼기에 족하다. 그게 난 중의 난 정방이라는 걸 이제야 알았으니 기쁨은 배로 늘었다. 그 난을 올 봄 난원에 입원을 시켰다. 오랜 세월 보살펴온 정성이 수포로 돌아가는 게 아닐까 하는 조바심으로 가슴이 아렸다.

아이들이 모두 떠나버린 단독 주택이 너무 헐거워 이태 전에 아파트로 이사를 했다. 함께 온 난들은 7층 고공의 새 환경에 적응하기가 힘겨웠는지 시름시름 앓더니, 지난 겨울엔 동해凍害까지 입어 살아있는 놈들까지도 건강을 잃었다.

　단독 주택에서 살 때엔 늦은 봄부터 가을 초입까지는 정원 나무그늘에 놓아두었다. 낮이면 적당한 햇살과 바람을 벗하고, 밤이면 이슬을 마시며 달이나 별과 밀어를 속삭였다. 늦가을부터는 거실 남창 가에서 따스한 햇볕을 받으니, 잎은 늘 진초록으로 싱그러워 보는 이를 즐겁게 하였다.

　아파트의 여건은 사뭇 달랐다. 겨울이면 햇볕이 잘 드는 서재 남쪽 베란다에 난 분들을 놓고 한 달에 한두 번 물을 주고 베란다와 서재의 샛문은 닫아놓았다. 방으로 흘러드는 냉기를 차단하기 위함이었다.

　그게 탈이었다. 겨울의 한복판에서 한 달쯤 지난 뒤 문을 열고 살펴보았더니. 몇 개의 분에서 밤색으로 변한 잎들이 보이질 않은가. 그러나 수명을 다한 퇴촉으로 생각하고 잘라내어 물을 주고는 샛문을 또 닫아놓았다. 좁은 베란다에 밤이면 냉기가 고이는 것도 모르고….

　그로부터 한 달쯤 뒤였을까. 난들이 심각한 고통 속에서 신음하고 있음을 발견한 것이다. 숨이 끊긴 것들은 뽑아내어 버리고, 살아 있는 것들은 미지근한 물로 온 몸을 적셔 주며 생기를 회복시키려 했으나 상처가 너무 깊은 탓인지 웃음을 보여주지 않았다.

　사라오름에 봄기운이 찾아올 무렵, 냉해가 심한 대여섯 분은 입원시키고 비교적 상태가 좋은 나머지는 거실 북쪽 베란다로 서둘러 옮겨놓았다. 햇볕이 잘 들지는 않았지만 눈 가까이 두고 보살피려 함이었다. '천연 미네랄 22'를 3~4일 간격으로 뿌려 주며 정을 쏟았다. 그러나 봄이 다 갈 무렵까지도 싹을 틔우지 않으니 마음만 초조로울 뿐이었다.

　여름이 문턱을 넘어 들어올 무렵의 어느 날, 드디어 몇 개의 분에서 새 생명들이 뾰족이 고개를 내민 것이다. 오랜 기다림 끝에 얻어진 새

싹을 대하니, 환희의 미소가 절로 나왔다.
 문득 "하늘이 때를 주고 땅이 기름지다 해도 인화가 없으면 생명을 키울 수 없다天時不如地利 地利不如人和."는 맹자의 말씀이 떠오른다.
 모든 생명은 화합에서 태어나고 자란다. 하늘을 거스르고 땅을 거스르고, 자연을 거스르면 죽음을 부른다. 천지 운행의 순리에 따라 더불어 살면 생명은 영원해 진다. 난과 나의 화합, 그것은 자연과 인간의 화합이요 물아일체物我一體가 아닌가.
 고층 아파트에 격리되어 있으면서도 싹을 틔워낼 수 있음은 무슨 힘인가. 구운 흙 서너 줌, 물 한 움큼, 바람 한 점, 햇빛 한 줄기에 정 한 아름이 어우러진 때문이다. 인간과 자연과의 화해일 수밖에 없다.
 "우주 속의 모든 사물이 따로따로 존재하는 것 같지만 내적으로는 모두 연결되어 있다."라고 한 화엄사상을 떠올려 본다. "자연은 살아있는 인격체요 한 생명"이라고 천지 부모설天地父母說을 갈파한 선각자 해월의 말에도 귀 기울여 본다.
 우주 속의 생명은 모두 하나다. 천지의 조화가 없이는 생명은 태어날 수 없을 것이다. 거대한 코끼리나 고래, 미물인 하루살이나 송사리, 아프리카의 거대한 수림, 길섶의 보잘 것 없는 잡초에 이르기까지 천지 조화의 산물이 아닌 게 어데 있으랴. 이 위대한 진리 앞에 머리를 조아리지 않을 자 그 누구란 말인가.
 지배의 권능을 부여받았다고 생각하는 사람들은 과학을 지배의 도구로 삼아 지구를 황폐화시키더니, 그것도 모자라 우주 정복의 깃발을 내두르고 있다. 나라마다 이 대열에 동참하기 위해 안간힘이다. 우주의 파괴는 가속이 붙고 있다. 지구와 인간의 불화, 우주와 인간의 불화다.
 이 오만한 인간들은 생명의 탄생까지 조작하려 하고 있지 않은가.

인간 게놈의 해독, 유전자의 조작, 인간 복제 등등, 순리를 거스르는 무서운 일들이 벌어지고 있다. 자신의 생명을 탄생시킨 하늘과 땅의 권능에 도전하는 인간, 창세기의 혼돈이 다가오는 듯 싶다.

끝없이 펼쳐진 하늘을 본다. 하늘에 맞닿은 드넓은 바다, 의연히 하늘로 머리를 치켜들고 정좌한 산, 어느 것도 말이 없다. 모든 생명을 끌어안은 하늘이여! 땅이여! 신비의 생명 근원이여! 하나됨을 찬탄하지 않을 수가 없다.

드디어 난들의 웃음소리를 듣는다. 가녀린 새싹들의 미소, 그것들과 함께 생명을 나누고 있음을 깨닫는다. 온 생명들의 연계된 장엄한 화엄세계의 아름다움이 펼쳐지고 있음이다.

문학평론

서사문학은 물의 제의祭儀와 상상력想像力의 유산

신승행

서사문학은 물의 제의祭儀와 상상력想像力의 유산

필자 소개

한국문인협회 회원, 한국문학비평가협회 이사, 국제펜클럽 회원(현)
제주산업정보대학 교수(현)
시집 『섬바다 숨비소리』 『문풍지』. 저서 『언어와 문학의 만남』

서사문학은 물의 제의祭儀와 상상력想像力의 유산
샤머니즘과 제주문학을 중심으로

신승행

1. 머리말

　물은 생명의 원천이면서 두려움의 존재인 것이다. 창세기에는 홍수 전설 속의 주인공 노아Noah를 통하여 인간을 다스렸다는 기록이 나타난다. 150일 동안의 홍수 그래서 방주方舟에 의하여 이어진 오늘의 인류사가 바로 그것이며 또한 샤머니즘의 원류로 알고 있는 바이칼Baikal 호수의 두려움이 또한 그러한 것들이다. 즉, 세계에서 가장 깊은 바이칼호를 앞에 놓고 퉁구스Tungus인들은 빌고 있었다는 것이 그것이다. 어째서 인간들은 물을 앞에 놓고 빌고 있었을까 하는 것이다. 이것이 바로 생명을 의식한 두려움의 실체였던 것이다.
　우리 나라 서사문학 역시 이러한 시점에 바탕을 두면서 형상화되어 나타나고 있다. 삼국시대 설화들이 변용되어 조선시대에 소설로 발전된 것처럼, 제주문학 역시 이러한 설화들이 근간이 되어 문학 창작에 원천이 되었던 것도 사실이다. 여기에는 물과 제의祭儀가 주종을 이루는 애니미즘Animism을 바탕으로 샤머니즘Shamanism과 금기禁忌가 함께 존재하고 있었다. 이렇게, 물은 생명을 만들었고 섭리의 상징적 존재로 우리 생활에는 불가분의 관계로 언제나 상존하는 것이다. 문학에 있어서의 물의 상상력은, 심리적 정신적으로 그 형상화의 범주가 다변적으로 나타나고 있으면서 제반 정서의 근원을 이루고 있기 때문에 그 이유 역시 여기에 기인하고 있다는 논리다. 그래서, 강물은 세월과 연계된 삶과 죽음을 이미지image화 시키는 요소로 나타나기도 하고, 호수는 추억이나 사색의 연장선으로 미화되어 형상화될 수도 있으며, 빗물은 그리움이나 슬픔으로, 안개나 이슬은 자기 성찰로, 바다는 두려움이나 기다림의 공간으로 형상화되어 나타나는 것이다. 이러한 정황들을 정리하면 다음과 같은 도해도 가능할 것이다.

삶과 죽음 + 물과 생명
-------------------------- = 갈등적 구조성립
(형상화 공간)

이러한 시점에서 물의 힘은, 존재의 근원을 파고 들어가 원초적인 것과 영적인 것을 물의 상상력에 의하여 조율되는 것이다. 이것이 바로 애니미즘dl요 또한 문학의 실체인 것이다. 그렇다면 샤머니즘에 나타난 물과 금기와의 관계는 어떤 것일까?

2. 샤머니즘과 물의 정체성

제주의 무속에 있어서 '물'은 직·간접적으로 민간신앙의 원천이 되고 있으면서 제의祭儀에 있어서 필수적 금기禁忌의 대상이 되고 있음을

발견할 수 있다. 즉, 물을 사용하여 목욕재계하고 제의의 공간을 정화시켜 정성을 통한 상징적 원의原義를 되찾고자 했던 경우들이 그러한 것들이다.

그 한 예로, 주부가 매일 첫 새벽에 샘물을 길어다가 먼저 제상祭床에 올리는 정화수를 들 수 있겠고, 부엌신인 조왕신 아니면 뒤뜰 장독대나 마당에서까지 정화수를 올려놓고 가족들의 무병과 장수를 신에게 비는 의식들이 그것이다. 그리고 동제洞祭에서는, 제관이 먼저 목욕재계한 후 마음을 다스리고 온갖 정성을 다하여 정화수 세 그릇을 떠 놓는다. 이러한 예는 무당들도 마찬가지였다. 무당들은, 잠자리에서 일어나는 즉시 몸 주신을 모시는 신단에 옥수玉水를 올리고 문안드리고서 거동하는 것이 그들의 무업巫業인 것이다.

참고로, 경기도 외딴 섬 풍도의 당제堂祭 샘물, 덕적도·소야도·위도의 당제 샘물, 충남 서산 황도의 서낭당 당제와 샘물 기타 여러 군도에서도 금기와 물에 대한 흔적은 존재한다. ―김태곤의 <물의 제의적 원의 상징原義象徵> pp.123~138에서 참조

이러한 물에 대한 원의는, 던데스Alan Dundes가 밝히는 북미 인디언 설화에서도 잘 나타난다. ― 장주근(경희대 민속학)의 논문 〈제주도 당신 신화의 구조와 의미〉에서 참조

그 설화의 예를 들면,

A) "괴물이 세계의 물을 다 가두었다"라는 말이 논증 대상으로 눈길을 끌고 있다.
B) "영웅이 괴물을 죽이고 물을 방출했다"라는 말 역시 맥을 같이 하고 있지 않는가.

단순한 논조로 버릴 수도 있는 내용이었지만, 역시 여기에서의 물은 무속적 기반으로 강하게 작용하고 있다는 사실을 접할 수 있었다.

A)인 경우,　　괴물 ＋ 물
　　　　　---------------- = 물은 생명의 원천적인 존재 (두려움)
　　　(두려움의 실체)

B)인 경우,　　영웅 ＋ 물
　　　　　---------------- = 물은 생존권의 절대적인 존재 (지배욕)
　　　(지배욕의 실체)

물은 이렇게 일상적인 것처럼 보이지만, 생명과 죽음을 앞에 놓고 어둠과 밝음을 일깨워 주는 환원된 공간으로 존재하는 것이다. 또한 상징적인 시간 역할로도 접근할 수 있다. 더욱 한결같은 것은, 늙은 뱃사공 카론Charon은, 강물을 통하여 삶과 죽음의 세월 곧 이승과 저승을 오가면서 심리적 갈등을 조장하고 있다는 사실이다. 이렇게 물 신앙과 무속적 제의는 이곳 제주에서도 많이 나타난다. 설문대할망이 바다에서 출현하는 예라든가. 제주시 이도2동 13번지 대동샘 옆 동백나무 숲에 있는 높이 75cm의 석상이 있는데, 이 석상을 가리켜 물할망이라고 부르고 있다. 때문에, 샘물이 마르지 않게 보살펴 주는 신이라 하여 제를 지낸다. 제주시 용담동에도 마을 샘물이 끊이지 않게 보살펴 주는 물할망신神이 있었다. ― (金泰坤 1982. 韓國巫俗圖錄 P.197~)

따라서, 용연 일각에서 구전되고 있는 용머리 기우제에서는, 지나던 한 도인이 그 곳을 지니다 말고, 비단 다섯 필을 높이 걸도록 한 다음 "龍"字를 대필하였더니 그 용자가 갑자기 실제의 용이 되어 하늘로 승천하여 즉각 비를 내려줘서 긴 가뭄을 면케 하였다는 설화가 전해지고 있다. 이처럼 물과의 상관관계는 회귀와 생명을 상징하는 것이기 때문에 우리들의 일상적인 삶에는 물론 심리적 정서나 문학에도 많은 영향을 주었던 것이 사실이다.

3. 물과 샤머니즘의 미학

제주 문학에 있어서 샤먼巫堂이나 금기에 관련된 작품들을 보면, 많은 금기의 속성과 지혜 같은 것들이 서로 조화를 이루면서 서사적으로 묘사되었음을 발견할 수 있다. 특히 서사敍事 분야에서는, 1993년에 발표된 오성찬의 〈잡초 이야기〉가 있는데, 이것 역시 제주의 전설인 〈서귀진 변인태〉(현용준, 제주도 전설, 1976)를 현대 감각에 맞도록 인용 구성한 소설이다. 즉 음흉하고 거짓말 잘하는 변인태는, 한라산을 넘는 과정에서 조방장의 부인을 겁탈하고 되레 그 부인을 협박하여 돈을 뜯어내는 이야기를 소설화한 것이다.

〈용마의 꿈〉(1983), 〈김녕 사굴 본풀이〉(1984)도 설화의 근간이 되는 뱀과 수심방의 굿을 통하여 전설의 진위를 백성들에게 검증케 하는 것인데 이것 역시 제주설화를 변용하여 개작한 것이다. 또한 죽은 영혼을 건지는 굿에 왕사리 바다가 등장하는 샤먼 활동 역시 눈 여겨 살펴 볼 수 있겠지만 여기에서는 현기영의 〈바람 타는 섬〉을 중심으로 더욱 구체적으로 살펴보고자 한다.

그의 작품은, 〈변방에 우짖는 새〉·〈바람 타는 섬〉·〈순이 삼촌〉 등 많은 작품들이 있지만 그의 소설은 그것 자체로 하나의 굿처럼 샤먼을 많이 끌어 드렸다. 이 소설 역시, 북제주군 구좌읍 하도, 세화리에 거주하고 있는 해녀들의 일상적인 삶과 소망을 그린 것인데, 1932년 1월 잠녀 항일운동을 배경으로 전개시킨 작품이다. 섬島과 고독과 가난으로 고립된 일제치하의 고통스러운 사회상, 그리고 일제의 억압으로부터 발생하는 제반 삶의 비극을 바다를 향해 토로하는 작품이다. 이러한 시점에서 마음에 맺힌 가난과 갈등들을 샤먼과 금기에 의해 해소시켜 보려는 몸부림을 목격하게 된다. 세찬 풍파에 시달리는 일상적인 삶 속에서 더욱 마음 아픈 것은 그 치욕과 억울함, 이런 것들이 바로 마음의 응어리로 드러난 것이다.

> 잠녀들이 동서로 내달아 물가에 일렬로 늘어서자 망태멘 상군 잠녀들이 맨발로 물에 들어서서 휙휙 좁씨를 뿌렸다. "좁씨를 뿌립네다. 곡식 풍년 주십서, 소라씨, 전복씨 뿌립네다. 소라, 전복 많이 열게 해줍서, 제발 세화리 잠수들 좀 살게 해줍서."
> 좁씨를 부린 상군 잠녀들이 일제히 물러나자, 이번엔 이 백 명 잠수들이 일제히 백지에 싼 한 줌 밥덩어리를 바다를 향해 힘껏 내던졌다.
> ― 〈바람 타는 섬〉 중에서

정화수에 숯과 고추를 띄우기도 하고 정화수를 무당이 들고 굿판 주변을 도는 행위 같은 것들도 예로 접근할 수 있겠지만, 더욱 안타까운 것은 우선은 가난에서 벗어나고 싶어하는 주민들의 현실적 소망을 빌고 비는 물의 신앙으로 볼 수밖에 없는 대목이다.

> 도아가 금춘의 도움을 받으며 급히 빈 바구니에 김이 모락모락 나는 흰쌀로 지은 밥 다섯 그릇을 넣어 뱃머리에 갖다 놓고 그 앞에 엎드렸다. 배 요동질에 쓰러지지 않도록 한 손으로 돛대 밑동을 꽉 잡고서, 다른 잠녀들도 두 손 모으고 뱃머리를 향해 고개를 숙였다. 용왕님께 축원을 올리는 도아의 낭랑한 음성이 솟구쳐 올랐다.
> "동의 청룡, 서의 백룡, 남의 적룡, 북의 흑룡, 중앙의 황룡, 여러 용신님네, 비록 소찬이나마 정성들여 올리오니 부디 우리 불쌍한 세화리 잠녀들 무사히 이 바다 건너게 해 주시옵기 소원입네다."

나머지 잠녀들도 함께 낮은 음성으로 축원 올리면서 머리를 연방 조아렸다.
　　　　　　　　　— 〈바람 타는 섬〉중에서

　역시 물은 신앙의 대상이 되었지만 그렇게 간절한 것이었다. 물과 제의의 상관적 관계는 이렇게 바다나 강이나 샘에서 출발하는 것이 일반적인 경우인데 특히 용신龍神 만큼은 물 신앙의 상징적 존재로서 우리들 삶에 있어서 없어서는 안될 정신적 지주로 볼 수밖에 없는 것이다. 그 예를 보면,

　　"그러면 삼촌, 사수 바다는 바람이 잔잔해도 이상하게 파도가 센데 왜 그러는고 예?"
　　하고 한 잠녀가 고개를 갸우뚱하면서 물었다.
　　"글쎄, 그것사 천 길 만 길 깊은 바다니깐 속내는 알 수 없지만, 아마도 바닷속 깊은 골짜기로 흐르는 센 물살 때문이 아닐까? 개울물도 좁고 깊은 여울목엔 물결이 높게 일어나는데 같은 이치일 거라."
　　퉁먹어 뾰로통해 있던 도아가 품앗이한다고 얼른 되받아 내쏜다.
　　"그게 아니우다. 얕은 물엔 새가 놀고 깊은 물엔 용이 논다고, 바닷속 용왕님이 크게 숨쉬기 때문에 물결이 큰 거주, 천 길 만 길 깊은 바다인데 용궁이 없을 리가 있수꽈?"
　　… 중략 …
　　여덟 길 깊은 물 속이었는데, 한 무리에 붉은 산호 떼가 바람에 쏠리는 숲처럼 조류를 타고 설레고 있었다. 가슴이 섬직 했다. 내가 너무 깊이 들어왔나? 저 아름다운 산호 숲에는 죽은 잠녀들의 넋이 깃들여 있다는데…… 혹시 용궁 들어가는 길목은 아닐까?
　　　　　　　　　— 〈바람 타는 섬〉중에서

　바로 물에 대한 상상력이 그것이다. 모진 세파에 언제나 버릴 수 없는 생명에 대한 일련의 두려움인 것이다. 이것은, 집단적 정서를 지향

하고 있으면서 그 역할의 기폭제는 결국 일상적 삶을 공유하게 하는 성격을 지니고 있는 것이다. 이러한 공유성은 연대 의식을 낳게 하고 믿음을 만들었다.

그리고, 바닷가 불턱에서 벌어진 넋들이 굿은 자연히 죽은 남편의 억울한 혼령을 진혼하는 사설로도 곁들여져 있었다. 먼저 구성진 사설로 저승을 관장하는 여러 신들을 차례차례 청해 모셔놓고, 북 장단 맞춰 춤과 노래로 기쁘게 해준 다음, 삼일 전에 저승길 떠난 외로운 혼령의 가련한 정황을 설명한 뒤 부디 저승으로 안착하게 해 주십사 하는 기원을 올린다. 그리고, 그 혼령은 비명에 죽어 저승에 못 가고 음습한 허공중에 엉겨 떠도는 무수한 억울한 혼령들 속에 있을지 모르므로 다 함께 청해 불러 진혼해 주기도 하였다.

> 그 동안 얼마나 고생이 많았느냐, 참말로 고맙고 고맙다. 병들어 객사 죽음 할 몸, 고향 땅에 데려와 이렇게 묻어 주었으니, 그보다 더 고마울 데가 어디 있겠느냐.
> 설운 열 여덟 살아, 이제랑 울지 말라, 나는 이제 아무 여한도 불만도 없다. 내 명이 짧아 죽은 걸, 내 사주 내 팔자 글러 죽은 걸, 누구를 원망하리. … (중략) …
> 소리 죽여 끅끅 흐느끼던 정심이 마침내 목놓아 울고, 구경꾼들도 얼굴에 눈물이 질펀했다.
> ─ 〈바람 타는 섬〉 중에서

샤먼巫堂은 이렇게 개인적·집단적 정서의 저변만을 암시하고 있지 않고 한 발 더 나아가 개인적 집단적 갈등이 발생하게 된 과정까지도 다시 재기한다. 이는 억압되어 드러내지 못했던 시대적 갈등을 보여주는 과정인 것이다. 말하고 싶어도 말하지 못하는 마음의 응어리를 작가는 제주의 역사라는 시대적 소재를 통해서 풀어내고 있다. 〈바람 타는 섬〉은 제주도 세화, 하도 마을을 배경으로 시작한 것도 이를 증명하고 있는 것이다. 일제시대 한 사람의 여성으로, 생활인潛女으로서 일상적이고 주변적인 이야기를 그린 것이다. 섬이라는 자연적 환경으로 인한 비참한 삶을 끌어내고 있으며, 그러면서 나약하나마 서서히 타오르는 잠녀들의 일제에 대한 저항과 생존권을 건 필사의 투쟁의식이 또한 묘사되고 있다. 이는 제주 백성으로서 아주 절박하고 참된 가치를 향한 집단적 항변이었다. 이 작품 곳곳에서 민요와 타령 노래가 많이 나온다. 이것은 단순한 목적성이 아니라 개인의 심리적 억압을 해소하고 있는 사실로도 간과할 수 없는 것이다.

>당귀신도 아무 소용이 없었다. 여옥은 임종 때 짚동같이 퉁퉁 부은 아버지의 얼굴에 소리없이 흐르는 눈물을 차마 잊을 수 없다. 어부가 배를 팔고 막일꾼으로 나서지 않으면 안 되는 막된 세상, 왜놈의 발동선들이 저인망 그물로 어장 바닥을 쓸어 가는 판에 ······
>
>어떤 새는 밤에도 울고
>어떤 새는 낮에도 울리
>이 새 저 새 날 닮은 새야
>밤낮 몰라 울어예는구나
>
>― 〈바람 타는 섬〉 중에서

샤머니즘에서 무당이 말하는 비극은 대립과 갈등을 조장하기 위한 것이 아니라 당시의 시대적 갈등을 심리적 현실적으로 묘사함으로써 극적인 효과도 기대할 수 있는 것이다.

>A) 우리들은 제주도의 가이없는 잠녀들
>　비참한 살림살이 세상이 안다

비오는 날 눈 오는 날 바람 부는 날에도
저 바다 물결 위에 시달리는 몸

B) "그래, 이건 우리가 이긴 싸움이야. 감옥에 간다고 패배한 게 아니지. 적은 우리의 몸을 가둘 수는 있어도 우리의 정신은 가둘 수 없어."
"물론이지. 이건 장구한 싸움이야. 우리 앞에도 우리 뒤에도 싸움은 면면히 이어지는 거지."
"아암, 우린 새끼를 낳기 위해 뱀에게 일부러 먹혀 죽는 두꺼비라구. 뱀에게 먹혀 죽은 두꺼비는 독을 뿜어 뱀을 죽이고, 그 속에서 새끼들이 태어나 시체를 먹이로 자라는 거지."
— 〈바람 타는 섬〉 중에서

현기영 소설 〈바람 타는 섬〉에 나타나는 A)의 경우는, 제주 섬사람들 특히 가난한 잠녀潛女들이 세찬 바다와 싸워가면서 살아가는 모습을 생동감 있게 그리고 있는데, 그러나 시달림의 상황은 어쩔 수 없는 것이었다. 어쩌면 주인공이 죽음을 맞이하거나 도망자의 신세가 되어버린 것이다. 그러나 B)에서의 그들은 그들의 생존을 억압하던 구조를 타파하고 새로운 상생의 세계를 만들고자 하는 것이다. 그러므로, 이 작품의 행적은 결코 비극이라 말할 수는 없다. 〈순이 삼촌〉에 나오는 주인공의 죽음이나 〈변방에 우짖는 새〉의 주인공의 죽음도 그들은 공동체의 카타르시스catharsis나 해원解寃을 획득하기 위한 과정이지 결코 비극적이라 할 수 없다는 것들 역시 그의 소설이 간접적으로 지적하는 특성이라 감히 말할 수 있을 것이다.

결국, 샤먼을 통하여 은원恩怨을 풀고자 하는 것은 사자를 위한 의례가 아니고, 그것은 산자를 위한 의례이며 과정이라는 논리에 접할 수 있다. 현대를 살아가는 제주인을 위한 의례인 것이다. 제주의 서사문학은 이렇게 샤머니즘 성격을 절묘하게 접근시키면서 현재와 만나고 있음을 알 수 있다.

4. 결 론

물은 결국 생명의 원천이면서 두려움의 대상이 되고 있었음을 이미 지적한 바 있다. 때문에 우리 인간들은 샤먼shaman 즉 무당을 중심으로 하는 제의식祭儀式에서 없어서는 안 될 삶의 덕목인 것이다. 그래서, 목욕재계하는 금기와 정화수로 문학은 이와 깊은 연관성을 지니고 있는 것이다. 문학에 있어서 물을 통한 상상력의 세계는 말할 수 없을 정도로 다변적이면서 심리적 정신적 원의原義의 상징으로 형상화의 세계를 깊이 있게 다루고 있는 것이다.

물과 생명 + 물과 두려움 = 샤먼(巫堂)을 통한 정화작용

이렇게 현기영의 소설에 나타나는 샤머니즘은, 오직 산 자를 위한 의례이며 일종의 카타르시스적인 회귀과정으로 간주할 수도 있을 것이다. 말하자면, 공포에 눌려 있는 제주 섬사람들의 슬픔이나 한숨 같은 그러한 감정을 해방시켜 독자들에게 쾌감을 주고자 하는 정화 시각의 한 단면으로도 가능한 것이다.

일제 치하의 혹독한 감시 속에서 전개된 뼈저린 고통과 한숨과 그리고 모진 억압과 수탈 속에서 죽어간 숱한 사람들을 위로하기 위한 시대적 수난을 바다를 앞에 놓고 전개한 것이다.

이렇게 현기영의 〈바람 타는 섬〉은 고통받는 시대적 상황 때문에 등장된 바다와 잠녀들의 행보는 물론 섬사람들의 끈기와 삶을 조명하기

위한 일종의 함성인 것이다. 물과 제의와의 관계는 여기서 그 가치를 지니고 있다. 또한 서사문학의 위상과 정체성을 다각적으로 모색할 수도 있었던 것이다.

* 이 원고는, 한국문학비평가협회가 주관하는 문학 세미나(2001.9)에서 발표한 내용임.

제주섬의 바람

2004년 12월 20일 1판 1쇄 인쇄
2004년 12월 30일 1판 1쇄 발행

엮은이 • 오 성 찬
펴낸이 • 푸른사상사
책임편집 • 제주펜 출판소위원회

등록 제2-2876호
서울시 중구 을지로3가 296-10 장양B/D 202호
대표전화 02) 2268-8706(7) 팩시밀리 02) 2268-8708
메일 prun21c@yahoo.co.kr / prun21c@hanmail.net
홈페이지 //www.prun21c.com
ⓒ 2004, 오성찬 외
ISBN 89-5640-290-6-03810

값 23,000원